HOW
JAPAN'S ECONOMY
GREW SO FAST

EDWARD F. DENISON AND WILLIAM K. CHUNG

HOW
JAPAN'S ECONOMY
GREW SO FAST

The Sources of Postwar Expansion

THE BROOKINGS INSTITUTION
Washington, D.C.

Library of Congress Cataloging in Publication Data:
Denison, Edward Fulton, 1915–
How Japan's economy grew so fast.
Includes bibliographical references and index.
1. Japan—Economic conditions—1945–
I. Chung, William K., joint author.
II. Brookings Institution, Washington, D.C.
III. Title.
HC462.9.D3837   330.9'52'04   76-10836
ISBN 0-8157-1808-x
ISBN 0-8157-1807-1 pbk.

1 2 3 4 5 6 7 8 9

THE BROOKINGS INSTITUTION is an independent organization devoted to nonpartisan research, education, and publication in economics, government, foreign policy, and the social sciences generally. Its principal purposes are to aid in the development of sound public policies and to promote public understanding of issues of national importance.

The Institution was founded on December 8, 1927, to merge the activities of the Institute for Government Research, founded in 1916, the Institute of Economics, founded in 1922, and the Robert Brookings Graduate School of Economics and Government, founded in 1924.

The Board of Trustees is responsible for the general administration of the Institution, while the immediate direction of the policies, program, and staff is vested in the President, assisted by an advisory committee of the officers and staff. The bylaws of the Institution state: "It is the function of the Trustees to make possible the conduct of scientific research, and publication, under the most favorable conditions, and to safeguard the independence of the research staff in the pursuit of their studies and in the publication of the results of such studies. It is not a part of their function to determine, control, or influence the conduct of particular investigations or the conclusions reached."

The President bears final responsibility for the decision to publish a manuscript as a Brookings book. In reaching his judgment on the competence, accuracy, and objectivity of each study, the President is advised by the director of the appropriate research program and weighs the views of a panel of expert outside readers who report to him in confidence on the quality of the work. Publication of a work signifies that it is deemed a competent treatment worthy of public consideration but does not imply endorsement of conclusions or recommendations.

The Institution maintains its position of neutrality on issues of public policy in order to safeguard the intellectual freedom of the staff. Hence interpretations or conclusions in Brookings publications should be understood to be solely those of the authors and should not be attributed to the Institution, to its trustees, officers, or other staff members, or to the organizations that support its research.

Foreword

SINCE World War II, the economies of Japan and most other industrially advanced nations have grown faster than that of the United States. Americans have been intrigued by this comparison for two decades. Many have a favorite explanation for what they term the sluggishness of American economic growth even though the level of output per worker in the United States remains well above that of any other large country.

In the 1960s Edward F. Denison systematically explored and sought to explain differences in the economic growth rates of the United States, Belgium, Denmark, France, West Germany, the Netherlands, Norway, the United Kingdom, and Italy. The investigation also encompassed analyses of the reasons for international differences in levels of output per worker, because information on levels of output was found essential to an understanding of differences in rates of growth. That study, *Why Growth Rates Differ: Postwar Experience in Nine Western Countries,* by Edward F. Denison assisted by Jean-Pierre Poullier, was published by Brookings in 1967.

Soon after the publication of *Why Growth Rates Differ,* William K. Chung, a naturalized American economist educated in Taiwan under the Japanese administration and fluent in the Japanese language, began a similar inquiry into growth in Japan, adapting Denison's "growth accounting" technique to Japanese experience. At that time, and for most of the period he worked on the present study, Chung taught economics at Denison University. He joined the staff of the Bureau of Economic Analysis of the U.S. Department of Commerce in 1973.

In 1972 Brookings organized a comprehensive investigation of the Japanese economy by a group of Japanese and American analysts under the leadership of Hugh Patrick and Henry Rosovsky, two American economists who have studied Japan for many years. To investigate the sources of Japanese growth, they arranged for the collaboration of Denison and Chung, who contributed a chapter on that topic to the Brookings book, *Asia's New Giant: How the Japanese Economy Works,* edited by Hugh Patrick and Henry Rosovsky and published in February 1976. Denison and Chung found it difficult to present their findings comprehensively in a single chapter, however, and it was clear that their research warranted separate publication. This volume is thus a sequel to *Asia's New Giant.* It is the second, *Industrial Organization in Japan,* by Richard E. Caves and Masu Uekusa, published by Brookings in June 1976, being the first.

This work reflects its authors' admiration for Japan's economic achievement. Yet it stresses that the extraordinarily rapid growth of the Japanese economy in the postwar period was made possible to a significant extent by the economic backwardness of Japan in relation to the United States at the beginning of the period.

The authors' research benefited greatly from its integration into the broader Brookings study, which fostered association with the other contributors to *Asia's New Giant,* cooperation with the Japan Economic Research Center, and assistance from the Japanese Advisory Committee (comprising Saburo Okita, Kazushi Ohkawa, and Tsunehiko Watanabe) and from many other Japanese who were consulted.

The authors are greatly indebted to the Economic Planning Agency of Japan, which provided office space and cooperation in securing information during their visit to Japan in the summer of 1973, and especially to Takeo Takahashi, Tadashi Kusuda, Naohiro Yashiro, and other members of the agency's staff who answered inquiries about the Japanese economy and statistics and furnished or arranged access to unpublished data. The guidance of Shozo Ichino, Hisao Kanamori, Tsutomu Noda, Kazushi Ohkawa, Miyohei Shinohara, and Tsunehiko Watanabe was invaluable. The Center for Econometric Data Development and Research in Tokyo made available the detailed and unpublished estimates of industrial employment prepared by Ichino and of industrial capital stock prepared by Kusuda. Gardner Ackley, Jack Alterman, Jerome A. Mark, Hugh Patrick, Jean-Pierre Poullier, and Henry Rosovsky made useful comments on the manuscript. Key K. Kobayashi of the Library of Congress was of great assistance in locating data. The authors owe a special debt to David Schwartzman, who was instrumental in bringing them together and had originally suggested to Chung that he investigate Japanese growth sources.

The authors acknowledge the manifold contributions to the project of Genevieve B. Wimsatt, research assistant, and Erna S. Tracy and Margaret

H. Su, senior secretaries, and they are grateful to Florence Robinson for preparing the index.

The Brookings study of the Japanese economy was supported by a grant from the Andrew W. Mellon Foundation. The Bureau of Economic Analysis of the U.S. Department of Commerce provided funds for the preparation of estimates of the sources of Japanese economic growth, presented in table 4-6 on page 38. For this reason these estimates may be freely reproduced, with credit to this book as the source.

The views in this book are those of the authors and should not be ascribed to the staff members, officers, or trustees of the Brookings Institution, to the Andrew W. Mellon Foundation, or to the Bureau of Economic Analysis.

GILBERT Y. STEINER
Acting President

June 1976
Washington, D.C.

Contents

Appendixes

Text Tables

Appendix Tables

HOW
JAPAN'S ECONOMY
GREW SO FAST

CHAPTER ONE

Introduction

JAPAN has emerged from the poverty which crushes most of the world's peoples and joined the small group of affluent developed nations. Long before World War II Japan had become a world power, and productivity and living standards had risen above levels prevalent outside Europe, the United States, and the British dominions. But economic gains have been far greater in the postwar period. From 1953, when Japanese output had regained its prewar peak, to 1973 total national income multiplied 5.43 times and national income per person employed 4.06 times.[1] This growth performance is unmatched in any other country, free market or socialist—at least this is so if one excepts such special cases as the oil states and Israel.

Population grew 1.1 percent a year from 1953 to 1973. Though above rates in most European countries and only moderately below the Japanese rate of 1.3 percent from 1900 to 1953, postwar Japanese population growth was much below that of most of the rest of the world, and of Asia. As the number of deaths dwindled, a concurrent fall in the birthrate resulting from birth control and easy and legal access to abortion prevented a postwar population explosion. With the drop in the proportion of children in the population, per capita output multiplied 4.35 times, even more than output per worker.

The rapidity with which output increased in Japan after World War II surprised Japanese and Western observers alike. This book provides estimates of the sources of that growth and comparisons with other countries.

We begin, in chapter 2, by comparing Japan's 1970 output and consumption with that of five other industrial countries. In chapter 3 a summary record

1. Based on national income measured in 1965 prices and computed by United States deflation techniques, as explained later. Data from 1952 through 1971 are shown in table 3-3, column 2. The preliminary estimate for 1973 is ¥55,184 billion when Okinawa is excluded as it is in earlier years. Because of a recession, 1973 national income was not exceeded in 1974 or 1975, according to preliminary estimates.

1

of Japanese economic growth is provided, first verbally, with emphasis on the important machinery manufacturing industries, and then by introducing time series for national income and employment. Estimates of the sources of growth in Japan and elsewhere are provided in chapter 4, followed in chapter 5 by an overview of "how Japan grew so fast," which summarizes the findings drawn from these estimates. The details of series for the factors of production, and discussions of their trends, are then introduced—for labor in chapter 6, and for capital in chapter 7. The next three chapters take up additional determinants of long-term growth: chapter 8, advances in knowledge; chapter 9, reallocation of resources; and chapter 10, economies of scale.

Chapter 11 turns to the question, what determinants are responsible for the level of output per worker being much lower in Japan than in the United States? and compares the answer with results obtained when determinants responsible for nine other advanced countries being below the United States were estimated. Finally, this question is addressed: if Japan wished to maintain its high postwar growth rate during the coming decades, could it do so? To provide perspective, the concluding chapter sets out, first, to divide the contributions of the various sources to postwar growth between the amounts that are "sustainable" and the amounts that are "transitional," and then to indicate how long the transitional contribution could continue at the previous rate before it would be exhausted. Appendixes provide supplementary information and describe the derivation of our estimates.

Most of the text and tables contained in chapters 1–12 has also been published, in much the same form, as chapter 2 of *Asia's New Giant*.[2] The appendixes, which provide supplementary information and describe the derivation of our estimates of sources of growth and sources of international differences in output levels, appear only in the present volume. So does chapter 11, which examines the reasons that output per person employed was much lower in Japan than in the United States in 1970, and scattered material in other chapters, including estimates of the sources of growth of national income per person employed.

Because our investigation was part of a multi-author Brookings Institution study of the Japanese economy, we felt no obligation to discuss all aspects of that economy ourselves, even though nearly all impinge upon growth in one way or another. Characteristics of political, social, and economic institutions that are peculiar to Japan are examined in other parts of *Asia's New Giant* and, of course, in many other sources.

We have examined Japanese growth in the same analytical framework

2. Hugh Patrick and Henry Rosovsky, eds., *Asia's New Giant: How the Japanese Economy Works* (Brookings Institution, 1976).

that one of us has applied to other countries. Indeed, one focus of the present study is the addition of Japan to comparisons in an earlier book, *Why Growth Rates Differ,* which examines eight Western European countries and the United States.[3] Comparison of Japanese experience with that in other advanced nations is a central theme of this book. After publication of *Why Growth Rates Differ,* a later study, *Accounting for United States Economic Growth,* introduced a number of improvements in techniques for estimating sources of growth.[4] These improvements were retained in preparing the estimates for Japan insofar as the data required to implement them could be derived.

One of these improvements, segregation of the output of employees of general government, private households, and institutions, not only provides better estimates but also (in combination with data for sectors already isolated) permits separate estimates of the sources of growth of national income originating in the nonresidential business sector. These estimates are of particular interest because nonresidential business is much more homogeneous than the economy as a whole.[5] They are provided for Japan in this book. However, the United States is the only other country for which such data are available so most international comparisons refer to the whole economy.

There is no way to describe or analyze growth without introducing estimates and assumptions. Nearly all numbers presented are estimates—either those of a Japanese government agency or our own. Our use of the data also requires assumptions. We can describe the data used, the assumptions introduced, the problems encountered, and sometimes our impression of reliability, but must leave it to the reader to bear in mind that almost all series are approximations and some are subject to the possibility of a considerable percentage error.

3. Edward F. Denison, assisted by Jean-Pierre Poullier, *Why Growth Rates Differ: Postwar Experience in Nine Western Countries* (Brookings Institution, 1967); hereafter *Why Growth Rates Differ.*

4. Edward F. Denison, *Accounting for United States Economic Growth, 1929–1969* (Brookings Institution, 1974); hereafter *Accounting for Growth.* Improvements are summarized on pages 2–4. That book, rather than *Why Growth Rates Differ,* provides the data for the United States that are reproduced in this volume. Estimates from the two sources are compared in *Accounting for Growth,* appendix S.

5. Its production is sold on the market, and market transactions establish the value of this output in current prices. Value in constant prices is obtained by dividing current values by price indexes, or by an equivalent procedure. Thus output is measured in a way that is generally uniform and statistically independent of input measures. Nearly all production is carried on by business enterprises which are organized for profit; use various types of labor, capital, and land in their operations; and must seek to combine these factors in proportions which minimize their costs if they are to achieve their goal of profit maximization.

CHAPTER TWO

Level of Output Compared with Other Countries

A RECENT STUDY by Kravis, Kenessey, Heston, and Summers, which was sponsored by the Statistical Office of the United Nations, permits comparisons of 1970 output and consumption in the six largest developed free market economies.[1] The investigation was based on direct comparisons of prices and quantities so that the use of exchange rates, a poor measure of purchasing power parity, was unnecessary. The study was made with care and provides information of exceptional quality. Measuring output of government, education, health services, and other difficult areas posed the usual problems, but the comparisons are easily the best available for any recent date.

Output data refer to gross domestic product at market prices. Gross domestic product differs from our preferred output measure, national income, in that it is gross of capital consumption, excludes net receipts of property income from abroad, and uses market prices rather than factor costs as weights. But international comparisons are not ordinarily affected greatly by the difference between these measures.

Output per Person Employed

Table 2-1 compares four measures of output and consumption in the five other countries with the corresponding measure in the United States. The

1. Irving B. Kravis, Zoltan Kenessey, Alan Heston, and Robert Summers, *A System of International Comparisons of Gross Product and Purchasing Power,* United Nations International Comparison Project: Phase One (Johns Hopkins University Press for the World Bank, 1975).

first is gross domestic product (GDP) per person employed, a crude measure of productivity.

Comparisons based on four sets of price weights are provided: (1) Outputs of the United States and the other country in 1970 are valued in U.S. prices. Japanese GDP per person employed is then found to be 55.2 percent of the level in the United States. (2) Outputs of the United States and the other country are valued in the prices of the other country. Based on Japanese prices, GDP per person employed in Japan is only 44.3 percent of the level in the United States. (3) Because there is no inherent reason to choose between price weights of one country and the other in general purpose comparisons, the geometric means of these two measures, Irving Fisher's "ideal" index, is often used. Japanese GDP per person employed is then 49.5 percent of that of the United States. (4) The authors of the UN report developed an "international" system based on linking comparisons between countries at adjacent levels of development. It meets circular tests, such that if country A's output, for example, is twice that of B, and B's three times that of C, A's must always be six times that of C. Japanese GDP per person employed is 49.9 percent of that of the United States by this measure. In all comparisons in table 2-1 the international and ideal indexes yield fairly similar results.

By 1970 GDP per person employed in Japan had approached the lower bound of the range observed in developed Western countries. The gaps be-

Table 2-1. *International Comparisons of Gross Domestic Product and Consumption, Various Measures, 1970*

Percentages of U.S. values

Measure	Price weights	United States	Japan	France	West Germany	United Kingdom	Italy
GDP per person employed	United States	100.0	55.2	79.1	73.3	60.4	61.6
	Other country	100.0	44.3	65.6	61.5	51.2	49.2
	Ideal index	100.0	49.5	72.1	67.2	55.6	55.1
	International	100.0	49.9	72.6	68.2	53.7	52.8
GDP per capita	United States	100.0	68.1	81.8	80.3	67.9	53.5
	Other country	100.0	54.6	67.8	67.3	57.5	42.7
	Ideal index	100.0	61.0	74.5	73.6	62.5	47.8
	International	100.0	61.5	75.0	74.7	60.3	45.8
Consumption per capita	United States	100.0	56.4	76.7	67.5	70.0	55.0
	Other country	100.0	39.9	60.5	56.0	57.9	42.0
	Ideal index	100.0	47.4	68.1	61.5	63.6	48.1
	International	100.0	48.3	67.9	61.2	62.2	46.0
Total GDP	United States	100.0	34.4	20.3	23.9	18.6	14.2
	Other country	100.0	27.6	16.8	20.0	15.7	11.4
	Ideal index	100.0	30.8	18.5	21.9	17.1	12.7
	International	100.0	31.1	18.6	22.2	16.5	12.2

Sources: Derived from GDP per capita, consumption per capita, and population data in Irving B. Kravis and others, *A System of International Comparisons of Gross Product and Purchasing Power*, United Nations International Comparison Project: Phase One (Johns Hopkins University Press for the World Bank, 1975), pp. 6, 171–78, and from employment figures in Organisation for Economic Co-operation and Development, *Labour Force Statistics, 1961–1972* (Paris: OECD, 1974), tables 1 and 2 for individual countries.

tween the Japanese figures and those for Italy and the United Kingdom were of only moderate size at all price weights. Other countries of Northern Europe and North America still stood well above Japan. This was true not only of the countries listed in the table but also of the Scandinavian and Benelux countries, Switzerland, Canada, and probably others. By the international price weight comparisons, the United States exceeded Japan in GDP per person employed by 100 percent. France did so by 45 percent, Germany by 37 percent, the United Kingdom by 8 percent, and Italy by 6 percent.[2]

Hours of work are unusually long in Japan, and output per man-hour compares less favorably with other countries than output per person employed. On the other hand, Japan compares more favorably in nonagricultural industries than in the whole economy.

It is apparent that output per worker in Japan was far below that in countries of Northern and Western Europe and North America throughout the period of rapid Japanese growth which this book examines. It was substantially below the level even of Italy in most of the period. Exploration of reasons for international differences in output levels is deferred to chapter 11, but the facts about the Japanese position must be borne in mind in interpreting Japan's postwar growth experience.

Output per Capita

Japan ranks considerably higher in GDP per capita than in GDP per person employed. Of the countries listed in table 2-1 Japan had much the highest percentage of the population employed in 1970—49.2 percent as against 44.9 in the United Kingdom, 43.7 in West Germany, 41.3 in France. 39.9 in the United States, and 34.7 in Italy. (However, the Japanese percentage exceeded only slightly the highest in Western countries—47.9 in both Denmark and Sweden.)[3] With Japan and Italy at opposite extremes in the percentage working, Japan was far above Italy in GDP per capita of the whole population—34 percent according to the international price weight measure. It was approximately equal to the United Kingdom. According to this measure the United States was 63 percent above Japan, France 22 percent above, and West Germany 21 percent above.

2. Data for West Germany cited in this study cover the Federal Republic (including the Saar) and West Berlin in all years.
3. These comparisons are computed from Organisation for Economic Co-operation and Development, *Labour Force Statistics, 1961–1972* (Paris: OECD, 1974).

Consumption per Capita

Japanese per capita consumption compared much less favorably with the other countries despite the low proportion of Japanese output devoted to national defense. This is because of the very high proportion devoted to gross capital formation. By the international price weight measure, per capita consumption in all countries shown in table 2-1 except Italy exceeded that in Japan by at least 27 percent. The Japanese advantage over Italy was only 5 percent whereas its per capita GDP was 34 percent higher.[4]

Total Gross Domestic Product

The Japanese economy is the third largest, after those of the United States and the Soviet Union, of all countries. The margin between Japan and the second and fourth countries is considerable. Abram Bergson put the GNP of the USSR in 1965 at 57.5 percent of that of the United States when valued in dollars and 35.0 percent when measured in rubles.[5] Another calculation, also based on data assembled by Bergson, puts the GNP of the USSR, valued in dollars, at 56.5 percent of the United States in 1960 and 64.8 percent in 1970.[6] These estimates compare with 34.4 and 27.6 as the 1970 Japanese

4. The per capita consumption comparison is based on the International Comparison Project classification. To improve international comparability each category of current expenditures is allocated either to consumption or to government purchases in all countries regardless of whether it is actually paid by private or public expenditure in any particular country. For example, all current expenditures for housing, health, education, and recreation are classified as consumption even though parts of these expenditures are government purchases and so classified in the national accounts of the countries.

5. Soviet estimates, according to Zoltan Kenessey, imply a moderately higher relative position for the USSR in 1968, 62.8 percent, based on national income measured in dollars. For these comparisons, see Abram Bergson, "The Comparative National Income of the USSR and the United States," in D. J. Daly, ed., *International Comparisons of Prices and Output,* Studies in Income and Wealth, vol. 37, Conference on Research in Income and Wealth (Columbia University Press for National Bureau of Economic Research, 1972), p. 182, and comment by Zoltan Kenessey, p. 196 of the same publication.

6. Data are from Abram Bergson, *Soviet Post-War Economic Development* (Stockholm: Almquist and Wiksell, 1974), pp. 69, 71, 79. Total GNP is employment times GDP per person employed. GDP per person employed in U.S. prices in 1960 was extrapolated to 1970 by the growth rate of GDP per person employed in national prices. Bergson's data for Soviet growth are slight adjustments of estimates by Stanley H. Cohn, "General Growth Performance of the Soviet Economy," in *Compendium of Papers on*

percentages of U.S. GDP based on comparisons in dollar and yen prices, respectively. The GDP of West Germany, the fourth largest country, in 1970 was only 23.9 percent of that of the United States based on comparisons in dollars and 20.0 percent in marks. Depending on the price weights used, Japanese GDP exceeded that of West Germany by 38 to 44 percent.

Similar comparisons for earlier years are not available. But it appears that Japan has been the third largest of the world's economies and the second largest market economy since about 1965.[7] This ranking is unlikely to change soon because the Japanese economy is much smaller than that of the USSR and much bigger than that of West Germany.

Japanese output has fluctuated sharply since 1970, so updated comparisons would depend substantially on the year chosen. But it is clear that the relative Japanese position has continued to improve, at least if the effects of short-term business fluctuation are eliminated.

Some inkling of the immensity of the Japanese economic achievement in moving from Asian to Western productivity standards during the past century is suggested by data for India, also taken from the UN study by Kravis and others. Based on international price weights, the per capita GDP of Japan in 1970 was $2,952; this compares with $342 for India, the second most populous of the Asian nations (after China). The gap dwarfs the percentage difference between Japan and even the richest of other large nations, France at $3,599 and the United States at $4,801.

Output per Worker in Manufacturing

Productivity comparisons for groups of products or industry divisions would be interesting but are generally unavailable. However, one study, which covers manufacturing, is of separate interest. Yukizawa found that in 1967 gross physical output per worker (including salaried employees) in manufacturing industries was 57.8 percent as big in Japan as in the United States if products were combined by U.S. weights and 49.3 percent as big if products were combined by Japanese weights. These compare with the all-

---

the Economic Performance of the Military Burden in the Soviet Union, Submitted to the Subcommittee on Foreign Economic Policy of the Joint Economic Committee, 91:2 (Government Printing Office, 1970), pp. 9–17.

7. This statement is based on extrapolation of the 1970 gross domestic product of each country in international prices (from table 2-1) by its gross domestic product in its own constant prices. This calculation shows that Japan passed France in 1960, the United Kingdom in 1962, and West Germany temporarily in 1964 and again in 1966.

industry estimates for GDP per worker in 1970 of 55.2 and 44.3. Yukizawa's investigation, which is modeled on earlier Anglo-American comparisons conducted by M. Frankel and L. Rostas, is based on direct comparisons of output in those manufacturing industries which are best suited for such comparisons. They covered one-fourth of the value added in manufacturing in the United States and one-third in Japan.[8]

The all-industry productivity gap in 1970 would be considerably narrowed if agriculture were excluded. On the other hand, trends in the two countries were such that a comparison for 1967 would necessarily yield a wider gap than a 1970 comparison, and this effect is accentuated by the fact that in 1970 the demand situation was exceptionally favorable to high productivity in Japan and exceptionally unfavorable in the United States. Differences in methodology between the studies yielding the estimates have unknown but possibly large effects. For these reasons an attempt to infer how the international gap in manufacturing compares with the gap in the average non-agricultural industry is impractical. It is clear, nonetheless, that there was a gap in manufacturing, as in other industries, and that it was big.

8. With the United States as 100, Yukizawa's results yield indexes of 37.5 in 1958–59, 39.7 in 1963, and 57.8 in 1967 if based on U.S. weights, and 31.6 in 1958–59, 34.0 in 1963, and 49.3 in 1967 if based on Japanese weights. Yukizawa provides similar figures for sixty separate products (fifty-nine in 1967). Kenzō Yukizawa, *Japanese and American Manufacturing Productivity: An International Comparison of Physical Output per Head,* Discussion Paper 087 (Kyoto University, March 1975).

CHAPTER THREE

The Record of Growth

THE JAPANESE growth rate from around 1890, or even earlier, to World War II was one of the world's highest, in the neighborhood of 3.5 percent a year. The rate, moreover, was generally rising, though marked by alternating "long swings" of faster and slower growth. In the postwar years, all advanced countries, not just Japan, experienced acceleration of prewar rates, but the acceleration was much greater in Japan. Superimposed on a high prewar rate of increase, this resulted in a postwar Japanese growth rate much above rates in other countries.[1]

War and Recovery

World War II deprived the Japanese empire of nearly half its 1930 land area, that in Taiwan, Korea, and southern Sakhalin. According to Tsuru's estimates, it also cost the domestic economy more than nine-tenths of its merchant marine, one-fourth of its housing, and one-fifth of its industrial plant, machinery, equipment, and other durables. In all, Tsuru judges, one-fourth of the national wealth vanished during 1941–45. In the wake of this massive destruction, repatriation of 5 million military and civilian personnel stationed overseas intensified the acute shortages of food, clothing, housing,

1. See Kazushi Ohkawa and Henry Rosovsky, *Japanese Economic Growth: Trend Acceleration in the Twentieth Century* (Stanford University Press, 1973), for the timing and an interpretation of Japanese growth rate changes. Long-term comparisons of Japan and other countries appear in Simon Kuznets, *Modern Economic Growth—Rate, Structure, and Spread* (Yale University Press, 1966), p. 65. See also Kazushi Ohkawa, "National Product and Expenditure, 1885–1969," in Kazushi Ohkawa and Yujiro Hayami, eds., *Economic Growth—The Japanese Experience Since the Meiji Era*, Japan Economic Research Center Paper 19 (Tokyo, February 1973), vol. 1, pp. 138–39.

and other daily necessities; together with natural increase repatriation raised the population by some 8 million, or 11 percent, by the end of 1948.[2]

Agricultural production, down disastrously in 1945, was recovering sharply by the following year but did not regain the 1933–35 average until 1950. Even then it was well below the level of 1936–40 and insufficient to meet the needs of the expanded population. American food shipments helped Japan through the period of tight food supplies. Industrial output recovered much less quickly; in fact, from 1945 to 1946 it dropped by more than one-half to a level only one-fifth of the 1939–44 average and less than one-quarter of even the 1934–36 average. The Japanese government extended rounds of credit to firms in basic industries to help them attract idle resources and expand production. But credit expansion was followed by soaring prices rather than the hoped-for rehabilitation and recovery. Large government deficits contributed to the inflation. The year-to-year increase in the wholesale price index was 364 percent in 1946, 196 percent in 1947, 166 percent in 1948, and still as much as 63 percent in 1949.[3] Gains in industrial production, though substantial if expressed as percentage changes from the prior year, were meager compared to the previous decline; even in 1949 output was only two-fifths of the 1939–44 level.

By the end of 1948, however, the occupation authorities (the Supreme Commander of the Allied Powers, or SCAP) had become determined to see Japan converted from a liability to an economic asset for the free world. Soon thereafter a set of economic stabilization policies, popularly known as the Dodge Line for Joseph Dodge, financial adviser to SCAP, was introduced and implemented. Government budgets were forcefully brought into surplus, and credit expansion and bank lending were slashed. Prices and wages began to stabilize as the fiscal and monetary restrictions took effect.

The Dodge Line, like the currency reform in West Germany, marked the end of economic disorder and laid a solid foundation for recovery and growth. When conflict flared up in Korea in the summer of 1950, the Japanese economy was ready to take effective advantage of the special demand situation

2. Economic conditions during the immediate postwar years are presented in detail in Shigeto Tsuru, *Essays on Japanese Economy* (Tokyo: Kinokuniya Bookstore Co., 1958), part 1; Hugh T. Patrick, "The Phoenix Risen from the Ashes: Postwar Japan," in James B. Crowley, ed., *Modern East Asia: Essays in Interpretation* (Harcourt Brace Jovanovich, 1970); and Kozo Yamamura, *Economic Policy in Postwar Japan* (University of California Press, 1967).

3. Wartime price controls lapsed at the end of the war. The Ministry of Finance instituted controls on selected major items in March 1946 but this did not halt the price rises, as the percentages cited indicate.

created by U.S. needs for military procurement in the area. By mid-1951 the country had become the major workshop and arsenal for the UN troops in Korea. By 1952, when the World War II peace treaty went into effect, the Japanese economy had evolved from the stage of rehabilitation and reconstruction into an era of normality. Price levels had stabilized, industrial production was 15 percent above the 1934–36 average (though it was not to exceed the wartime high until 1955), and the market mechanism had resumed its ordinary functions of guiding production and distribution.

Industrial Production

Though postwar Japanese growth was broadly based, it featured the rapid growth of manufacturing output—as had growth in the 1920s, when textiles and other light manufacturing industries spearheaded economic development, and in the 1930s, when the pressure of military requirements resulting from the movement of Japanese armies into Manchuria and northern China caused steel, machinery, chemicals, and other heavy industries, along with electric power, to dominate industrial expansion. The tempo of these industries increased until the outbreak of war in the Pacific in December 1941. By the time Japan recovered its independence in 1952, the heavy industries were ready to resume a leading role in industrialization.

Table 3-1 indicates the magnitude of the expansion of production in manufacturing as a whole and in various manufacturing industries. The growth rate of manufacturing output from 1953 to 1971, 14.0 percent, surpassed the rate of national income growth of 8.8 percent (or 9.2 percent, depending on the method of deflation) in the whole economy, and even the rate of 11.1 percent in the nonagricultural nonresidential business sector as a whole.[4]

Within manufacturing the growth rate was highest in the important machinery group, and if any portion of the economy can be said to be the "leading sector," this was it in postwar Japan. The machinery industries consist of electrical and nonelectrical machinery, transportation equipment (including automobiles), and precision instruments. Then small, they were themselves almost wholly equipped with new capital facilities in the 1950s. Sales of their products benefited from the long boom in capital expenditures by Japanese business generally, from foreign purchases (especially of ships), and from swelling demand for motorcycles, household durables, and eventually automobiles. We shall sketch the development of some of these industries.

4. National income growth rates are shown in table 3-5, below.

Table 3-1. *Production Indexes of Selected Manufacturing Industries, 1953, 1961, 1966, and 1971, and Growth Rates, 1953–71*

	Indexes (1953 = 100)			Growth rate (percent)
Industry	1961	1966	1971	
All manufacturing	311.4	521.8	1,056.9	14.0
Iron and steel	337.2	549.2	1,060.0	14.0
Machinery[a]	516.0	923.2	2,489.6	19.6
Chemicals	302.7	625.0	1,200.5	14.8
Petroleum and coal products	404.4	840.7	1,926.9	17.9
Rubber	315.8	424.7	743.2	11.8
Paper and pulp	275.6	413.2	665.0	11.1
Textiles	210.7	316.4	463.5	8.9

Sources: Computed from Ministry of Foreign Affairs, *Statistical Survey of Japan's Economy* (1972), p. 19, except that indexes for petroleum and coal products, paper and pulp, and rubber were secured from Bank of Japan, *Economic Statistical Annual of Japan* (1963), pp. 217–18, and the 1972 edition of the same publication, pp. 213–14, and for rubber in the years 1963–71 from Economic Planning Agency, *Keizai yōran* [Economic Statistics in Brief] (1973), p. 128.

a. The machinery industry is composed of general machinery, electrical machinery, transportation equipment, and precision instruments.

The government has heavily protected and subsidized shipbuilding since the turn of the century. By 1935 Japan was the third largest shipbuilder, with 11 percent of the world's total.[5] After the postwar hiatus in activity, successive credit injections by the Japan Development Bank, starting in 1951, set the shipbuilding industry on a course of swift recovery, and long-term growth soon resumed. Japanese shipbuilders, benefiting from cheap labor and technological innovations, were in a supreme position in international competition when the closing of the Suez Canal in 1956 created a booming demand for supertankers, and again as the supertanker gave way first to the giant tanker in the late 1950s and then to the mammoth tanker of 80,000 to 100,000 gross tons during the 1960s. In the early 1970s they were building monster tankers of 470,000 gross tons and expanding facilities so as to be able to construct ships of 1,000,000 gross tons. Japan became the world's leading shipbuilder in the 1950s, but even in 1960 produced only one-fifth of the world's tonnage. By 1971 Japan's production was almost seven times its 1960 production and equaled almost half of the world's tonnage; it had increased from 500,000 gross tons in 1955 to 12.0 million in 1971.[6]

In the 1950s, when automobile ownership was still a symbol of affluence, motorcycles won acceptance as the most popular means of daily transporta-

5. Ichirō Yano, ed., *Nihon kokusei zue* [A Graphic Survey of Japan] (1967), p. 342.
6. Data in this paragraph exclude ships of less than 100 gross tons. World totals exclude the USSR and China. Data are from Yano, *A Graphic Survey of Japan,* 1967 edition, p. 342; 1971 edition, p. 349; and 1973 edition, pp. 340–42.

tion. Motorcycle production jumped from 2,600 units in 1950 to 195,500 in 1955, 1,368,000 in 1960, and 2,447,000 in 1966. Though it then tapered off for a time, it rose again to reach 3,565,000 in 1972.[7] Japan displaced France as the largest motorcycle manufacturer. One of every twelve Japanese owned a motorcycle in 1966.

The automotive industry joined the group of growth industries later. Even though domestic markets were completely closed to imports of passenger cars, progress was slow during the 1950s for two reasons: highway systems and other infrastructures related to automobile traffic were not sufficiently developed, and household incomes were too low to permit the general use of cars. The domestic market did not grow to sufficient size in the 1950s to enable manufacturers of passenger cars to reach production volumes corresponding to break-even points.

In the early sixties the situation changed completely. The government stepped up spending for highways and related facilities. Use of advancing technology enabled Japanese automobile producers to cut prices while consumer incomes were rising sharply, and car ownership came within the reach of many people. Although trade restrictions on foreign cars were somewhat liberalized in the mid-1960s, tariffs on imported cars remained very high. Moreover, the Japanese automotive industry was by then so well established that foreign auto makers would have found the Japanese market hard to penetrate even in the absence of protection. Indeed, with their competitive position sharpened by cheap labor, technical competence, and economies of large-scale production, the Japanese car manufacturers wedged into markets abroad.

Passenger car production in Japan grew more than 155-fold from 1955 to 1970, truck production 46-fold, and bus production about 9-fold. Since 1967 Japan has ranked as the second largest producer in the world, second only to the United States. In 1972 annual production exceeded 4 million passenger cars, more than one-seventh of total world production.

Equipping a nation of 100 million with modern household appliances for the first time, when accomplished in two decades or less, creates a huge market. This happened in Japan. In the mid-1950s hardly anyone owned electric cleaners, electric washers, electric refrigerators, or television sets; in the 1970s, nearly everyone did. The speed with which domestic markets for these products moved from original equipment toward dependence on replacement is indicated by the fact that from 1964 to 1971 alone the percentage of households with electric washers jumped from 61 to 94, with electric

7. Data in this and the several following paragraphs are from Yano, *A Graphic Survey of Japan,* 1973 edition, chapter 37, unless otherwise indicated.

refrigerators from 38 to 91, and with electric cleaners from 27 to 74.[8] The percentage with television sets had passed 90 by the mid-1960s. From 1955 to 1972 production of electric washers went from 461,000 to 4,204,000, of electric refrigerators from 31,000 to 3,454,000, of electric cleaners from 51,000 to 3,972,000, and of television sets from 137,000 to 13,035,000. Growth of transistor radios, cameras, sewing machines, and watches was no less outstanding. By 1967 Japan was the world's largest producer of television sets, radios, cameras, and sewing machines, and held or was approaching second place in washers, refrigerators, cleaners, and watches.

The enormous growth of the sales of these products stemmed from the increasing affluence of the Japanese and the cost saving and consequent price reductions made possible by sharply rising volume. Sales promotion through the mass media, patterned closely on American techniques, had a bandwagon effect, helping to shift consumption patterns toward consumer durables. With so favorable a home market as a base and aided by low wages at prevailing exchange rates, producers were able to reinforce growth by penetrating foreign markets, especially for television sets.

Such examples illustrate the breadth as well as the almost incredible tempo of growth in the machinery industries. We need add only that private purchases of producers' durables and nonresidential construction, which consist in important part of products of other branches of the machinery industries, jumped, when measured in 1965 prices, from ¥1.1 billion in 1953 to ¥5.1 billion in 1965 and ¥14.0 billion in 1972.[9]

Since the machinery industries are large users of steel, and such other steel-using industries as construction were also booming, swiftly rising demand for steel was assured. It was met by domestic production despite Japan's poor endowment of iron ore, coke, and, initially, scrap. Technological innovations so improved the competitive position of Japanese steel mills that they not only precluded foreign steel from Japanese markets but even made large inroads into foreign markets. Continuous improvements in marine transport facilities reduced transportation costs, and raw materials were brought from such distant sources as India, Malaysia, Chile, Canada, and the United

8. National Life Research Institution, *Kokumin seikatsu tōkei nenpō* [Annual Statistical Report on National Standards of Living] (1970), pp. 120–21, and 1973 edition, pp. 98–99.

9. These estimates are from the Economic Planning Agency's national income statistics. Production data for a wide variety of types of industrial and electrical machinery are also available. Scanning series for even a brief period (the years 1966 through 1970 are shown in Bureau of Statistics, Office of the Prime Minister, *Japan Statistical Yearbook, 1971* [1972], pp. 200–07) conveys an impression of extremely quick and general expansion.

States.[10] Steel ingot production leaped from 7.7 million tons in 1953—just equal to the previous peak in 1943—to 16 million in 1959, 28 million in 1961, 62 million in 1967, and 97 million in 1972. Since 1964 Japan has been the third largest manufacturer (after the United States and the USSR).

Petroleum refining is another large and fast-growing industry that is almost entirely dependent on imported raw material and in which Japan has stood third to the United States and the Soviet Union since 1964 (though with a far wider gap than in steel). Some 99.6 percent of the crude oil consumed in Japan in 1971 was imported; this compares with 79.1 percent in 1935, 82.5 percent in 1950, and 99.1 percent in 1965.[11] Thriving on the growing demand for them for industrial use, electric power generation, house heating, and motorists' needs, petroleum and coal products grew at an annual rate of 17.9 percent from 1953 to 1971 (see table 3-1).

As in other countries, chemicals developed into a leading growth industry. Heavy industries greatly increased their consumption of basic chemical compounds such as sulphuric acid, caustic soda, soda ash, and dyes. Organic chemical products, especially petroleum chemicals, have been gradually replacing the nonorganic chemicals in importance.

The textile, paper and pulp, and rubber industries grew less than the average for all manufacturing. But by standards in other parts of the world the growth rates of 9 to almost 12 percent in these industries are high.

Other Industries

Nonmanufacturing industries have of course shared in growth; indeed, most seem to have expanded output at a high rate. The volume of goods handled by retailers increased by perhaps 10.5 percent a year from 1954 to 1970, and wholesale trade by over 11 percent.[12] The general pattern in con-

10. In 1971 imports represented 98 percent of total domestic consumption of iron ore, 7 percent of scrap, and 81 percent of coke. See Yano, *A Graphic Survey of Japan,* 1973 edition, p. 277.

11. Yano, *A Graphic Survey of Japan,* 1973 edition, p. 299.

12. The rates cited are growth rates of retail and wholesale sales deflated by the implicit deflator for household expenditures, exclusive of "fuel and light" and "housing." (Sales data are from Census of Wholesale and Retail Trade as reported in Bureau of Statistics, *Japan Statistical Yearbook, 1961,* p. 229, and *1972,* p. 284; the implicit deflator is computed from Economic Planning Agency estimates of consumption in current and constant prices.) Wholesale sales increased more than retail sales, as would be expected since other GNP commodity components grew more than consumption. EPA estimates of "value added" in commerce, measured in 1965 prices, grew even more— 13 percent a year.

struction, electric power, and most branches of transportation, communication, finance, and service industries was one of buoyant expansion. Exceptions were the primary industries—agriculture, lumbering and forestry, fisheries, and mining—in which growth of output was slow after the initial recovery from immediate postwar disruption. Output of all but fisheries seems actually to have turned downward in the late 1960s.

Measurement of National Income

Our main concern is with the growth of output in the economy as a whole —specifically, of national income—and the changes that produced this growth. National income, which is also called "the net national product valued at factor cost," is a measure of the net output of goods and services produced by the nation's economy. It differs conceptually from "net national product valued at market prices" only in that each component of output is valued by the factor cost of producing it rather than by its market price.

The factor cost of a product—the earnings of labor and property derived from its production—differs from its market price in two ways: indirect business taxes incorporated in its market price are eliminated whereas subsidies (which are not part of its market price) are included. Factor cost valuation is, in principle, a little more convenient than market price valuation for analysis of productivity changes. If the earnings of resources are the same in all activities, a mere shift in the allocation of resources from a lightly taxed to a heavily taxed commodity (or from a subsidized to an unsubsidized one) raises the real product at market prices whereas such a shift leaves product at factor cost unchanged. Analysis of a market price measure of net output would necessitate adding a purely statistical "source" of growth to represent the effect upon the market price series of shifts in the composition of output between lightly and heavily taxed or subsidized commodities. The contribution of these shifts, which may be positive or negative, would be the difference between the growth rates of the two measures.[13]

For data we rely on the Economic Research Institute of the Economic Planning Agency of Japan.[14] However, we have of necessity made our own

13. Table 3-3, column 1, and table C-3, column 1, provide statistically comparable estimates of national income at factor cost and net national product at market prices, both valued in 1965 prices.

14. Specifically the principal sources were *Annual Report on National Income Statistics, 1973* (1973), *Revised Report on National Income Statistics, 1951–1967* (1969), *Shōwa 40-nen. Kaitei kokumin shotoku tōkei (Suikei shiryōshū)* [Sourcebook of Revised National Income Statistics, Base Year 1965] (1970), and EPA worksheets.

estimates for some details in order to fill gaps in the EPA data. We have also adjusted series to improve comparability with those for the United States and other Western countries.

Table 3-2 shows national income in current prices, table 3-3, national income measured in constant prices of 1965. In these tables total national income is divided among three small sectors and one large sector. Each of the small (or "special") sectors has the characteristic that measured output results from use of only one factor of production.

National income originating in the largest of the three special sectors con-

Table 3-2. *National Income in Current Prices, by Sector and Industrial Branch, 1952–71*

Billions of yen

			National income originating in				
		General government, households,			*Nonresidential business*		
Calen-dar year	*Total national income* (1)	*institutions, and foreign governments* (2)	*Services of dwellings* (3)	*Inter-national assets* (4)	*Total* (5)	*Agricul-ture* (6)	*Nonagri-cultural industries* (7)
1952	5,019	519	119	−2	4,383	861	3,522
1953	5,850	627	161	−8	5,070	858	4,212
1954	6,576	709	199	−14	5,682	1,042	4,640
1955	7,124	764	244	−15	6,131	1,252	4,879
1956	7,870	808	278	−14	6,798	1,152	5,646
1957	9,230	875	323	−18	8,050	1,216	6,834
1958	9,582	934	372	−14	8,290	1,216	7,074
1959	10,610	1,004	471	−13	9,148	1,295	7,853
1960	12,850	1,145	553	−12	11,164	1,343	9,821
1961	15,204	1,373	640	−17	13,208	1,445	11,763
1962	17,393	1,623	744	−33	15,059	1,603	13,456
1963	19,954	1,939	862	−43	17,196	1,746	15,450
1964	22,859	2,300	1,074	−70	19,555	1,835	17,720
1965	25,620	2,741	1,300	−68	21,647	2,115	19,532
1966	29,450	3,143	1,520	−67	24,854	2,397	22,457
1967	35,065	3,537	1,727	−64	29,865	2,954	26,911
1968	41,717	4,071	1,957	−91	35,780	3,135	32,645
1969	48,210	4,716	2,236	−103	41,361	3,158	38,203
1970	57,520	5,638	2,592	−75	49,365	3,293	46,072
1971	64,326	6,628	3,084	−17	54,631	3,081	51,550

Sources: Columns 1 and 6, see text and appendix B for derivation; column 2, table A-1, column 1, plus table A-2, columns 1–3; column 3, table A-4, column 8; column 4, table A-3, column 3; column 5, column 1 minus columns 2, 3, and 4; column 7, column 5 minus column 6.

Table 3-3. *National Income in Constant Prices, by Sector and Industrial Branch, 1952–71*

Billions of 1965 yen

							National income originating in		
	Total national income		General government, households, institutions, and foreign governments				Nonresidential business		
Calendar year	Japanese deflation procedures (1)	U.S. deflation procedures[a] (2)	Japanese deflation procedures (3)	U.S. deflation procedures[a] (4)	Services of dwellings (5)	International assets (6)	Total (7)	Agriculture (8)	Nonagricultural industries (9)
1952	8,907	9,446	1,594	2,133	636	−1	6,678	1,400	5,278
1953	9,667	10,170	1,638	2,141	672	−7	7,364	1,497	5,867
1954	10,372	10,855	1,680	2,163	720	−12	7,984	1,714	6,270
1955	11,210	11,705	1,713	2,208	742	−12	8,767	2,150	6,617
1956	11,838	12,313	1,718	2,193	760	−11	9,371	1,962	7,409
1957	13,083	13,533	1,720	2,170	801	−14	10,576	2,026	8,550
1958	13,780	14,136	1,764	2,120	879	−13	11,150	2,116	9,034
1959	14,912	15,233	1,825	2,146	982	−13	12,118	2,327	9,791
1960	16,989	17,305	1,879	2,195	1,023	−12	14,099	2,242	11,857
1961	18,770	19,007	2,037	2,274	1,125	−16	15,624	2,210	13,414
1962	20,418	20,617	2,193	2,392	1,163	−33	17,095	2,208	14,887
1963	22,234	22,370	2,377	2,513	1,192	−41	18,706	2,060	16,646
1964	24,340	24,434	2,549	2,643	1,235	−68	20,624	2,102	18,522
1965	25,613	25,613	2,734	2,734	1,300	−68	21,647	2,115	19,532
1966	28,009	27,900	2,908	2,799	1,367	−65	23,799	2,185	21,614
1967	31,798	31,607	3,050	2,859	1,451	−63	27,360	2,455	24,905
1968	36,141	35,840	3,217	2,916	1,575	−89	31,438	2,502	28,936
1969	40,030	39,596	3,409	2,975	1,674	−98	35,045	2,375	32,670
1970	44,424	43,848	3,605	3,029	1,774	−72	39,117	2,216	36,901
1971	46,907	46,193	3,798	3,084	1,926	−21	41,204	1,987	39,217

Sources: Column 1, sum of columns 3, 5, 6, and 7; column 2, sum of columns 4, 5, 6, and 7; column 3, sum of table A-1, column 2, and table A-2, columns 4, 5, and 6; column 4, see appendix C; column 5, table A-4, column 14; column 6, table A-3, column 7; column 7, sum of columns 8 and 9; columns 8 and 9, 1965 values in current prices, from table 3-2, extrapolated by corresponding values of net national product in constant prices, from table C-3, columns 4 and 5 (see appendix C for explanation).

a. U.S. deflation procedures differ from Japanese only in general government, households, institutions, and foreign governments. For each component of this sector, 1965 national income in current prices was extrapolated by employment.

sists of the output of employees of general government, private households, nonprofit institutions, and foreign governments.[15] In current prices, the value of national income originating in this sector is simply the compensation of employees of these entities, which employ all labor that is not used in the business sector.

Dwellings represent a large fraction of the capital stock. They contribute to the value of output by providing services to their occupants. National income originating in the "services of dwellings" sector measures the net contribution that the stock of dwellings makes to the national income. It consists

15. The "foreign governments" component is confined to Japanese employed in Japan by foreign governments. Japanese employees of the U.S. armed forces are the main component. See appendix A for estimates.

of property income (monetary and imputed) derived from dwellings. Put differently, it is the gross rental value of occupied dwellings minus all expenses (including depreciation) except property income. Thus it measures the value of the net output of dwellings and their sites.

National income originating in the "international assets" sector consists of investment income received from abroad less investment income paid to abroad; for Japan it is negative in all years.

All other national income originates in nonresidential business. It consists of production by enterprises that sell their products at a price, other than the "value added" of dwellings. Government enterprises such as postal, telephone, and electric services and government-operated railroads are included. The tables divide national income originating in nonresidential business between agriculture and nonagricultural industries. Forestry (except general government activities) and fisheries, industries of some importance in Japan, are classified as nonagricultural industries within nonresidential business.

Nearly all the data needed to construct the current price series which are shown in Table 3-2 were available from the EPA. The main exception was compensation of employees of private nonprofit institutions in the fields of health and education, which the EPA does not isolate and we estimated in order to obtain estimates by sector. Total national income, which equals net domestic product at factor cost plus net factor income received from abroad, scarcely differs from the EPA series.[16] Appendixes A and B describe the estimates in detail.

The only series in constant prices that the EPA publishes is gross national product at market prices. That series is obtained by deflating a current price GNP series that is estimated as the sum of expenditures (i.e., from the product side of the national accounts). We replaced it with a series obtained by applying the same deflator to the current price GNP series that is obtained as the sum of EPA estimates of income and other charges against GNP (i.e., from the income side of the national accounts). The series are conceptually identical but statistically different. Of the two we believe that the series from the income side is the more nearly consistent with employment data and hence with our total input series, and that its use consequently yields a more accurate series for output per unit of input. Its use also preserves statistical consistency with national income in current prices. This GNP series was then divided among the sectors and between agricultural and nonagricultural nonresidential business. Capital consumption in current prices, as estimated by the EPA, was deflated and the resulting estimates for each sector and for

16. The only difference is the coverage of net factor income from abroad; see p. 143.

agricultural and nonagricultural residential business were deducted from GNP to secure net national product at market prices. The three special sectors, agriculture, and nonagricultural nonresidential business were then reweighted with 1965 factor cost weights to secure national income in 1965 prices. More detailed reweighting would have been desirable but the necessary data were unavailable. Appendixes A and C fully describe the constant price series. Appendix C also provides series for GNP and net national product (NNP) at constant market prices for each sector.

Columns 1 and 2 of table 3-3 show alternative series for national income in constant prices; the difference is in general government, households, institutions, and foreign governments. The output of this sector in current prices is valued by employee compensation in both the United States and Japan but the two countries use different procedures to measure output in constant prices. In the United States and most other countries the current price estimates are deflated by series for average compensation of employees to secure constant price series—or, equivalently, base year expenditures are simply extrapolated by employment. We have applied this method to secure the estimates shown in table 3-3 as "based on U.S. deflation procedures."[17] The series shown as "based on Japanese deflation procedures" is our estimate of the corresponding amount that the EPA includes in its constant price series for Japan.[18] This series and each of its components rise more than the corresponding series based on U.S. deflation procedures.[19]

The series based on U.S. deflation procedures will be emphasized not because we prefer them in all respects—we do not—but because we wish to

17. Six components were treated separately (see p. 156). "U.S. deflation procedures" refers to procedures in use in the United States before the revision in the U.S. national income and product accounts introduced by the U.S. Department of Commerce in the January 1976 issue of *Survey of Current Business*.

18. Estimation was necessary because the EPA does not deflate all components separately. See appendix A. Note that GNP and national income are the same in this sector.

19. In general government the compensation of employees is deflated by the weighted average of indexes of the pay of employees in certain grades that are based on education and experience. This fixed-weight index rises less than the average earnings of all employees of general government combined because of shifts in employment composition toward the higher pay grades. Thus real output rises more than when average earnings are used as the deflator. The series for the compensation of employees of private households and of various types of private nonprofit institutions are deflated by price indexes for consumer goods and services. This procedure ascribes to persons employed by households and institutions increases in output per worker roughly similar to those achieved in the production of the goods and services whose price indexes are selected. Finally, the compensation of employees of foreign governments is deflated by the price of exports, which has changed little in comparison with the increases experienced in average pay, so output rises much more than employment.

compare Japanese growth and its sources with experience in other countries.

Isolating general government, households, institutions, and foreign governments permits one to state immediately the amount of the increase in total national income, measured by either procedure, that was created by the addition to labor employed by this sector. From 1961 to 1971, for example, such labor contributed ¥810 billion, or 3 percent, of the ¥27,186 billion increase in national income in 1965 prices that is obtained by U.S. deflation procedures. Similarly, national income originating in the "services of dwellings" sector measures the contribution that was made by residential capital and land to the increase in total national income in 1965 prices. From 1961 to 1971 this contribution was ¥801 billion, or 3 percent of the total increase. The third small sector, "international assets," consists of the excess of the deflated value of receipts of property income from abroad over payments of property income to foreigners, a series which has been persistently negative. From 1961 to 1971 it declined by ¥5 billion, −0.02 percent of the total change in constant price national income.

The rest of national income originates in the "nonresidential business" sector. This sector consists almost entirely of enterprises that buy and sell for a price and whose output consequently can be measured by market transactions. It accounted for 89 percent of 1971 national income measured in 1965 prices, and for 94 percent of the increase in national income from 1961 to 1971. The main task of growth analysis is to distribute the growth of output in this sector among its sources.

Measurement of Employment and Output per Worker

Table 3-4 shows our estimates of employment, classified by sector and also by class of worker. Tables 3-3 and 3-4 together permit the calculation of national income per person employed. Appendix D describes the detailed derivation of employment estimates; we describe them here in a more general fashion.

In Japan, as in most other countries, employment data have been collected and processed by various agencies and individuals, and the analyst must choose from among alternative sources. Our first consideration is to secure maximum statistical consistency between our employment and output series. This dictates use of employment estimates prepared and published by the Economic Planning Agency as part of the estimation process that also yields the compensation of employees component of the EPA national income series. The EPA employment estimates, however, cover only wage and salary

Table 3-4. *Employment by Sector, Industrial Branch, and Class of Worker, 1952–71*
Thousands

			Nonresidential business					
				Nonagricultural industries				Addendum:
		General government, households, institutions,				Wage and	Self-employed and	nonagricultural
Calendar year (1)	Total employment (2)	and foreign governments (2)	Total (3)	Agriculture (4)	Total (5)	salary workers (6)	family workers (7)	wage and salary workers[a] (8)
1952	37,199	3,033	34,166	13,394	20,772	12,739	8,033	15,772
1953	39,376	3,068	36,308	14,035	22,273	13,411	8,862	16,479
1954	39,862	3,120	36,742	13,695	23,047	13,798	9,249	16,918
1955	41,047	3,196	37,851	14,046	23,805	14,392	9,413	17,588
1956	41,715	3,180	38,535	13,615	24,920	15,553	9,367	18,733
1957	42,778	3,152	39,626	13,160	26,466	16,925	9,541	20,077
1958	43,000	3,078	39,922	12,709	27,213	18,059	9,154	21,137
1959	43,273	3,112	40,161	12,072	28,089	18,947	9,142	22,059
1960	44,345	3,175	41,170	11,959	29,211	20,053	9,158	23,228
1961	44,640	3,266	41,374	11,630	29,744	20,848	8,896	24,114
1962	45,381	3,407	41,974	11,337	30,637	22,035	8,602	25,442
1963	45,824	3,547	42,277	10,720	31,557	22,808	8,749	26,355
1964	46,517	3,695	42,822	10,312	32,510	23,669	8,841	27,364
1965	47,453	3,795	43,658	9,900	33,758	24,883	8,875	28,678
1966	48,528	3,889	44,639	9,544	35,095	26,101	8,994	29,990
1967	49,545	3,966	45,579	9,290	36,289	26,889	9,400	30,855
1968	50,365	4,041	46,324	9,077	37,247	27,639	9,608	31,680
1969	50,757	4,118	46,639	8,787	37,852	28,104	9,748	32,222
1970	51,289	4,183	47,106	8,242	38,864	29,121	9,743	33,304
1971	51,421	4,253	47,168	7,509	39,659	29,998	9,661	34,251

Sources: See appendix D.
a. Sum of columns 2 and 6.

workers and even for this group exclude persons employed in agriculture, forestry, and fisheries as well as Japanese employed by foreign governments. We have used data from the Labor Force Survey (conducted by the Bureau of Statistics of the Office of the Prime Minister and similar to the Current Population Survey in the United States) for employment not covered by the EPA series.[20] To divide total wage and salary employment between the sec-

20. For 1952 the estimate for wage and salary workers was also based on the labor force series because EPA data were not available. Questions and procedures used in the Labor Force Survey have been changed from time to time. The series used here has been adjusted to conform to the labor force series published since 1967.

Table 3-5. *Selected Growth Rates, 1953–71*

Percent per year

Item	Total national income			Employment			National income per person employed		
	1953–71	1953–61	1961–71	1953–71	1953–61	1961–71	1953–71	1953–61	1961–71
Japanese deflation procedures									
Whole economy	9.17	8.65	9.59	1.49	1.58	1.42	7.56	6.96	8.05
United States deflation procedures									
Whole economy	8.77	8.13	9.29	1.49	1.58	1.42	7.17	6.45	7.75
Nonresidential business	10.04	9.86	10.18	1.46	1.65	1.32	8.45	8.08	8.75
Agriculture	1.59	4.99	−1.06	−3.42	−2.32	−4.28	5.18	7.49	3.37
Nonagricultural industries	11.13	10.89	11.32	3.26	3.68	2.92	7.63	6.95	8.17
Wage and salary workers	...	...	...	4.57	5.67	3.71	...	...	...
Self-employed and unpaid family workers	...	...	...	0.48	0.05	0.83	...	...	...

Source: Computed from tables 3-3 and 3-4.

tors, our own estimates (described in appendix A) were used for general government, households, institutions, and foreign governments.

Estimates of employment in 1952, and especially the composition of employment in that year, are very uncertain.

Growth Rates

We shall focus on growth from 1953 to 1971 and in the subperiods 1953–61 and 1961–71.[21] It was probably in 1953 that national income first exceeded the prewar peak. The decade for which the Ikeda administration announced the target of doubling national income started in 1961, and that year subdivides the postwar period as well as any other, though perhaps no better than 1960. We end with 1971 because it was the last year for which detailed national accounting information could be obtained when we undertook the project.[22]

Table 3-5 shows the principal growth rates for these periods, which can be computed from tables 3-3 and 3-4. We are chiefly concerned with explaining the high rates for total national income growth in the whole economy based on U.S. deflation procedures—8.8 percent over the whole period, 8.1 percent in 1953–61 and 9.3 percent in 1961–71—and with the even higher rates for total national income originating in the nonresidential business sector, which approximate 10 percent in all these periods.[23]

21. However, estimates for 1952 are shown in all annual tables. They are less reliable than those for later years.

22. Use of 1970, 1972, or 1973 as the terminal year would yield growth rates that are slightly higher because 1971 was a year of moderate recession. Use of 1974 or 1975, when recession was deeper than in 1971, would yield lower rates.

23. Growth rates for the whole economy are lower than those usually quoted; the latter are based on GNP measured from the expenditure side of the accounts and deflated according to Japanese procedures. The growth rate of GNP, as published in the Japanese national accounts, was 10.15 percent from 1961 to 1971. In this particular period estimates from the income side of the accounts yield a still higher rate for GNP, 10.46 percent. (The direction of difference between the growth rates of these two series varies with the particular years compared.) This rate is lowered to 9.74 percent by deducting depreciation, to 9.59 percent by using factor cost weighting, and finally to 9.29 percent by substituting U.S. for Japanese deflation procedures. Appendix C provides continuous series for various output measures.

CHAPTER FOUR

Estimates of the Sources of Growth

THE SIZE of any nation's output is governed by many determinants, and changes in these determinants cause its output to change. Analysis of the sources of growth seeks to measure the size of the contribution to the growth rate of the national income made by changes in each determinant. Techniques for preparing such estimates were developed by one of us in three studies of Western nations, and previously applied by the other to Japanese experience.[1] The estimates presented here for Japan are wholly new.[2] In

---

1. Edward F. Denison, *The Sources of Economic Growth in the United States and the Alternatives Before Us,* CED Supplementary Paper 13 (Committee for Economic Development, 1962), *Why Growth Rates Differ,* and *Accounting for Growth;* and William K. Chung, "Study of Economic Growth in Postwar Japan for the Period of 1952–1967: An Application of Total Productivity Analysis" (Ph.D. dissertation, New School for Social Research, New York, 1971).

2. Previous investigations were of course consulted. Especially worthy of mention are detailed estimates of the contributions of inputs, and of output per unit of input as a whole, by Hisao Kanamori, "What Accounts for Japan's High Rate of Growth?" *Review of Income and Wealth,* Series 18 (June 1972), pp. 155–71, and unpublished supplementary "Explanation of Estimation"; estimates of growth sources in manufacturing and the whole economy by Tsunehiko Watanabe and F. Egaizu, "Gijutsu shinpo to keizai seichō" [Technological Advance and Economic Growth] in Motoo Kaji, ed., *Keizai seichō to shigen bunpai* [Economic Growth and Resource Allocation] (Iwanami Shoten, 1967), pp. 121–51, esp. p. 130; estimates of the contribution of labor input by Tsunehiko Watanabe, "Improvement of Labor Quality and Economic Growth—Japan's Postwar Experience," *Economic Development and Cultural Change,* vol. 21 (October 1972), pp. 33–53 (estimates by Watanabe and Egaizu from the Japanese-language *Economic Studies Quarterly* of March 1968 are included); and analysis by Kazushi Ohkawa and Henry Rosovsky, *Japanese Economic Growth: Trend Acceleration in the Twentieth Century* (Stanford University Press, 1973), much of which is along similar lines though results are not presented in the form of sources of growth tables. Our main

derivation and presentation they follow very closely those provided for the United States in *Accounting for Growth*.

Several tables that will be used to analyze the Japanese experience are introduced here. Some are needed for estimates of the sources of growth, others provide the estimates themselves, and the remainder compare the sources of growth in Japan and other countries.

Income Shares

Table 4-1 provides percentage distributions of the national income earned in nonresidential business among the classical factors of production—labor, reproducible capital, and land; earnings of capital are divided between inventories and nonresidential structures and equipment. No attempt was made to isolate returns to risk or entrepreneurship or other forms of "pure profit"; such income is included in the earnings of capital and land. The derivation of these estimates is fully described in appendix E and summarized here without qualifications.

Labor earnings consist of all compensation of employees in nonresidential business together with 68.3 percent of agricultural proprietors' income and 89.2 percent of nonagricultural proprietors' income. These percentages of proprietors' income result from the assumption (applied separately for agriculture and nonagricultural industries) that the earnings of labor provided by proprietors' and unpaid family workers fell short of the average earnings of paid labor in the whole economy by the same percentage that earnings of capital and land used by unincorporated enterprises fell short of the earnings of corporate capital and land. This percentage shortfall is small in nonagricultural proprietorships but large in agriculture. Estimates of labor earnings in Japan are necessarily affected appreciably by the procedure used to allocate proprietors' income because proprietors' income is large.[3]

Nonlabor earnings in each of three parts of nonresidential business (agriculture, nonagricultural corporations, and nonagricultural proprietorships) were allocated among nonresidential structures and equipment, inventories,

---

results and those of these writers seem to be broadly consistent where we estimate the contributions of the same determinants. However, see also p. 85, note 2, and pp. 229–34 with respect to gains from the reallocation of resources.

3. We estimate that in 1970 labor earnings represented 71.3 percent and nonlabor earnings 28.7 percent of nonresidential business national income. The unallocated percentages were: compensation of employees, 51.7 percent; proprietors' income, 23.2 percent; and "pure" property shares, 25.1 percent.

Table 4-1. *Percentage Distribution of National Income Originating in Nonresidential Business, by Income Share, 1952–71*

Calendar year	National income[a] (1)	Labor (2)	Nonresidential structures and equipment (3)	Inventories (4)	Land (5)
1952	100.00	79.11	10.08	5.39	5.42
1953	100.00	79.47	10.53	5.77	4.23
1954	100.00	78.02	11.12	6.05	4.81
1955	100.00	79.39	9.66	5.13	5.82
1956	100.00	79.09	10.47	5.66	4.78
1957	100.00	74.88	13.38	7.41	4.33
1958	100.00	76.31	12.44	6.72	4.53
1959	100.00	76.06	12.64	6.71	4.59
1960	100.00	72.08	15.44	8.15	4.33
1961	100.00	71.48	15.95	8.36	4.21
1962	100.00	72.86	15.00	7.74	4.40
1963	100.00	74.33	14.07	7.17	4.43
1964	100.00	74.44	14.04	7.03	4.49
1965	100.00	76.33	12.80	6.29	4.58
1966	100.00	75.52	13.08	6.71	4.69
1967	100.00	73.80	13.44	7.62	5.14
1968	100.00	72.44	14.40	7.92	5.24
1969	100.00	72.07	14.43	8.33	5.17
1970	100.00	71.28	14.82	8.82	5.08
1971	100.00	73.13	13.96	8.32	4.59

Sources: See appendix E.
a. Excludes corporate transfers to households and private nonprofit institutions.

and land in proportion to the value of assets. This procedure assumes that, within each part of the sector, the ratio of earnings to asset values is the same for the various types of asset.

After the data of table 4-1 are smoothed to minimize the effects of business fluctuations (appendix table E-2), they provide weights that are used to combine labor, the two types of capital, and land to obtain a series measuring total factor input in nonresidential business. This choice of weights is based on the proposition that, if a small percentage increase in the number of units of all of the factors would raise the sector's output by x, the same percentage increase in the number of units of any one factor would raise output by x times the share of that factor in total earnings.

The reasoning is as follows. Total earnings of each factor are the product of the number of units of the factor and its price, or earnings, per unit, while the marginal product of each factor is the extra output that would be added by one additional unit of that factor when the quantities of the other factors are held constant. To minimize costs, enterprises must combine factors in such proportions that the marginal products per unit of the several factors are proportional to their prices, or earnings, per unit; this condition is presumed to be satisfied.

The United States is the only other country for which estimates for nonresidential business have been prepared. In two periods the shares compare as follows:

	1952–59		1960–68	
	Japan	United States	Japan	United States
Nonresidential business national income	100.0	100.0	100.0	100.0
Labor	77.8	81.2	73.7	80.2
Nonresidential structures and equipment	11.3	11.1	14.3	11.9
Inventories	6.1	4.2	7.4	4.0
Nonresidential land	4.8	3.5	4.6	3.9

Table 4-2 compares the shares of labor earnings in the whole economies of eleven countries in two time periods. (Neither period is the same for all the countries; in most countries the first ends in 1959, the second in 1964.) In the 1950s Japan had one of the highest labor shares; since 1960 its labor share has been one of the lowest. Up to the time the data stop, at least, Japan is the only country in which the labor share dropped appreciably.

The data for Japan are necessarily crude, if only because of the importance of proprietors' income, a mixed share that must be allocated between labor and property. Our results nevertheless support the general belief that since 1960 the labor share has been lower than in most other countries. Our use of the data implies that it was earnings of capital and land rather than monopoly profit or other elements of pure profit that were correspondingly large. It is the estimated shares of inventories (especially), of dwellings, and of nonresidential land that are relatively high in Japan; that of nonresidential structures and equipment is not exceptional.

Of course, the most striking feature of table 4-2 is the broad similarity of income shares in all countries and both time periods despite large differences in factor proportions and other conditions.[4] Later we shall observe that earnings differentials among groups of workers classified by age, sex, or amount

4. Because table 4-2 refers to the whole economy rather than just nonresidential business, labor shares are considerably affected by the size of the three special sectors, each of which consists entirely of either labor or nonlabor income.

Table 4-2. *Labor Earnings as a Percentage of National Income
for the Whole Economy, by Country, Various Periods, 1950–71*[a]

Country	Period	Labor share	Period	Labor share
Japan	1952–59	77.6	1960–71	72.7
Belgium	1950–59	72.6	1960–64	74.9
Canada	1950–62	77.3	1963–67	78.4
Denmark	1950–59	75.2	1960–62	75.5
France	1950–59	76.8	1960–64	78.6
West Germany	1950–59	73.5	1960–64	74.0
Italy	1950–59	72.0	1960–62	72.0
Netherlands	1950–59	73.8	1960–64	76.1
Norway	1950–59	72.7	1960–64	78.3
United Kingdom	1950–59	77.6	1960–64	78.4
United States	1950–59	79.9	1960–68	79.3

Sources: For Japan, computed from national income by sector in current prices in table 3-2 and from table 4-1; corporate transfers to households and private nonprofit organizations are excluded from national income. For Canada, Dorothy Walters, *Canadian Growth Revisited, 1950–1967*, Staff Study 28 (Economic Council of Canada, 1970), p. 59. For the United States, computed from data underlying Denison, *Accounting for Growth*, tables 3-1 and J-1, pp. 18 and 260. For other countries, computed from data underlying Denison, *Why Growth Rates Differ*, table 4-1, p. 38.

a. Figures given are averages of percentages for the years in the periods shown.

of education also are broadly similar in Japan and advanced Western countries. These earnings differentials will be used as weights to combine groups of workers in our derivation of an index of labor input, because cost minimization implies that the marginal products of different types of workers—as well as of labor as a whole, capital, and land—are proportional to their earnings per unit. Thus reliance on proportionality between earnings and marginal products is a pervasive element in our methodology.

Convention is thought to influence wage patterns in Japan importantly, and to some extent to affect price setting too; this is suspected of introducing a divergence between relative earnings and relative marginal products. If one believed this divergence were sufficiently serious, he might prefer to discard Japanese earning data and substitute as "shadow prices" the earnings and price weights from a country, such as the United States, where the divergence is presumed less severe. United States prices would then be used to estimate the price and wage ratios that would prevail in Japan if the economy were more competitive. Because income shares and earnings weights in the two countries are not so very different, such a substitution would not alter our results greatly. Their similarity to patterns in other countries suggests that insofar as Japanese earnings are set by conventions the conventions tend to codify differentials that would be present in any case.

Indexes of Inputs in Nonresidential Business

Only the barest description of the remaining tables will be provided in this chapter. Their meaning will be amplified in later chapters which discuss the sources of growth substantively. Appendixes describe their derivation and the sources of data.

Table 4-3 shows indexes of labor input in nonresidential business and the

Table 4-3. *Indexes of Sector Labor Input for Nonresidential Business, 1952–71*

1965 = 100

| | | | | | Efficiency of an hour's work as affected by changes in hours due to | | | |
| | | | | Age-sex composi- | | Specified | Amount | |
Calen-dar year (1)	Employ-ment (1)	Average weekly hours (2)	Total weekly hours (3)	tion of total hours (4)	Intra-group changes (5)	inter-group shifts (6)	of educa-tion (7)	Labor input (8)
1952	78.26	99.49	77.86	98.11	97.22	98.81	93.31	68.47
1953	83.16	98.88	82.24	98.24	96.97	98.68	93.81	72.52
1954	84.16	100.46	84.55	98.44	96.29	98.25	94.31	74.26
1955	86.70	99.34	86.12	97.84	96.22	98.25	94.82	75.53
1956	88.27	101.11	89.26	98.18	95.39	98.30	95.33	78.34
1957	90.76	102.63	93.16	98.48	95.28	98.55	95.84	82.56
1958	91.44	102.99	94.18	98.21	95.54	98.69	96.36	84.04
1959	91.99	103.36	95.09	98.44	95.70	98.95	96.88	85.88
1960	94.30	103.68	97.78	99.04	95.62	99.04	97.40	89.33
1961	94.77	103.51	98.10	99.18	96.11	99.87	97.91	91.44
1962	96.14	101.88	97.97	99.07	98.16	99.97	98.43	93.75
1963	96.84	100.90	97.72	99.31	98.94	99.97	98.95	94.98
1964	98.09	101.01	99.07	99.73	99.32	99.98	99.47	97.59
1965	100.00	100.00	100.00	100.00	100.00	100.00	100.00	100.00
1966	102.25	100.19	102.44	100.12	100.02	100.01	100.53	103.14
1967	104.40	101.11	105.57	100.26	99.56	99.77	101.06	106.25
1968	106.11	100.37	106.51	100.61	100.71	99.76	101.59	109.37
1969	106.83	100.43	107.30	101.24	100.93	99.83	102.13	111.78
1970	107.90	99.91	107.82	101.64	101.41	99.87	102.67	113.95
1971	108.04	99.36	107.36	102.12	101.81	99.98	103.22	115.19

Sources: Column 1 is computed from column 3 of table 3-4, column 3 is the product of columns 1 and 2, and column 8 is the product of columns 3 through 7. Columns 2, 4, 5, and 6 are described in appendixes F and G, and column 7 in appendix H.

component series that were multiplied to obtain it.[5] Employment, average hours, and total hours worked are shown in the first three columns; appendixes D, F, and G explain how they were obtained. These series are only the starting point for labor input measurement because the total hours worked by employed persons are not a homogeneous mass. Hours worked by persons in different demographic groups (five age groups are distinguished for each sex) or who have received different amounts of education (ten educational levels are distinguished for each sex) are not considered to represent the same amount of labor input. Rather, the relative amounts of labor contained in an average hour worked by different demographic or education groups are measured as proportional to the average hourly earnings of persons in the groups. This procedure assumes that earnings are proportional to marginal products, as will tend to be the case if employing enterprises seek to minimize their costs. Changes in the average labor input content of an hour worked resulting from changes in the demographic and educational composition of total hours worked are measured by the indexes in columns 4 and 7, respectively. Appendixes G and H describe the sources and methods used to obtain them.

Other columns refer to the effect on output of changes in average hours. As appendix G explains more fully, we consider that a change in the average hours of all workers in nonresidential business combined yields a proportional change in labor input if it results from a shift in the proportion of part-time workers or female workers or from a change in average part-time hours, but not if it is a consequence of two other types of change. First, reductions in the average hours of a homogeneous group of full-time workers tend to raise output per hour, preventing total work done from declining in proportion to the decline in hours; when full-time hours are extremely long, as in most activities in Japan during most of the period covered, the offset may be complete. Column 5 implements our assumptions about the strength of the offset, which are the same as were used in the analysis of U.S. growth.[6]

5. Labor input is the same in nonresidential business as it is in the whole business sector because no labor is classified in the services of dwellings sector, as defined.

6. Full-time workers in nonresidential business were divided among agricultural workers, nonagricultural self-employed and unpaid family workers, and nonagricultural wage and salary workers, and each of these three groups was further divided by sex to secure six full-time groups in all. So long as average weekly hours (as shortened by inclusion of vacation and holiday weeks) exceeded 52.7 for any male group and 49.0 for any female group, changes in average full-time hours were assumed not to affect output per worker. The assumption covered all cases except nonagricultural wage and salary workers after 1967 and, for females only, in two earlier years. Between these levels and levels of 42.7 for males and 39.0 for females, changes in average hours are assumed to be partially offset by changes in work done per hour—almost entirely offset at the upper end of the range, which is all that is observed in Japan, and to only a small extent at the lower end.

Second, column 6 offsets changes in the average hours worked in nonresidential business which result from shifts in the distribution of full-time workers of each sex among nonagricultural wage and salary employment, agricultural employment, and nonagricultural self-employment. Even though their average hours differ, we consider that full-time workers in the three groups provide the same amount of labor input if they work the average numbers of hours for their group and their other characteristics are similar.

Table 4-4 supplements the index of labor input used by nonresidential business with indexes of the sector's inputs (holdings) of inventories, fixed

Table 4-4. *Indexes of Sector National Income, Inputs, and National Income per Unit of Total Factor Input for Nonresidential Business, 1952–71*
1965 = 100

			Indexes of inputs					
Calendar year	Sector national income in 1965 prices (1)	Labor (2)	Inventories (3)	Nonresidential structures and equipment (4)	All reproducible capital (5)	Land (6)	Total factor input (7)	Sector national income per unit of input (8)
1952	30.85	68.47	25.87	38.66	33.49	100.00	59.83	51.56
1953	34.02	72.52	28.31	39.92	35.30	100.00	63.14	53.88
1954	36.88	74.26	29.52	41.52	36.75	100.00	64.74	56.97
1955	40.50	75.53	31.72	43.20	38.68	100.00	66.18	61.20
1956	43.29	78.34	35.78	44.88	41.39	100.00	68.90	62.83
1957	48.86	82.56	41.59	47.37	45.24	100.00	72.91	67.01
1958	51.51	84.04	46.41	50.58	49.07	100.00	75.07	68.62
1959	55.98	85.88	49.72	54.13	52.54	100.00	77.40	72.33
1960	65.13	89.33	54.52	58.72	57.20	100.00	81.18	80.23
1961	72.18	91.44	64.52	65.00	64.82	100.00	84.98	84.94
1962	78.97	93.75	74.00	72.86	73.24	100.00	89.02	88.71
1963	86.41	94.98	80.97	81.60	81.38	100.00	92.07	93.85
1964	95.27	97.59	91.21	90.67	90.85	100.00	96.22	99.01
1965	100.00	100.00	100.00	100.00	100.00	100.00	100.00	100.00
1966	109.94	103.14	107.66	109.38	108.79	100.00	104.15	105.56
1967	126.39	106.25	121.85	120.26	120.83	100.00	108.78	116.19
1968	145.23	109.37	142.08	134.30	137.06	100.00	114.16	127.22
1969	161.89	111.78	162.87	151.52	155.53	100.00	119.40	135.59
1970	180.70	113.95	189.01	172.46	178.29	100.00	125.03	144.52
1971	190.35	115.19	213.74	195.48	201.92	100.00	129.80	146.65

Sources: Column 1 is computed from column 7, table 3-3. Column 2 is column 8, table 4-3. Columns 3 and 4 are described in appendix I. Column 5 is the weighted average of columns 3 and 4. Column 6 is estimated not to have changed. Column 7 is the weighted average of columns 2, 3, 4, and 6. Column 8 is column 1 divided by column 7. Weights used to construct columns 5 and 7 appear in table E-2. See text for method of calculation.

Table 4-5. Indexes of Sector Output per Unit of Input, Nonresidential Business, 1952–71

1965 = 100

Calendar year	Output per unit of input (1)	Gains from reallocation of resources from		Reduction of international trade barriers (4)	Effects of irregular factors			Economies of scale		Advances in knowledge and n.e.c.[a] (10)
		Farming (2)	Nonfarm self-employment (3)		Effect of weather on farm output (5)	Changes in intensity of utilization of employed resources resulting from		With output measured in U.S. prices (8)	Associated with income elasticities (9)	
						Work stoppages (6)	Fluctuations in intensity of demand (7)			
1952	51.56	89.95	94.81	99.97	99.99	99.97	104.68	86.30	86.36	77.55
1953	53.88	90.59	94.49	99.97	98.87	100.00	105.04	87.27	88.04	78.91
1954	56.97	91.13	94.44	99.97	99.94	100.00	105.36	88.17	88.82	80.30
1955	61.20	91.49	94.76	99.97	103.62	100.00	104.79	89.33	89.10	81.70
1956	62.83	92.61	95.57	99.97	99.97	100.00	105.05	89.99	90.37	83.14
1957	67.01	93.75	96.12	99.97	99.47	100.00	105.81	91.43	91.37	84.60
1958	68.62	94.61	97.04	99.97	100.15	100.00	101.53	91.89	92.94	86.09
1959	72.33	95.79	97.47	99.97	101.51	100.00	100.46	92.93	93.34	87.60

Year										
1960	80.23	96.32	97.99	99.97	100.46	100.00	105.29	94.73	95.19	89.14
1961	84.94	96.75	98.45	99.97	100.31	100.00	105.72	95.92	96.66	90.72
1962	88.71	97.33	99.11	99.97	100.57	100.00	104.77	97.05	97.45	92.32
1963	93.85	98.36	99.27	99.98	99.89	100.01	105.01	98.09	98.88	94.48
1964	99.01	99.13	99.51	99.99	100.16	100.00	103.68	99.29	100.16	97.20
1965	100.00	100.00	100.00	100.00	100.00	100.00	100.00	100.00	100.00	100.00
1966	105.56	100.67	100.31	100.01	99.95	100.01	99.62	101.25	100.77	102.87
1967	116.19	101.16	100.07	100.02	100.79	100.01	102.06	103.11	102.22	105.83
1968	127.22	101.71	99.94	100.03	100.81	100.01	105.25	105.11	103.04	108.86
1969	135.59	102.04	99.94	100.06	100.51	100.00	106.32	106.60	104.16	111.99
1970	144.52	102.76	100.20	100.09	100.26	100.00	106.72	108.14	105.21	115.20
1971	146.65	103.67	100.58	100.12	99.90	100.00	103.03	108.86	105.80	118.50

Sources: Column 1 is column 8 from table 4-4. Columns 2 through 4 are described in appendix J, columns 5 and 6 in appendix K, columns 7 and 10 in appendix M, and columns 8 and 9 in appendix L.

a. Not elsewhere classified.

capital (the index is a weighted average of gross and net stock, with gross stock given three-fourths of the weight), and land.[7] The inventory and gross fixed capital stock series, which are described and discussed in appendix I, are based on data from the Economic Planning Agency. The quantity of land available for use is estimated not to have changed. Total factor input is a weighted index (based on income share weights, with weights changed in each pair of years) of the series for labor, capital, and land. The table also shows the index of output (as measured by sector national income) per unit of factor input.

Indexes of Determinants of Output per Unit of Input

There are many determinants of output per unit of input. Table 4-5 shows indexes for the effects of these determinants, which are classified in nine categories. These indexes are measured on a scale such that a difference of, say, 1 percent in the value of an index in any year would change total national income in nonresidential business by an estimated 1 percent. The meaning of the individual series, insofar as it is not self-evident, is explained in later chapters as well as in appendixes J to M. The appendixes also describe the derivation of the data.[8]

7. Inventories and fixed capital held by government enterprises are deliberately omitted. With the capital stock of government enterprises increasing less than the stock of private firms, and their earnings close to zero, omission of their stock is necessary to avoid understating the contribution of capital to the growth rate. The situation in Japan is nearly the same as that in the United States (where earnings of government enterprises are simply omitted from national income); the problem is discussed in *Accounting for Growth*, pp. 273–74.

8. It may be useful to compare table 4-5 with the corresponding table, 6-1, in *Accounting for Growth*. Columns 2, 3, 5, and 6 were obtained by procedures similar to those followed for the corresponding series in the U.S. estimates. Column 9, which has no U.S. counterpart, was secured by a procedure similar to that for European countries described in *Why Growth Rates Differ*, pp. 243–45. The derivation of column 8 has elements of the methodology from both of these previous studies. Column 4 is a judgmental series.

Columns 7 and 10 are obtained by a different procedure than in earlier studies. As is well known, there are notable swings in output per unit of input as a result of changes in the intensity of use of employed resources stemming from fluctuations in the intensity of demand. In the case of the U.S. estimates, an index for the effects of such fluctuations (corresponding definitionally to column 7 of table 4-5) was independently estimated. The index of the effects of the incorporation of advances in knowledge into production together with those of miscellaneous unmeasured determinants (corresponding definitionally to column 10 of table 4-5) was obtained by division of output per unit of input by all the other components (that is, as the residual). For Japan, an index of the joint effects of the determinants covered by columns 7 and 10 was secured by dividing

Sources of Growth in Japan

Table 4-6 provides estimates of the sources of growth of national income in the nonresidential business sector and in the economy as a whole. Using growth rates and the contribution of each determinant to the growth rate to present results in such tables has a number of advantages, one of which is the possibility of comparing periods of different lengths. The contribution of each determinant is the estimated amount by which the growth rate would have been lowered if there had been no change in that determinant while all others changed as they did.[9]

The estimates for nonresidential business in table 4-6 are obtained by dividing the growth rate of output (from table 3-5) between total factor input and total output per unit of input in proportion to their growth rates (calculated from table 4-4); dividing the contribution of total output per unit of input among its determinants in proportion to the growth rates of the nine individual component indexes (calculated from table 4-5); dividing the contribution of total factor input among labor, inventories, nonresidential structures and equipment, and land in proportion to their contributions to the growth rate of total factor input (roughly, the product of their growth rates, calculable from table 4-4, and their weights, given in table E-2);[10] and, finally, dividing the contribution of labor among its components in proportion to the growth rates of the individual indexes in table 4-3.[11]

Estimates of the sources of growth of national income in the whole economy are easily calculated from those for nonresidential business and the esti-

---

column 1 by columns 2–6, 8, and 9. After studying its behavior, we assumed (1) that the average value of the demand-intensity index (column 7) was the same in three pairs of years: 1952–53, 1962–63, and 1970–71; and (2) that the index for advances in knowledge and n.e.c. grew at a constant rate, equal to the rate from 1952–53 to 1962–63, from the beginning of 1952 to the end of 1962, and thereafter at a constant rate equal to the rate from 1962–63 to 1970–71. These assumptions permitted calculation of column 10, and column 7 was obtained by division. See appendix M for further explanation and comments on the sensitivity of our results to errors in these assumptions.

9. Estimates are computed to two decimal points to avoid rounding discrepancies in further calculations. This practice, of course, has no implications as to accuracy.

10. See appendix E, pp. 175–76, for an exact description.

11. The estimate for each component is slightly higher than would be obtained by simply measuring the contribution of total input, total output per unit of input, and each component of output per unit of input as the growth rate of its index, and each component of input as the product of the growth rate of its index and its average weight (using the labor weight for all labor input components). The sum of such estimates would fall a little short of the actual growth rate because of the statistical interaction terms.

Table 4-6. *Sources of Growth of Actual National Income, Nonresidential Business and Whole Economy, 1953–71*

Growth rates and contributions to growth rates in percentage points

Item	Nonresidential business			Whole economy[a]		
	1953–71 (1)	1953–61 (2)	1961–71 (3)	1953–71 (4)	1953–61 (5)	1961–71 (6)
National income	10.04	9.86	10.18	8.77	8.13	9.29
Total factor input	4.18	3.88	4.43	3.95	3.53	4.35
Labor	1.99	2.30	1.75	1.85	1.91	1.78
Employment	1.14	1.30	0.99	1.14	1.14	1.09
Hours	0.27	0.48	0.14	0.21	0.38	0.11
Average hours	0.02	0.45	−0.31	0.01	0.35	−0.27
Efficiency offset	0.21	−0.09	0.44	0.18	−0.06	0.38
Intergroup shift offset	0.04	0.12	0.01	0.02	0.09	0.00
Age-sex composition	0.17	0.09	0.22	0.14	0.07	0.19
Education	0.41	0.43	0.40	0.34	0.33	0.35
Unallocated	...	...	...	0.02	−0.01	0.04
Capital	2.19	1.58	2.68	2.10	1.62	2.57
Inventories	0.89	0.75	1.00	0.73	0.57	0.86
Nonresidential structures and equipment	1.30	0.83	1.68	1.07	0.64	1.44
Dwellings	...	...	...	0.30	0.42	0.27
International assets	...	...	...	0.00	−0.01	0.00
Land	0.00	0.00	0.00	0.00	0.00	0.00
Output per unit of input	5.86	5.98	5.75	4.82	4.60	4.94
Advances in knowledge and n.e.c.[b]	2.39	1.84	2.83	1.97	1.42	2.43
Improved resource allocation	1.15	1.40	0.95	0.95	1.08	0.82
Contraction of agricultural inputs	0.78	0.87	0.72	0.64	0.67	0.62
Contraction of nonagricultural self-employment	0.36	0.53	0.22	0.30	0.41	0.19
Reduction in international trade barriers	0.01	0.00	0.01	0.01	0.00	0.01
Economies of scale	2.36	2.47	2.28	1.94	1.90	1.96
Measured in U.S. prices	1.29	1.25	1.33	1.06	0.96	1.14
Income elasticities	1.07	1.22	0.95	0.88	0.94	0.82
Irregular factors	−0.04	0.27	−0.31	−0.04	0.20	−0.27
Effect of weather on farming	0.06	0.19	−0.04	0.05	0.14	−0.04
Labor disputes	0.00	0.00	0.00	0.00	0.00	0.00
Intensity of demand	−0.10	0.08	−0.27	−0.09	0.06	−0.23

Sources: Derived from tables 3-3, 4-1, 4-3, 4-4, and 4-5.

a. Growth rates based on U.S. deflation procedures. See table 3-5 for rates based on Japanese deflation procedures.

b. Not elsewhere classified.

mates of constant price national income by sector in table 3-3. Changes in output in sectors other than nonresidential business can be ascribed to a single factor: in general government, households, institutions, and foreign governments, to labor; in the services of dwellings, to capital (the stock of dwellings); and in international assets (the net flow of property income from abroad), also to capital (international assets).[12] The change in total national income that arises in nonresidential business is allocated among determinants in proportion to their contributions to the growth rate in nonresidential business. Table 4-6 is the most important of our tables, and the main product of our growth investigation.

Sources of Growth in Eleven Countries

We have available for comparison estimates of the sources of growth of total national income in a postwar period of at least twelve years' duration, computed on a substantially comparable basis, for two North American and eight Western European countries. To improve and simplify the comparisons, table 4-7 introduces several adjustments to the growth rates of Japan and the other countries to eliminate, insofar as possible, irrelevant influences from comparisons of growth sources. Thus not only Japan but also Belgium and France adopt deflation procedures that are not followed in the remaining countries and that raise the growth rate; the effects are eliminated in row 2. An adjustment of the Canadian series to allow for a different treatment of the statistical discrepancy is also included here. Rows 3 and 4 eliminate the effects of irregular factors on the growth rates of output per unit of input.

The remaining adjustments were made because the analysis of European growth rates begins with 1950 and in the early 1950s—perhaps up to about 1953—output changes in certain European countries were greatly affected by factors directly related to World War II. To eliminate some of the effects, unusual gains in West Germany from balancing the capital stock after wartime destruction and division of the country, and in three other countries from modernizing the stock after the war, are eliminated in row 5.

The adjustments in line 6 are perhaps more speculative. For the European countries separate estimates of growth sources are available for 1950–55 and 1955–62, and the 1950–55 residual estimates of the contributions of ad-

12. In the first of these sectors, changes in output (measured by U.S. deflation procedures) that would have occurred if output had changed in proportion to employment in the sector as a whole are ascribed to employment; the small remainder, which results statistically from changes in mix, to unallocated factors.

Table 4-7. *Derivation of Standardized Growth Rates of Total National Income, by Country, Various Periods, 1948–71*

Growth rates and contributions to growth rates in percentage points

Item	Japan, 1953–71	United States, 1948–69	Canada, 1950–67	Belgium, 1950–62	Denmark, 1950–62	France, 1950–62	West Germany, 1950–62	Italy, 1950–62	Netherlands, 1950–62	Norway, 1950–62	United Kingdom, 1950–62
1. National income	9.17	3.85	5.15	3.20	3.51	4.92	7.26	5.96	4.73	3.45	2.29
2. Differences from U.S. in deflation procedures[a]	0.40	...	0.33	0.17	...	0.23	...	...	...	...	...
3. Effect of weather on farming[b]	0.05	−0.01	−0.03	0.00	−0.07	−0.01	0.00	0.01	0.02	−0.02	0.00
4. Intensity of demand[b]	−0.09	−0.14	−0.10	0.00	0.22	0.00	0.00	0.00	0.19	0.00	−0.09
5. Capital adjustments (pre-1955)[c]	...	...	...	...	0.04	...	0.30	...	...	0.04	...
6. Other special pre-1955 adjustments[d]	...	...	...	...	−0.31	...	0.69	0.35	0.45	...	...
7. National income, standardized rate[e]	8.81	4.00	4.95	3.03	3.63	4.70	6.27	5.60	4.07	3.43	2.38

Sources: For Japan, tables 3-5 and 4-6; for the United States, Denison, *Accounting for Growth*, p. 127; for Canada, Walters, *Canadian Growth Revisited*, p. 37 (weighted average of 1950–62 and 1962–67 periods); for European countries, Denison, *Why Growth Rates Differ*, pp. 302–16.

a. Differences are in deflation of employee compensation in general government, households, institutions, and foreign governments, and in construction. For Canada, includes half the statistical discrepancy between output series.

b. Only the effect on output per unit of input is measured here. The effect of a third irregular factor, labor disputes, was zero in the only countries in which it was explicitly estimated.

c. Includes "balancing of the capital stock" in West Germany and "reduction in the age of capital" in Denmark, West Germany, and Norway.

d. Difference between 1950–62 and 1955–62 contributions of advances in knowledge and its application, general efficiency, and errors and omissions.

e. Row 1 minus rows 2–6.

vances in knowledge and n.e.c. in Germany and Italy, the defeated Western powers, are large. We believe this simply reflects the restoration of a functioning economy and balanced production during the period from 1950 to 1952 or 1953. For the comparisons here, we have adjusted the German and Italian growth rates for 1950–62 downward by the amounts of the difference between the 1950–62 and 1955–62 residuals.[13] The 1950–55 residual was also especially large in the Netherlands and unusually small in Denmark. We have similarly substituted 1955–62 for 1950–62 residuals for these countries in the belief that the unusual 1950–55 figures, if not related to the war, probably result from imperfections of the data.[14]

Table 4-8 shows the sources of growth of the standardized growth rates derived for each country in table 4-7. Table 4-9, derived from table 4-8, shows the amount by which the standardized growth rate of Japan in 1953–71 exceeds the standardized rate of each of the other countries in the period specified (row 18), and the amount by which the contribution of each determinant fell below its contribution to Japanese growth in 1953–71.

A standardized output series has uses other than international comparisons, and we provide a continuous annual series for Japan in appendix N.

Some of the countries we compare had growth rates in 1953–71, the period for which Japanese growth is analyzed, that differed considerably from their rates in the periods to which tables 4-7 and 4-8 refer. We do not have 1953–71 growth rates of actual or standardized national income for some of these countries but can provide estimates of the 1953–71 growth rates of actual net national product at market prices, based on each country's own deflation procedures.[15] They are as follows (page 45):

13. Correspondingly, in table 4-8 the 1955–62 estimate for "advances in knowledge and n.e.c." is substituted for the 1950–62 estimate.

14. Some of these adjustments should logically be accompanied by further adjustments to the European estimates for the contributions of economies of scale. They have not been made, but would be too small to affect any interpretation of Japanese growth.

15. Rates for Belgium, Denmark, France, Italy, West Germany, the Netherlands, and the United Kingdom are computed from series for net national product valued at 1963 market prices given in Statistical Office of the European Communities, *National Accounts Aggregates 1951–1972* (Brussels, 1973).

For Japan the rate is computed from the series for net national product valued at 1965 market prices shown in table C-3 of this study.

For the United States the rate is computed from the series for net national product valued at 1972 market prices from Department of Commerce, Bureau of Economic Analysis, *Survey of Current Business,* January 1976.

The rate for Canada was computed from a series constructed as follows. Index values of net national product at 1961 factor cost ("net national income") in 1950, 1955, and 1967 were computed from growth rates shown in Dorothy Walters, *Canadian Growth Revisited, 1950–1967,* Staff Study 28 (Economic Council of Canada, 1970), p. 3. To

Table 4-8. *Sources of Growth of Standardized Growth Rate of National Income, Whole Economy, by Country, Various Periods, 1948–71*
Percentage points

Item	Japan, 1953–71	United States, 1948–69	Canada, 1950–67ᵃ	Belgium, 1950–62	Denmark, 1950–62	France, 1950–62	West Germany, 1950–62	Italy, 1950–62	Netherlands, 1950–62	Norway, 1950–62	United Kingdom, 1950–62
Standardized growth rate	**8.81**	**4.00**	**4.95**	**3.03**	**3.63**	**4.70**	**6.27**	**5.60**	**4.07**	**3.43**	**2.38**
Total factor input	**3.95**	**2.09**ᵇ	**3.02**	**1.17**	**1.55**	**1.24**	**2.78**	**1.66**	**1.91**	**1.04**	**1.11**
Labor	1.85	1.30	1.85	0.76	0.59	0.45	1.37	0.96	0.87	0.15	0.60
Employment	1.14	1.17	1.82	0.40	0.70	0.08	1.49	0.42	0.78	0.13	0.50
Hours of work	0.21	−0.21	−0.20	−0.15	−0.18	−0.02	−0.27	0.05	−0.16	−0.15	−0.15
Age-sex composition	0.14	−0.10	−0.13	0.08	−0.07	0.10	0.04	0.09	0.01	−0.07	−0.04
Education	0.34	0.41	0.36	0.43	0.14	0.29	0.11	0.40	0.24	0.24	0.29
Unallocated	0.02	0.03	0.00	0.00	0.00	0.00	0.00	0.00	0.00	0.00	0.00
Capital	2.10	0.79ᵇ	1.14	0.41	0.96	0.79	1.41	0.70	1.04	0.89	0.51
Inventories	0.73	0.12	0.10	0.06	0.15	0.19	0.33	0.12	0.22	0.13	0.09
Nonresidential structures and equipment	1.07	0.36	0.87	0.39	0.66	0.56	1.02	0.54	0.66	0.79	0.43
Dwellings	0.30	0.28ᵇ	0.30	0.02	0.13	0.02	0.14	0.07	0.06	0.04	0.04
International assets	0.00	0.03	−0.12	−0.06	0.02	0.02	−0.08	−0.03	0.10	−0.07	−0.05

Land										
0.00	0.00	0.00	0.00	0.00	0.00	0.00	0.00	0.00	0.00	0.00
Output per unit of input, standardized										
4.86	1.91[b]	1.96	1.86	2.08	3.46	3.49	3.94	2.16	2.39	1.27
Advances in knowledge and n.e.c.[c]										
1.97	1.19	0.66	0.84	0.75[d]	1.51	0.87[d]	1.30[d]	0.75[d]	0.90	0.79
Improved resource allocation										
0.95	0.30	0.64	0.51	0.68	0.95	1.01	1.42	0.63	0.92	0.12
Contraction of agricultural inputs										
0.64	0.23	0.54	0.20	0.41	0.65	0.77	1.04	0.21	0.54	0.06
Contraction of nonagricultural self-employment										
0.30	0.07	0.10	0.15	0.18	0.23	0.14	0.22	0.26	0.23	0.04
Reduction of international trade barriers										
0.01	0.00	0.00	0.16	0.09	0.07	0.10	0.16	0.16	0.15	0.02
Economies of scale	1.94	0.42	0.66	0.51	0.65	1.00	1.61	1.22	0.78	0.57	0.36
Measured in U.S. prices	1.06	0.42	0.63	0.40	0.42	0.51	0.70	0.62	0.55	0.45	0.27
Income elasticities	0.88	...	0.03	0.11	0.23	0.49	0.91	0.60	0.23	0.12	0.09

Sources: Same as Table 4-7.
a. Details may not add to totals because of rounding.
b. The −0.01 percentage point contribution of the "dwellings occupancy ratio" is included in the contribution of "dwellings" for comparability with other countries.
c. Not elsewhere classified.
d. Estimate for 1955–62 period.

Table 4-9. Contributions of the Sources to Growth of Standardized Total National Income, Shortfalls from Japan in 1953–71

Percentage points

Source of growth	United States, 1948–69	Canada, 1950–67[a]	Belgium, 1950–62	Denmark, 1950–62	France, 1950–62	West Germany, 1950–62	Italy, 1950–62	Netherlands, 1950–62	Norway, 1950–62	United Kingdom, 1950–62
1. Employment	−0.03	−0.68	0.74	0.44	1.06	−0.35	0.72	0.36	1.01	0.64
2. Hours of work	0.42	0.41	0.36	0.39	0.23	0.48	0.16	0.37	0.36	0.36
3. Age-sex composition	0.24	0.27	0.06	0.21	0.04	0.10	0.05	0.13	0.21	0.18
4. Education	−0.07	−0.02	−0.09	0.20	0.05	0.23	−0.06	0.10	0.10	0.05
5. Unallocated labor input	−0.01	0.02	0.02	0.02	0.02	0.02	0.02	0.02	0.02	0.02
6. Inventories	0.61	0.63	0.67	0.58	0.54	0.40	0.61	0.51	0.60	0.64
7. Nonresidential structures and equipment	0.71	0.20	0.68	0.41	0.51	0.05	0.53	0.41	0.28	0.64
8. Dwellings	0.02	0.00	0.28	0.17	0.28	0.16	0.23	0.24	0.26	0.26
9. International assets	−0.03	0.12	0.06	−0.02	−0.02	0.08	0.03	−0.10	0.07	0.05
10. Total factor input, lines 1 to 9	1.86	0.95	2.78	2.40	2.71	1.17	2.29	2.04	2.91	2.84
11. Advances in knowledge and n.e.c.[b]	0.78	1.31	1.13	1.22	0.46	1.10	0.67	1.22	1.07	1.18
12. Contraction of agricultural inputs	0.41	0.10	0.44	0.23	−0.01	−0.13	−0.40	0.43	0.10	0.58
13. Contraction of nonagricultural self-employment	0.23	0.20	0.15	0.12	0.07	0.16	0.08	0.04	0.07	0.26
14. Reduction of international trade barriers	0.01	0.01	−0.15	−0.08	−0.06	−0.09	−0.15	−0.15	−0.14	−0.01
15. Total, lines 10 to 14	3.29	2.57	4.35	3.89	3.17	2.21	2.49	3.58	4.01	4.85
16. Economies of scale: growth of market measured in U.S. prices	0.64	0.43	0.66	0.64	0.55	0.36	0.44	0.51	0.61	0.79
17. Economies of scale: income elasticities	0.88	0.85	0.77	0.65	0.39	−0.03	0.28	0.65	0.76	0.79
18. Standardized growth rate	4.81	3.86	5.78	5.18	4.11	2.54	3.21	4.74	5.38	6.43

Source: Computed from table 4-8.
a. Detail may not add to totals because of rounding.
b. Not elsewhere classified.

Japan	9.3	Belgium	4.2
West Germany	5.5	Denmark	4.1
France	5.4	Norway	4.0
Italy	5.3	United States	3.2
Netherlands	5.0	United Kingdom	2.6
Canada	4.9		

If U.S. deflation procedures were uniformly followed, the Japanese rate would be reduced from 9.3 percent to 8.9 percent and rates for West Germany, France, Canada, Belgium, and perhaps other countries would be a little lower. The rates also are affected by different cyclical positions of the countries in 1953 and 1971. The U.S. rate, for example, would be raised from 3.2 percent to about 3.7 percent if it were calculated on the basis of potential rather than actual net national product.

The main reason these rates differ from those in table 4-7, row 1, is the difference in time periods. Others include the use of different base years for deflation, use of market price instead of factor cost weights, and data revisions after the rates shown in table 4-7 were computed.

---

obtain a 1953 value for this index, GNP in 1961 prices, as estimated by Statistics Canada, was used to interpolate (by proportional interpolation) between the 1950 and 1955 values. The same series was used to extrapolate from 1967 to 1971.

For Norway net national product at 1963 market prices for 1953–69 was obtained from Organisation for Economic Co-operation and Development, *National Accounts of OECD Countries, 1953–1969,* by deducting "depreciation and other operating provisions" from GNP. The 1969 value was extrapolated to 1970 by net national product at 1961 market prices, obtained from Norway Statistik Sentrabyra, *Nasjonalregnskap 1954–1970,* by deducting from net domestic product at 1961 market prices (p. 32) the value in 1961 prices of net "interest, dividends, etc." paid to abroad, obtained by dividing the current-price series for such payments (p. 32) by the implicit deflator for imports, calculated by dividing current price imports (p. 14) by constant price imports (p. 32). The 1970 estimate was extrapolated to 1971 by the excess of gross domestic product in 1970 purchasers' values, from OECD, *National Accounts of OECD Countries, 1961–1972,* p. 309, over net payments to abroad of property and entrepreneurial income, from p. 320 of the same source, deflated by the implicit deflator for imports.

CHAPTER FIVE

How Japan Grew So Fast: An Overview

HOW DID JAPAN obtain a postwar growth rate far above that experienced by any other advanced country? According to our results, the answer is not to be found in any single determinant of output. Rather, changes in almost all important determinants were highly favorable in comparison with other countries, and in none was the change particularly unfavorable.

We base this conclusion on our analysis of the sources of growth in Japan from 1953 to 1971 and the comparison with similar analyses for ten other advanced countries. These analyses are not for the same time periods as that for Japan; for eight European countries they cover 1950–62, for Canada 1950–1967, and for the United States 1948–69. The lack of more recent data for Europe is inconvenient but not a serious handicap. We make international comparisons to learn what is unusual about Japanese growth; for this purpose a sample of ten other countries, including all the large, advanced, free enterprise economies, is highly satisfactory even though the time periods differ.

For a preliminary summary, the contributions of groups of determinants to Japanese growth from 1953 to 1971 may be compared with the simple average of their contributions in the other ten countries.

After adjustments of growth rates to improve statistical comparability, to eliminate the effects of irregular factors on output per unit of input, and to screen out the effects of some early postwar recovery elements in certain European countries (table 4-7), the Japanese growth rate (8.8 percent a year) exceeded the average of the other ten (4.2 percent) by 4.6 percentage points. Of this difference 0.9 percentage points are accounted for by an above-average contribution from changes in employment, hours of work, and the distribution by age and sex of total hours worked, 1.2 percentage points by a greater contribution from capital, 1.0 percentage point by a greater contribution from the application of new knowledge to production, and 0.3 percentage points by greater than average contributions from the reallocation of resources away from agriculture and from nonagricultural self-employment. The contributions of these determinants (as well as of others whose contributions are not exceptionally large) are computed as if countries operate under conditions of constant returns to scale, which is by no means the case; we believe that economies of scale are important. Markets were growing much faster in Japan than the average for the other countries as a result of the growth sources already enumerated. Chiefly for this reason, economies of scale contributed 1.2 percentage points more to growth in Japan than to the average growth rate of the other ten countries.

The pervasiveness of the Japanese advantage is striking. *All* of the five groups of sources enumerated in the preceding paragraph made a larger contribution to growth in Japan in 1953–71 than to growth in *any* of the other ten countries in the periods analyzed, with the sole exception that Italy (1950–62) is estimated to have gained more from the reallocation of resources away from agriculture and nonfarm self-employment.

It may be noted that Japan gained only about an average amount from one of the principal remaining growth sources, increased education of the labor force, and a lower than average amount from another, the relaxation of barriers to international trade. Four countries gained more than Japan from education and eight gained more from the reduction of trade barriers. But the margins are not large.

Not only did Japan stand first in the contributions from most of the important growth sources; other countries tended not to stand high or low in all major determinants but rather to have a mixed ranking. The latter feature helps to explain why the Japanese growth rate exceeded others by so wide a margin.

The table below features the relative contributions of the sources to the growth of Japanese national income, a subject of interest quite apart from international comparisons. Summarized from table 4-6, it provides estimates for growth during our two subperiods. The contributions of irregular factors are eliminated so as to secure the growth rate of standardized national income.[1] Remaining determinants are consolidated into seven groups. These

---

1. The standardized series is not a potential output series. Unlike potential output series, it eliminates the effects on productivity of weather in agriculture and of labor disputes (in addition to those of fluctuations in demand, which are eliminated from both types of series). Table N-1 provides annual estimates of these effects. On the other

are ranked by the size of their contributions over the 1953–71 period as a
whole (which happens to be the same as the 1961–71 ranking).

	Growth rate or contribution to growth rate of national income			
	Percentage points		Percent of standardized growth rate	
Output measure or source of growth	1953–61	1961–71	1953–61	1961–71
National income (U.S. deflation procedures)	8.13	9.29	. . .	. . .
Irregular factors	0.20	−0.27	. . .	. . .
Standardized national income	7.93	9.56	100.0	100.0
More capital	1.62	2.57	20.4	26.9
Advances in knowledge and miscellaneous determinants	1.42	2.43	17.9	25.4
Economies of scale	1.90	1.96	24.0	20.5
More work done, with account taken of workers' characteristics except education	1.58	1.43	19.9	15.0
Less labor misallocated to agriculture and nonagricultural self-employment	1.08	0.81	13.6	8.5
Increased education per worker	0.33	0.35	4.2	3.7
Reduced international trade barriers	0.00	0.01	0.0	0.1

The growth rate was higher by one-fifth in 1961–71 than it had been in
1953–61 once the effect of irregular determinants has been eliminated.
Capital and advances in knowledge account for the acceleration. The contribution of capital increased greatly, by six-tenths, and that of advances in
knowledge even more, by seven-tenths.[2] The increase in labor input (except
education) and the reallocation of labor contributed less in the second period
than in the first, but the differences were much smaller. In subsequent chapters we will discuss each determinant. Here we anticipate certain findings.

hand, standardized national income does not eliminate the effect on total output of
differences between actual and potential labor input. We think there is no great difference in Japan between growth rates of standardized and potential national income in
these periods. In the United States the difference in 1948–69 is only 0.02 percentage
points. (In *Accounting for Growth*, p. 124, the growth rate of potential national income
is given as 4.02.)

2. These and similar statements later in this chapter assume that the net contribution of miscellaneous determinants, which is combined with that of advances in knowledge, did not change much.

The largest contribution to growth was made by capital. The main components of the capital stock increased at extraordinary rates; over the whole 1953–71 period the gross stock of private nonresidential structures and equipment grew at an average annual rate of 9.2 percent, the stock of inventories at 11.9 percent. This achievement required similarly large increases in annual gross investment, which were made possible by the combination of three developments, all large. They were the increase in total annual national income (or output), which is to say in the resources available for division between saving and consumption; a rise in the proportion of income saved; and a decline in the price of capital goods (including inventories) relative to the price of other components of the national product, presumably reflecting a decline in the relative production cost of capital goods.

The next largest contribution was made by advances in knowledge and miscellaneous determinants. This combination includes all growth sources, positive or negative, not separately estimated. Comparison of the estimates for Japan with estimates for other countries strongly suggests that the world's stock of knowledge was not advancing fast enough to contribute as much to growth as we estimate Japan secured from advances in knowledge and miscellaneous determinants. The probable explanation is that the average state of technology, business organization, and management practice—which has been not only well below (or behind) the efficiency permitted by the world's stock of knowledge concerning how to produce at low cost but also below average actual practice in the industrialized West—was moving closer to the technological and managerial frontier. There was, in other words, a major element of "catching up" in the contribution of this source. In making this statement we do not mean to distinguish sharply between the dissemination of knowledge and the elimination of other sources of inefficiency as ways of narrowing the productivity gap between Japan and Western countries.

Economies of scale made possible by expanding markets were the third largest source of growth. According to our estimates there were two reasons for their large size. First, the growth of total output, and therefore of the size of the market for the average commodity (whether the market was local, regional, national, or international), was very rapid. Second, among consumer goods the expansion of markets was especially large for commodities such as consumer durables that offered especially big opportunities for gains from scale economies as production expanded.

Because all components of labor input except education are closely interrelated they are combined in the preceding text table. This combination makes up the fourth largest growth source. Total man-hours worked in the whole economy increased at the high annual rate of 1.5 percent from 1953 to 1971. Average hours scarcely changed in this period; the growth rate of employment was also 1.5 percent. The growth rate of total hours worked was much higher in 1953–61, 2.2 percent, than in 1961–71, when it fell to 1.0 percent. Other components of labor input (in addition to education) raised labor input further in both periods.

The allocation of resources was substantially improved by reducing the proportion of the total labor supply that is inefficiently used in agriculture or consists of self-employed and unpaid family workers in nonfarm enterprises too small for efficiency. Agricultural employment fell from 35.6 percent of all employment in Japan in 1953 to 14.6 percent in 1971, while self-employed and family workers in nonagricultural industries slipped from 22.5 to 18.8 percent.[3] Because of this reallocation, nonagricultural wage and salary employment—the type of employment most closely related to the increase in the value of output—increased far more than total employment: by 108 percent from 1953 to 1971 as compared with 31 percent. The situation was not as favorable to growth as if total employment had risen by 108 percent with no change in allocation because the additional agricultural and self-employed workers who would then have been present in 1971 would have contributed something to 1971 output. But this lost contribution was much less than that actually made by the extra nonfarm wage and salary workers in their actual employment, so the gain from reallocation was large. We estimate that by the grouping in the preceding text table, it was the fifth largest source of growth.

Educational background is a very important determinant of the quality of labor, and the increase in the education of the labor force was a significant source of growth of national income. However, its contribution was dwarfed by those of the five preceding groups of output determinants. The last source listed in the text table above is the gain from the reduction of barriers to international trade. This gain was trivial because changes in trade barriers had little effect on trade in 1953–71.

Because most sources shared responsibility for the very high rate of Japanese growth, none contributed an unusually large percentage of the standardized growth rate in comparison with other countries. Indeed, the percentage distribution of growth by source in Japan was not so very different from that in the United States, where the growth rate was far lower. The chief differences in the United States in the 1948–69 period were that economies of scale contributed a smaller percentage (10.7) than in Japan and education a larger percentage (10.4).[4]

3. Numbers in this paragraph were calculated from table 3-4. Nonagricultural self-employment dropped much more when expressed as a percentage of nonagricultural employment.

4. See *Accounting for Growth*, p. 128, table 9-5, column 3.

National Income per Person Employed

Thus far attention has been confined to total national income. Estimates of the sources of growth of national income per person employed are provided in table 5-1. They are shown for both the nonresidential business sector and the economy as a whole.

For most output determinants contributions to the growth rates of national income per person employed are the same as contributions to total national income (shown in table 4-6), or would be the same were it not for trivial differences in statistical interaction terms. In this category are all components of output per unit of input and—because they are on a per-worker basis even in the total national income table—labor input components except employment. The employment component disappears from the classification. Capital inputs per person employed grew less than they did in the aggregate because employment was increasing, and they consequently contributed less to growth of national income per worker than of total national income. Land per worker became scarcer as employment increased, so its contribution to growth of output per worker was negative.

Table 5-2 summarizes for the economy as a whole the sources of growth of national income per person employed in our two subperiods, using the same groupings as were used earlier for total national income. As before, the groups of sources are ranked by the size of their contributions over the 1953–71 period as a whole.

The incorporation of new knowledge into the productive process is estimated to have been the most important source of growth of national income per person employed after 1961 (and, by a slight margin over economies of scale, in the 1953–71 period as a whole). Gains from economies of scale were the biggest growth source in 1953–61 and the third biggest after 1961. They were made possible by the growth of *total* national income as a result of changes in all other determinants, including employment. The increase in capital input per person employed was the second largest source of growth of output per worker after 1961 and the third largest over the whole period. Together, these three sources contributed 71.5 percent of the growth of standardized national income per person employed in 1953–61 and 81.9 percent in 1961–71. Almost as important as capital in the earlier period, but much less so after 1961, were gains from the reallocation of labor out of farming and nonfarm self-employment.

National income per worker grew much faster in Japan than elsewhere, and much more than in the United States. Its growth rate of 7.21 percent from

Table 5-1. *Sources of Growth of Actual National Income per Person Employed, Nonresidential Business and Whole Economy, 1953–71*
Percentage points

Item	Nonresidential business			Whole economy[a]		
	1953–71	*1953–61*	*1961–71*	*1953–71*	*1953–61*	*1961–71*
	(1)	(2)	(3)	(4)	(5)	(6)
National income	**8.45**	**8.08**	**8.75**	**7.17**	**6.45**	**7.75**
Total factor input	**2.63**	**2.13**	**3.03**	**2.38**	**1.88**	**2.84**
Labor	0.85	1.00	0.76	0.71	0.77	0.69
Hours	0.27	0.48	0.14	0.21	0.38	0.11
Average hours	0.02	0.45	−0.31	0.01	0.35	−0.27
Efficiency offset	0.21	−0.09	0.44	0.18	−0.06	0.38
Intergroup shift offset	0.04	0.12	0.01	0.02	0.09	0.00
Age-sex composition	0.17	0.09	0.22	0.14	0.07	0.19
Education	0.41	0.43	0.40	0.34	0.33	0.35
Unallocated	...	...	...	0.02	−0.01	0.04
Capital	1.85	1.21	2.33	1.73	1.17	2.21
Inventories	0.78	0.62	0.87	0.63	0.45	0.75
Nonresidential structures and equipment	1.07	0.59	1.46	0.87	0.42	1.26
Dwellings	...	...	...	0.23	0.31	0.20
International assets	...	...	...	0.00	−0.01	0.00
Land	−0.07	−0.08	−0.06	−0.06	−0.06	−0.06
Output per unit of input	**5.82**	**5.95**	**5.72**	**4.79**	**4.57**	**4.91**
Advances in knowledge and n.e.c.[b]	2.37	1.83	2.82	1.95	1.41	2.42
Improved resource allocation	1.15	1.39	0.95	0.95	1.07	0.82
Contraction of agricultural inputs	0.78	0.86	0.72	0.64	0.66	0.62
Contraction of nonagricultural self-employment	0.36	0.53	0.22	0.30	0.41	0.19
Reduction in international trade barriers	0.01	0.00	0.01	0.01	0.00	0.01
Economies of scale	2.35	2.46	2.26	1.93	1.88	1.94
Measured in U.S. prices	1.28	1.24	1.32	1.05	0.95	1.13
Income elasticities	1.07	1.22	0.94	0.88	0.93	0.81
Irregular factors	−0.05	0.27	−0.31	−0.04	0.21	−0.27
Effect of weather on farming	0.06	0.19	−0.04	0.05	0.15	−0.04
Labor disputes	0.00	0.00	0.00	0.00	0.00	0.00
Intensity of demand	−0.11	0.08	−0.27	−0.09	0.06	−0.23

Sources: Derived from tables 3-3, 3-4, 4-1, 4-3, 4-4, 4-5, and 4-6.
a. Growth rates based on U.S. deflation procedures.
b. Not elsewhere classified.

Table 5-2. *Condensed Classification of Sources of Growth of National Income per Person Employed, Whole Economy, 1953–61 and 1961–71*

Output measure or source of growth	Percentage points		Percent of standardized growth rate	
	1953–61	*1961–71*	*1953–61*	*1961–71*
National income per person employed (U.S. deflation procedures)	6.45	7.75	...	...
Irregular factors	0.21	−0.27	...	...
Standardized national income per person employed	6.24	8.02	100.0	100.0
Advances in knowledge and miscellaneous determinants	1.41	2.42	22.6	30.2
Economies of scale	1.88	1.94	30.1	24.2
More capital per worker	1.17	2.21	18.8	27.6
Less labor misallocated to agriculture and nonagricultural self-employment	1.07	0.81	17.1	10.1
Changes in working hours and characteristics of labor except education	0.44	0.34	7.1	4.2
Increased education per worker	0.33	0.35	5.3	4.4
Reduced international trade barriers	0.00	0.01	0.0	0.1
Less land per worker	−0.06	−0.06	−1.0	−0.7

Source: Table 5-1.

1953 to 1971 after the effects of irregular factors are eliminated compares with 2.42 percent in the United States from 1948 to 1969. A more interesting comparison is provided by data for the nonresidential business sector, the only sector where output per unit of input can increase. In this sector, the growth rates of output per person employed, after eliminating the effect of irregular factors, were 8.50 percent in Japan and 2.83 percent, or just one-third as much, in the United States. Contributions to these growth rates are summarized in table 5-3. It is evident that all of the first five groups of determinants listed contributed importantly to the explanation of why the Japanese growth rate was so much higher.

The percentage distributions are also of interest. Advances in knowledge were the largest source of growth in both countries, but accounted for 51 percent of the growth rate in the United States as against only 28 percent in Japan even though the actual contribution was larger in Japan by nearly two-thirds. Economies of scale stood second in both countries. In the United

Table 5-3. *Condensed Classification of Sources of Growth of National Income per Person Employed, Nonresidential Business, Japan, 1953–71, and the United States, 1948–69*

Output measure or source of growth	Percentage points			Percent of standardized growth rate	
	Japan, 1953–71	United States, 1948–69	Differ- ence	Japan, 1953–71	United States, 1948–69
National income per person employed (U.S. deflation procedures)	8.45	2.65	5.80	...	...
Irregular factors	−0.05	−0.18	0.13	...	...
Standardized national income per person employed	8.50	2.83	5.67	100.0	100.0
Advances in knowledge and miscellaneous determinants	2.37	1.44	0.93	27.9	50.9
Economies of scale	2.35	0.51	1.84	27.6	18.0
More capital per worker	1.85	0.40	1.45	21.8	14.1
Less labor misallocated to agriculture and nonagricultural self-employment	1.14	0.36	0.78	13.4	12.7
Changes in working hours and char- acteristics of labor except education	0.44	−0.34	0.78	5.2	−12.0
Increased education per worker	0.41	0.50	−0.09	4.8	17.7
Reduced international trade barriers	0.01	0.00	0.01	0.1	0.0
Less land per worker	−0.07	−0.04	−0.03	−0.8	−1.4

Sources: Japan, table 5-1. United States, Denison, *Accounting for Growth*, table 8-4, p. 114.

States the increased education of employed persons contributed almost as much as economies of scale, 18 percent, whereas in Japan education was responsible for less than 5 percent. Labor, capital, and land input together were responsible for almost two-fifths of the 5.67 percentage point difference between the adjusted growth rates of national income per person employed in the nonresidential business sectors of Japan and the United States, and components of output per unit of input for three-fifths.

CHAPTER SIX

Labor Input

WE NOW EXAMINE the separate sources of growth. In this chapter the components of labor input are considered.

Employment

Employment, shown in table 3-4, rose almost 31 percent from 1953 to 1971, equivalent to the high annual rate of 1.49 percent (1.58 percent in 1953–61 and 1.42 percent in 1961–71). Without changes in working hours or in the demographic composition or educational background of employed persons (all of which will be examined separately), an increase in employment of the size observed would have contributed an estimated 1.14 percentage points to the 1953–71 growth rate of total national income (table 4-6). This is much more than in seven of the ten other countries, a trifle less than in the United States (1948–69), and considerably less than in West Germany (1950–62) and, especially, Canada (1950–67), where the employment contribution was 1.82 percentage points (tables 4-8 and 4-9).

The Japanese employment increase from 39.4 million in 1953 to 51.4 million in 1971 is more than accounted for by the increase in the working-age population. Only 0.1 million of the 12.0 million increase in employment is ascribable to reduced unemployment; the rest is the consequence of a larger labor force. But the labor force increased much less than the adult population, especially after 1961. It equaled 70.0 percent of the population fifteen and over in 1953, 69.1 percent in 1961, and 65.0 percent in 1971—still a high figure by international standards. Corresponding percentages for males were 86.8, 84.9, and 82.2; for females 54.3, 54.3, and 48.8. If the participation rate had not changed, the employment increase from 1953 to 1971 would have been 17.2 million instead of 12.0 million. Changes in the age distribution of the adult population may have affected the overall participation rate, but the main reasons for the decline were extension of schooling and the decreasing importance of agriculture, which tended to lower the rates for teenagers and females.

The growth rate of employment in the United States was 1.55 percent from 1948 to 1969. This exceeds the 1953–71 rate of 1.49 in Japan, but it was achieved only by a very large increase in the employment of adult women, many available only for part-time work, and by a huge increase in the number of students holding part-time jobs. Such workers added a much lower than average amount to output; remaining components of labor input bring their special characteristics into the calculation.

Hours of Work

Japan and Italy (1950–62) were the only countries examined in which changes in working hours made a *positive* contribution to the growth rate. In Japan it amounted to 0.21 percentage points in 1953–71. (It was 0.38 points in 1953–61 and still as much as 0.11 points in 1961–71.) In most countries changes in hours subtracted appreciably from growth. As a result, the Japanese advantage was substantial: 0.36 to 0.48 percentage points in comparisons with all countries except France (0.23 points) and Italy (0.16 points).

Diminution of part-time employment, which served to raise average hours per person employed, was a main element in the favorable Japanese experience. In the business sector (including agriculture) full-time employment rose from 77.0 percent of total employment in 1953 to 82.5 percent in 1961 and 85.3 percent in 1971. The reduction of more than one-third in the part-time proportion resulted from the rapidly expanding demand for labor that made full-time jobs available to persons previously able to find only part-time work. The rise in the percentage of full-time employment in Japan is the reverse of the decline in the United States—from 88.9 percent of business employment in 1948 to 83.9 in 1969—which resulted from the increasing number of persons not previously in the labor force who desired only part-time work.

Reductions in full-time hours in Japan were only moderate, especially since they are much longer than in other advanced nations. Moreover, the hours of full-time workers, including even nonagricultural wage and salary workers, were so long that—as implied by the assumptions underlying the estimates for all the countries—the reductions that did take place were almost entirely offset by higher output per hour, the consequence of reduced fatigue and related effects.[1]

1. Estimates of the effects of changes in hours in nonresidential business are constructed in three parts which sometimes, as in table 4-6, are shown separately. "Average

Weekly hours per person employed are shown in the table below for full-time workers in the business sector in Japan at the initial and terminal dates of the periods, and in the United States in the nearest years for which data are available.[2] The workweek (even as shortened by the inclusion of vacation and holiday weeks) has been long. For nonagricultural wage and salary workers it averaged 8.7 hours longer in Japan in 1971 than in the United States in 1969 for males, and 9.5 hours longer for females.

	Average weekly hours worked					
	Japan			*United States*		
	1953	*1961*	*1971*	*1953*	*1961*	*1969*
Nonagricultural wage and salary workers						
Male	54.2	54.2	51.1	42.6	42.8	42.4
Female	52.7	51.7	47.5	39.5	39.0	38.0
Nonagricultural self-employed and unpaid family workers						
Male	61.1	61.7	57.5	53.1	53.9	53.1
Female	56.1	59.3	55.0	53.3	52.5	50.9
Agricultural workers						
Male	55.0	55.7	53.4	55.8	53.9	55.5
Female	52.5	54.0	52.5	48.5	47.9	48.8

Composition of Labor by Age and Sex

The proportions of total hours worked by males and females, and within each sex by individuals of different ages, change over time. An average hour worked has a different value in each demographic group. It was neces-

---

hours" show what the effect would be if changes in average hours altered labor input proportionally. The "efficiency offset" to intragroup changes cancels the portion of this estimate that results from changes in average hours within six groups of full-time workers to the extent, nearly complete in Japan, that offsetting efficiency gains are assumed to occur. The "intergroup shift offset" cancels the effect on average hours of changes in the employment weights of the six groups of full-time workers. For further explanation of the procedures, see appendixes F and G. See also Denison, *Accounting for Growth,* pp. 24–26, 31–33, 35–43, 47–48, 105–06, and 125.

2. Our basic data appear (for Japan, in tables F-1, F-2, and F-3) with overlapping time series for different periods. For this table we have linked so as to adjust all years to conform to the levels for the latest year shown. The 1953 estimate of 56.1 hours for female self-employed and unpaid family workers in Japan is erratically low. Estimates for 1952 and 1954 are 58.4 and 59.6, respectively.

sary to develop the index shown in table 4-3, column 4, to allow for the effect of changes in these proportions.

The calculation of such an index rests on the assumption that average earnings in the ten age-sex groups distinguished are proportional to the marginal products of labor, per hour worked, of these groups. If this assumption is correct, it is necessary and legitimate to consider an average hour worked by a demographic group whose average hourly earnings are twice as high as those of another group to represent twice as much labor input.

The assumption implies that an average hour's work by males thirty-five to fifty-nine years of age, for example, is 2.23 times as valuable as an average hour's work by females twenty to twenty-four years of age. The assumption is valid insofar as earnings differentials among age-sex groups reflect differences in the value of the work that is actually performed. It does not matter whether these differences result from differences in the value of the work the groups are able and willing to do (because of variations in skill, training, experience, and strength; in attitudes; in home, marital, and school responsibilities that inhibit the assumption of responsibility on the job or working at inconvenient hours; in continuity of labor force participation; and the like) or from failure to use abilities that are present. Such failure may occur because abilities are not recognized or because of discrimination in employment practices with respect to hiring, training, promotion, or dismissal so that one group or another cannot reach its full work capability. Potential abilities that are unused do not affect output; a newsboy might make a competent publisher but his unused potentiality has no more effect than if it did not exist.[3] An error is introduced into the calculation by discrimination only insofar as relative earnings are affected by differences in pay for identical work. Our use of earnings weights implies a judgment that this type of discrimination, failure to provide "equal pay for equal work" when all costs are taken into account, does not greatly affect differentials in earnings among age-sex groups.

Our willingness to make such a judgment was greatly influenced by the fact that average hourly earnings (which include bonus payments) vary by age and sex in much the same pattern as in other countries; by far the highest earnings accrue to males in the middle age ranges.[4] The earnings of females

3. An improvement over time in the allocation of workers (classified by age and sex or by other characteristics) among jobs could raise the average productivity of all workers and hence total output. If such a change occurred we would not wish to classify the gain as a contribution of labor input but instead as a contribution of output per unit of input (specifically, of improved resource allocation).

4. When expressed as percentages of the average hourly earnings of all age-sex groups combined, average earnings of eight of the ten age-sex groups we distinguish are almost the same in Japan and the United States. The Japanese percentages are above the Ameri-

average around half of the earnings of males, only moderately less than in the United States.

Postwar changes in the composition of total hours worked in the business sector in Japan were unusual. The percentage worked by females, after an initial increase from 38.0 in 1953 to 39.1 in 1955, dwindled steadily, falling to 38.5 in 1961 and 35.9 in 1971.[5] Probably because of extension of education, the percentages worked by teenagers, both males and females, dropped sharply, especially after 1967. Over the four-year period from 1967 to 1971 alone the percentage of total hours worked by teenagers dropped by nearly two-fifths, from 8.2 percent to 5.1 percent. The proportion of hours worked by males in the prime working ages increased steadily. These compositional shifts toward the age-sex groups with the highest earnings, and presumptively the highest marginal products, are estimated to have contributed 0.14 percentage points to the 1953–71 growth rate of national income in the economy as a whole, the largest figure among the eleven countries. The contribution rose from 0.07 points in 1953–61 to 0.19 points in 1961–71.

In the United States, in contrast, the dominant change was an increase in the proportion of total hours worked by females. In the business sector this percentage had already risen from 16.6 percent in 1929 to 22.3 percent in 1948. It was 24.3 in 1953, 26.1 in 1961, and 29.7 in 1969. (Despite the convergence of the Japanese and American percentages, it will be noted that the Japanese percentage remained much the higher.) With the contribution made to growth by changes in age-sex composition negative in the United States, this determinant contributed 0.24 percentage points to the difference between Japanese and U.S. growth rates.

Education of Employed Persons

Educational background exerts a decisive influence on the types of work an individual can perform and his proficiency in any particular occupation. The Japanese labor force has received as much education as the labor forces of Northwest Europe and Canada, or perhaps a bit more, moderately less than that of the United States, and considerably more than that of Italy. In the 1950s it had had much more education than is typical of countries at Japan's economic level at that time.

---

can for two groups, males fifteen to nineteen years of age (54 percent as against 36 percent) and males thirty-five to fifty-nine (145 percent as against 128 percent). Table G-1 provides a full comparison and notes differences between the countries with respect to dividing lines between age brackets.

5. Data cited in this paragraph are from tables G-2 and G-3. They have been adjusted to provide comparable series over time.

60 HOW JAPAN'S ECONOMY GREW SO FAST

The increase in the education of employed persons during the postwar period was of intermediate size in comparison with other advanced countries, as was the contribution of this change to the growth rate of national income. At 0.34 percentage points, this contribution exceeded that in six of the other countries (by as much as 0.23 percentage points) and fell short of that in four (but at most by only 0.09 points).

Table 6-1 shows percentage distributions of employed persons of each sex (excluding those still in school) among ten educational levels in 1950, 1960, and 1970 (columns 3 to 8). It also shows the estimated average number of years of education of persons in each education category (column 1) and the weight assigned to persons in each education category in constructing a labor input index (column 2). The weights are intended to represent the relative hourly earnings of persons employed in the business sector who differ only in amount of education. The basic earnings data distinguish only four educational levels, so considerable estimation was required to obtain additional detail. Despite the formality and rigidity of the wage structure in large firms in Japan, differences in earnings among education groups, like differences among broad demographic groups, are much like those in the United States and other countries.

Table 6-1. *Distribution of Employed Persons Not in School by Amount of Education, and Related Data, 1950, 1960, and 1970*

Education	Average years of education (1)	Weight (8 years = 100) (2)	Males 1950 (3)	Males 1960 (4)	Males 1970 (5)	Females 1950 (6)	Females 1960 (7)	Females 1970 (8)
No school	0	70	1.57	0.55	0.24	4.78	1.52	0.55
Elementary, junior high, youth training								
1–3 years	2	80	1.99	0.69	0.31	3.13	0.99	0.36
4 years	4	86	5.34	3.27	0.85	6.30	2.85	0.70
5–6 years	5.8	91	15.15	7.32	5.21	24.03	14.83	11.26
7–8 years	7.5	97	41.35	34.04	25.06	33.12	27.84	21.70
9 years	9	107	7.93	21.28	22.93	7.78	29.38	29.38
Middle school (old)a	10.7	117	16.29	13.43	10.16	16.75	11.80	9.28
Senior high school	12	122	3.79	9.92	21.41	2.37	11.04	21.37
Junior college and college preparatory school (old)a	14	147	3.91	4.05	4.04	1.64	1.90	4.08
University and postgraduate	17	172	2.68	5.45	9.79	0.10	0.43	1.32
Total	...	...	100.00	100.00	100.00	100.00	100.00	100.00
Average years of education	...	...	8.15	9.16	10.17	7.22	8.42	9.31
Average weight (8 years = 100)	...	...	103.71	109.34	115.52	98.66	104.29	109.20
Indexes (1950 = 100)								
Average years of education	...	...	100.00	112.39	124.79	100.00	116.62	128.95
Average weight	...	...	100.00	105.44	111.39	100.00	105.71	110.69

Sources: See appendix H.
a. Refers to types of schools eliminated by the 1947 reorganization of the school structure.

At the bottom of table 6-1 are estimates of average years of education (which do not enter directly into the calculation of sources of growth estimates) and the average weight implied by each distribution.

The upward movement in the distributions by amount of education is pronounced. By careful selection of breaking points, it can even be made to sound sensational. For example, the percentage of males with zero to six years of education plummeted from 24.0 in 1950 to 6.6 in 1970, and the corresponding percentage for females from 38.2 to 12.9. Males with twelve or more years of education jumped from 10.4 percent in 1950 to 35.2 percent in 1970, females from 4.1 percent to 26.8 percent. This mode of expression may give an exaggerated impression of changes, but increases in the average number of years of education are more representative and these amounted to 25 percent and 29 percent for males and females, respectively—quite considerable increases. Years of education, however, do not give a satisfactory indication of the economic significance of the change. The index of "educational quality" of labor, based on the use of relative earnings rather than years of school to compare groups, is the appropriate measure for growth analysis. It rose 11.4 percent for males and 10.7 percent for females over the same period.[6]

The upward movement in the education distributions results from the greater education of persons entering the labor force than had been attained by those who left it. Persons leaving the labor force in the early 1950s had received their education many years before. Changes in education back to the late nineteenth century would have to be described in detail for a full explanation of the postwar upward shift; here we can only sketch them.[7]

Three partially related types of development account for the shift. The first is the introduction and lengthening of compulsory education. Although a modern school system was promulgated in 1872 and a four-year requirement for compulsory education was established in 1886, enrollment data show clearly that enforcement of the four-year requirement was only gradually introduced and the nation did not approach full compliance before 1909. At about that time—in 1908—the requirement was raised from four years to six. In 1947 it went to the current nine years. Second, the school system has been reorganized from time to time in such a way that students reaching what might

6. Estimates for some countries, including the United States, allow for an increase in the number of days attended per year of education. No such allowance has been made for Japan except insofar as reduction in absenteeism may have reduced the years elapsed before a particular certificate or degree is obtained. Historical data on attendance are sparse, but it seems unlikely that more than a minor adjustment could be justified. See also appendix H.

7. Appendix H provides a somewhat fuller description.

be regarded as a certain point on the educational ladder obtained more years of education. One major reorganization was the introduction in 1947 of the American school system; among other changes, junior high school required three years, one more than the previous "upper elementary" school—both after six years of ordinary elementary school. Third, voluntary continuation of education after completing compulsory schooling has increased, the joint effect of growing desire and financial ability to continue schooling on the part of students and parents and of expansion of the educational establishment. Continuation on a massive scale is a new development of the postwar period; in this respect Japanese experience resembles that of the United Kingdom and some other countries of Western Europe.

Unallocated Labor Input

Contributions of the labor input components described so far, except employment, stem from changes within the business sector only. In general government, households, institutions, and foreign governments changes in output are measured by changes in employment (according to U.S. deflation techniques) so that other labor characteristics do not affect measured output. However, within this nonbusiness sector the change in output in each individual segment is measured by the change in employment in that segment, so that changes in the relative importance of segments that have different base-year values of output per worker may affect the growth rate. The "unallocated" component of labor input, calculated separately only for Japan and the United States, measures this effect. The amounts are too small to require discussion.

CHAPTER SEVEN

Capital Input

THE INCREASE in the stock of private capital contributed an estimated 2.10 percentage points to the growth rate of national income from 1953 to 1971. The contribution was much larger in 1961–71, at 2.57 percentage points, than in 1953–61, when it was 1.62 points. We first discuss the capital stock of firms—including inventories as well as structures and equipment—and offer some general comments on investment and saving. We conclude with additional remarks about dwellings and international assets.

Growth of Private Nonresidential Business Capital

The stock of private nonresidential business capital increased at a pace quite outside the range observed in other advanced countries.[1] The growth rate of the gross stock of nonresidential structures and equipment was 9.2 percent and that of inventories was 11.9 percent. The highest rates among the other ten countries listed in tables 4-7 to 4-9, those for West Germany in 1950–62, were 5.5 percent for the gross stock of nonresidential structures and equipment and 7.0 percent for inventories. Rates in West Germany, in turn, were well above those in the remaining countries.[2] Rates in the United States in 1948–69 were 3.5 percent both for gross stock of fixed capital and for inventories. Even in a short boom period such as 1964–69 these rates reached only 4.5 and 5.2.[3]

1. We must except Israel, where both gross and net stock of nonresidential structures and equipment in the private economy grew at an annual rate of 12.5 percent from 1950 to 1965, according to A. L. Gaathon, *Economic Productivity in Israel,* Praeger Special Studies in International Economics and Development (Praeger Publishers in cooperation with the Bank of Israel, 1971), p. 42. Israel, however, is a special case.
2. Capital stock growth rates are from the same sources as table 4-7.
3. Computed from Denison, *Accounting for Growth,* p. 54, table 5-2, columns 1 and 3.

Growth rates of private nonresidential business capital in postwar Japan were not only high but also rising. The following table provides growth rates of the gross stock of fixed capital and the stock of inventories in our two main subperiods and in four shorter periods:[4]

	Growth rates (percent)	
Period (calendar years)	Fixed capital (gross stock)	Inventories
1953–61	6.0	10.8
1961–71	11.8	12.7
1953–56	3.8	8.1
1956–60	6.7	11.1
1960–67	10.8	12.2
1967–71	13.1	15.1

Nonresidential business capital receives at least as much weight in total output in Japan as in the other countries, so these high growth rates resulted in a contribution to growth in Japan that was much greater than elsewhere (table 4-9). This was also true of the separate components, fixed capital and inventories. (The bigger difference is in the contribution of inventories, partly because they receive especially great weight in Japan.) The acceleration of capital stock growth rates combined with the previously noted increase in earnings weights to yield a 90 percent increase from 1953–61 to 1961–71 in the contribution of these two types of capital.

Rise in Annual Gross Investment by Private Business

To achieve the capital stock growth rates recorded, truly enormous increases were required in annual gross investment, measured in constant (1965) prices, and one may well ask how it was possible for Japan to expand investment so much. An increase in output available for division between consumption and saving, a higher saving rate, and a falling relative price for investment goods all *could* contribute to an increase in investment; for any particular type of investment, so could an increase in its share of total investment. To examine what actually happened to the quantity of any type of investment, its index can be regarded as the product of indexes of these four quantities or ratios that govern its behavior.

4. Dividing points between the shorter periods were selected to match jumps in the annual percentage increases in fixed capital. They are clearly delineated except that 1961 might be substituted for 1960.

Table 7-1. *Analysis of Indexes of Fixed Nonresidential Business Investment*

Description[a]	1960/53[b]	1971/60[b]	1971/53[b]
1. GNP (constant prices)	176.3	298.4	526.2
2. GPI/GNP (current prices)	152.2	106.0	161.4
3. FNBI/GPI (current prices)	104.3	88.1	91.9
4. Price ratio, GNP/FNBI	100.2	143.2	143.4
5. FNBI (constant prices)	280.3	399.5	1,119.8

Sources: Economic Planning Agency, *Annual Report on National Income Statistics, 1973* (1973), and *Revised Report on National Income Statistics, 1951–1967* (1969).

a. GNP, gross national product at market prices; GPI, gross private investment; FNBI, fixed nonresidential business investment.

b. Percentages, based on fiscal year data.

Table 7-1 provides such indexes for the largest component of gross private investment, fixed nonresidential investment by private business.[5] As shown in row 5, such investment, valued in 1965 prices, reached 280.3 percent of its 1953 level in 1960. In 1971 it reached 399.5 percent of its 1960 level and 1,119.8 percent of its 1953 level.

In this table, gross private investment is defined to include inventory accumulation by private business, private residential construction, and net foreign investment, in addition to gross fixed nonresidential investment by private business. Gross private investment is conceptually identical to gross national saving—private saving plus government saving—when government saving is defined as the government surplus on income and product account— i.e., as the excess of government receipts over expenditures. As explained below, expenditures include investment by government enterprises.

Consider first the change from 1953 to 1960. Row 1 shows that in 1960 gross national product in constant prices was 176.3 percent of 1953. This would have been the index of total gross private investment (of all types) valued in constant prices if there had been no change in either the proportion of the nation's gross output saved and invested or in relative prices. Actually, gross national saving (gross private investment) jumped from 18.05 percent of GNP in 1953 to 27.47 percent in 1960, an index of 152.2 as shown in row 2. This would have been the index of total gross private investment of all types valued in constant prices if there had been no change in the nation's gross output or in relative prices. As is customary in the calculation of saving rates, these percentages for saving are based on current-price data because decisions as to how much to save from income are presumed to be based on

5. Here we divide the 1953–71 period at 1960 rather than 1961 because some 1961 relationships were abnormal. Data in this section are based on the national accounts as reported by the Economic Planning Agency, and refer to fiscal years ending March 31 following the year named.

prevailing price relationships, not on the relative prices of consumption goods and investment goods operative in some past or (as in this case) future base year. Next, as shown in row 3, the percentage of total gross private investment (in current prices) that was allocated to fixed nonresidential business investment increased moderately, from 68.29 percent to 71.23 percent, or to an index of 104.3. Finally, as shown in row 4, the ratio of the average price of all output (GNP) to the price of fixed nonresidential business investment rose slightly, to an index of 100.2. Consequently, the quantity (constant-price value) of this type of investment would have risen slightly even if there had been no change in constant-price GNP, in the saving rate, or in the share of saving allocated to this type of investment.

Only the first two of the four indexes changed much, so that by this way of looking at the matter the rise from 1953 to 1960 in fixed nonresidential business investment was due mainly to the increase in GNP and the rise in the national saving (or total gross private investment) rate. Both changes were big.

The further rise in fixed nonresidential business investment after 1960 must be explained differently. With 1960 equal to 100, the 1971 index was 399.5. The increase in real GNP—to an index of 298.4—was again the biggest factor. But the further rise in the gross saving rate was small—from 27.47 to 29.13 percent, an index of 106.0. The share of nonresidential fixed investment in total investment actually dropped; the index was only 88.1. Although the annual share is somewhat erratic because of the volatility of two of the other components (inventory accumulation and net foreign investment), the 1960–71 drop was fairly representative of the downward trend, which stemmed from the swelling importance of residential construction.

The fourth index, the ratio of the implicit price deflator for GNP to the deflator for fixed nonresidential business investment, was 143.2 in 1971 (with 1960 equaling 100). This means that real fixed nonresidential business investment was 43 percent bigger in 1971 than it would have been if its relative price had not changed, provided that real GNP and the proportion of current dollar GNP devoted to such investment are considered to be unaffected by the change in relative prices. The drop in the relative price of fixed nonresidential business investment was persistent, and began even before 1960. A sizable drop occurred every year from 1957 to 1971. The declining relative price of investment goods was thus a major factor facilitating the sharp rise in real investment. This was not an international development, at least on any such scale. The 1960–71 index corresponding to the Japanese figure of 143.2 was only 102.7 in the United States.

When the whole period from 1953 to 1971 is considered, increases in three of the four series—real GNP, the gross saving rate, and the ratio of the price deflator for GNP to that for fixed nonresidential business investment—are all found to have contributed greatly to the rise in this type of investment. The decline in the share of total private investment devoted to fixed nonresidential business investment provided a moderate offset.

It is unnecessary to repeat all these calculations for investment in inventories, which fluctuates widely on an annual basis. Suffice it to note that the first two indexes in table 7-1 apply also to inventory investment, and that the price of goods held in private business inventories fell even more, relative to the GNP deflator, than did the price of fixed nonresidential business investment. In the case of inventories the drop was important in both periods. The index of the ratio of GNP prices to prices of goods held in private inventories was 124.5 in 1960 with 1953 taken as 100, 147.5 in 1971 with 1960 as 100, and 183.6 in 1971 with 1953 as 100.

Consideration of inventories thus strengthens the conclusion that the increase in real investment by business enterprises was facilitated enormously by the decline in the relative price of investment goods.[6]

Distribution of Investment and Saving

Important as was the change in relative prices, the rates of saving and investment command the most attention. Table 7-2 shows private gross investment and gross saving as percentages of GNP, together with detail to indicate the groups doing the investment and saving. Definitions and classification correspond approximately to those of the U.S. national income and product accounts.[7] Data shown are averages of the annual percentages for the fiscal years in each period.

Gross private investment rose from an average of 17.2 percent of GNP in 1952–54 to 30.5 percent of a vastly increased GNP in 1970–71. With one exception the increase was continuous between the periods shown in the table. From 1967 through 1971 roughly two-thirds of private investment, equal to 20 percent of GNP, was made by private corporations; this includes their fixed investment and additions to their inventories. Similar investment

6. However, this conclusion does not extend to residential construction, for which the price index rose a trifle more than the GNP deflator until 1965 and much more thereafter.

7. The Japanese national accounts show figures for total investment, total saving, and government saving that are higher by the amounts of government expenditures that they classify as gross government investment. Gross government investment ranged from 7.0 percent to 9.4 percent of GNP in the periods shown in table 7-1.

Table 7-2. *Gross Investment and Saving as Percentages*
of Gross National Product, Various Periods, Fiscal Years 1952–71
Annual averages

Fiscal years	Gross private investment				Gross private saving			Government surplus on income and product account			Statistical discrepancy (11)
	Total (1)	Corporate[a] (2)	Non-corporate[a] (3)	Net foreign (4)	Total (5)	Corporate[b] (6)	Non-corporate (7)	Total (8)	General government[c] (9)	Government enterprises[d] (10)	
1952–54	17.2	11.1	6.4	−0.3	16.5	7.4	9.1	−0.6	0.6	−1.1	1.3
1955–57	21.8	15.9	6.3	−0.4	22.8	9.2	13.5	−0.6	1.3	−1.9	−0.4
1958–60	24.3	17.3	6.5	0.5	24.9	11.0	13.9	−0.5	1.1	−1.6	−0.1
1961–63	27.2	21.6	6.7	−1.1	27.2	12.6	14.6	−0.1	2.0	−2.1	0.2
1964–66	25.5	16.6	8.2	0.7	26.6	12.5	14.1	−2.3	0.7	−2.9	1.2
1967–69	29.9	20.2	9.0	0.6	30.6	14.9	15.8	−1.1	1.8	−2.9	0.4
1970–71	30.5	19.7	8.9	1.9	31.9	15.6	16.3	−0.5	1.7	−2.2	−0.9

Sources: Derived from Economic Planning Agency, *Revised Report on National Income Statistics, 1951–1967*, pp. 10–11, 18–19, 20–21, 238–39, 258–59, and *Annual Report on National Income Statistics, 1973*, pp. 14–15, 20–21, 24–25, 222–23, 240–41.

a. The small "balancing item" appearing in tables for fixed investment by legal form of organization was allocated in proportion to other fixed investment.

b. Includes "damage of fixed capital by accident."

c. Equals "saving of general government" in the Japanese national accounts minus profit of government enterprises and gross fixed capital formation by general government.

d. Equals profit and depreciation of government enterprises less gross fixed capital formation and increase in stocks by government enterprises.

by unincorporated firms was only one-sixth as big, at about 3.5 percent of GNP, despite these firms' importance in production and employment.

Dwellings acquired by households and investment by nonprofit organizations accounted for the remaining 5.5 percentage points of the approximately 9.0 percent of GNP shown by table 7-2 to have been devoted to private non-corporate investment in 1967–71. The final investment component, net foreign investment, having been negative in three of the first four periods shown, turned positive in the last three.[8] In 1970–71 it averaged as much as 1.9 percent of GNP and over 6 percent of gross private investment.

Gross private investment is, by definition, equal to the sum of gross private saving and government saving when the latter is construed as the value of the government surplus on income and product account. This equality is missing in the actual data because the series for saving are statistically inconsistent with those for investment. The statistical discrepancy in the national income accounts must be added to saving or subtracted from investment to secure equality. Consequently, in table 7-2 column 1 equals the sum of columns 5, 8, and 11.

If they were consistently measured, private saving would have exceeded private investment in all periods because part of private saving was absorbed

8. This item is termed "net lending to the rest of the world" in the Japanese national accounts.

by a government deficit, as shown in table 7-2, column 8.[9] The nature of this deficit is brought out in columns 9 and 10. Receipts of general government exceeded general government expenditures (including outlays for construction and equipment), but the excess (column 9) was insufficient to finance fully the excess of capital outlays by government enterprises (including their inventory accumulation) over their depreciation charges and profits (column 10). The government deficit was usually modest, averaging only 0.82 percent of GNP from 1952 to 1971.[10] Hence nearly all private saving was available to finance private investment.

Gross private saving has behaved quite differently in the United States and Japan. In the United States it has been stable at around 16 percent of GNP throughout the postwar period, and indeed much longer if one excepts major wars and depressions. In Japan it started at about the same level, 16.5 percent, in 1952–54 but then rose sharply, reaching 31.9 percent in 1970–71. From 1961 through 1971 it averaged 28.8 percent (as against 15.8 percent in the United States). Both the level and increase in the Japanese gross private saving rate are extraordinary; the former exceeds the rate in any other major country.[11] Moreover, even though good comparable data are lacking to isolate depreciation allowances, which are included in gross saving, it is clear that the big excess of the gross saving rate in Japan over that in other major countries results from more net saving.

Both corporations and households contributed to the high rate of private saving. Columns 6 and 7 of table 7-2 show that in recent years corporations have contributed nearly half of gross private saving and households (including owners of unincorporated enterprises) a little more than half. Earlier the corporate share had been smaller. Other familiar saving rates besides the

9. In a few individual years government had a surplus on income and product account.

10. This percentage was larger than in the United States, where the deficit averaged 0.53 percent of GNP during the same period. However, investment by government enterprises was bigger in Japan, and such enterprises financed most of their investment from external sources.

11. Note that the figures cited are for the gross *private* saving rate. National saving rates of 30 percent or thereabouts are sometimes cited for a few Western countries but these include not only private saving and the government surplus on income and product account (i.e., gross private investment) but also expenditures for construction and durable equipment by both general government and government enterprises and sometimes (as in the Economic Planning Agency's national accounts for Japan) inventory accumulation by government enterprises. In Japan such goverment outlays averaged 9.0 percent of GNP in 1970–71. Adding them to gross private investment would bring the 1970–71 national saving or investment ratio up to 39.5 percent of GNP (or 40.5 percent when measured as the sum of components of saving). Their balancing addition to the surplus on income and product account would yield gross government saving equal to 8.5 percent of GNP.

percentages of GNP shown in the table may be mentioned. Net corporate saving averaged no less than 85 percent of corporate profits after tax from 1967 to 1971 while net personal saving averaged an equally remarkable 19.6 percent of disposable personal income.[12] Despite payment of only 15 percent of profits as dividends, corporate saving fell short of corporate investment by 4 or 5 percent of GNP in 1964–71 (column 2 less column 6). Earlier the gap was even larger. The deficiency (as well as the excess of government expenditures over receipts) was of course made good by the excess of noncorporate saving over noncorporate investment, including investment in owner-occupied houses. The transfer was largely effectuated by bank intermediation; new equity investment in corporations by individuals was small.

The reasons that corporate and personal saving were available in the amounts required to free resources for investment on the huge scale observed are by no means wholly clear, mainly because it is almost impossible to prove the accuracy or inaccuracy of many hypotheses, however probable or improbable they may seem.

A number of plausible partial explanations that have been suggested for the high personal saving rate may be mentioned.[13] First, there may be a tendency to base consumption on income of the past rather than on current income. Because personal income rose so sharply, even a moderate time lag would greatly raise the saving rate. Fortifying this possibility but not a requisite for its acceptance is the observation that Japan had long and recently been a low-income agrarian society; a few decades of rapid growth might not for everyone overcome a deep-seated feeling of poverty and accompanying adherence to traditional consumption habits. Second, bonuses, paid twice a year, comprise a larger fraction of wage and salary income than in other countries. For the wide range of workers covered by the Basic Survey on Wage Structure they equaled 23 percent of annual earnings in 1971 (30 percent of earnings other than bonuses).[14] It may be easier to save from such

12. The corporate percentage is 85 whether the inventory valuation adjustment is included or omitted. The capital consumption allowances deducted by the Economic Planning Agency to calculate profits (and hence net corporate saving) appear to be generous estimates in this period.

13. The high personal saving rate has been the subject of much speculation and investigation by Japanese economists. This paragraph is based chiefly on reviews and analyses of the literature by Toshiyuki Mizoguchi (but we are responsible for the selection and wording of the suggestions). See his *Personal Savings and Consumption in Postwar Japan* (Tokyo: Kinokuniya Bookstore Co., Ltd., 1970), and *Chochiku no keizaigaku* [Economics of Personal Savings] (Tokyo: Keisō Shobō, 1973).

14. These percentages are based on a comparison of twelve times total monthly contractual earnings during June 1971, from the 1971 survey, with annual special earnings (bonuses) paid during calendar year 1971 (or, for new employees only, the year ended June 1972) from the 1972 survey. Data from Bureau of Statistics, *Japan Statistical Yearbook, 1973/74*, p. 396.

infrequent payments than from regular weekly or monthly paychecks.[15] Third, proprietors' income, as well as the sum of proprietors' income and pure types of property income, are an unusually large part of personal income, and households headed by proprietors are an unusually large fraction of households; it is suggested that there is a higher propensity to save from this type of income than from wages and salaries, or by this category of households than by households headed by wage and salary earners. Fourth, the age distribution, which is unusually young, is favorable to saving if people save in order to support themselves after retirement.[16] Fifth, meagerness of social security benefits accentuates the need to save privately for old age. Sixth, a shortage of liquid assets, relative to rapidly rising income, might exert a strong pressure to save; similarly, pressure may be exerted upon the typical family not owning land to save in order to lift a ratio of accumulated net worth to income that is exceptionally low because of the rapid rise in income. The slow development of institutions providing consumer installment credit and mortgage loans intensified the need to increase asset holdings and net worth. Finally, it has been suggested that as a result of their moral education in the past the Japanese have a predisposition toward saving as a desideratum in itself.

The high corporate saving rate seems not really very surprising when one considers that, continuously, financing needs to grasp profitable investment opportunities were ample to absorb funds available from internal sources, that balance sheets showed such high ratios of debt to net worth that the pressure to add to stockholders' equity was strong, that financial markets were not such as to permit easy sale of new common stock issues, and that profits rose so rapidly that dividends increased substantially in most years despite the high saving rate.[17]

To understand the Japanese investment experience one also needs to know why business wished to undertake so much investment. We have already touched upon aspects of this question and will now approach it more systematically.

15. Bonuses may also help explain why the postwar rate was above the prewar rate and why the saving rate rose during the postwar period. Before World War II only white-collar workers received bonuses but in postwar Japan they have been paid to blue-collar workers as well. The fraction of earnings paid in bonuses has also risen gradually during the postwar period.

16. However, it is also argued that in Japan the saving ratio rises with age so that the age distribution is adverse to saving.

17. See Henry C. and Mable I. Wallich, "Banking and Income," in Hugh Patrick and Henry Rosovsky, eds., *Asia's New Giant: How the Japanese Economy Works* (Brookings Institution, 1976), for a discussion of corporate (as well as of personal) saving. These authors find a much higher dividend payout for big corporations than for smaller ones.

The Demand for Business Investment

Why was business investment demand so strong? Why did the rapid increase in capital stock resulting from so enormous a flood of investment fail to drive the rate of return so low that further investment would be discouraged, if not choked off? The following circumstances seem ample to explain sustained high investment in Japan, given the availability of saving.

1. A booming, fast-growing economy creates a strong demand for capital, and the Japanese economy grew faster than any other. The main reason investment grew so much is the obvious one: the demand for investment was derived from the expanding demand for end products which, in turn, stemmed from the rise in income created by the increase in production.

The expansion of investment from 1953 to 1971, big as it was, sufficed only to increase total capital input in the nonresidential business sector about as fast as the output of the sector. The increase was somewhat less than that of output before, and more after, 1961 and over the whole period somewhat less for fixed capital and somewhat more for inventories. Growth rates compare as follows:

	Nonresidential business national income	Input of reproducible capital		
		Total	Nonresidential structures and equipment	Inventories
1953–71	10.0	10.2	9.2	11.9
1953–61	9.9	7.9	6.3	10.8
1961–71	10.2	12.0	11.7	12.7

We are not suggesting merely that a spiral was under way in which increased investment raised output and higher output induced more investment. According to table 4-6, output determinants *other* than capital were responsible for some 78 percent of the 1953–71 growth of output in nonresidential business, and 71 percent even if a proportional share of the gains from economies of scale is transferred to capital. Had other determinants not been so extraordinarily favorable to output growth, capital would have increased less and it too would have contributed less to growth. For, with a smaller expansion of national income, the derived demand for capital would have been smaller. (Also, to revert to the determinants of saving, with lower GNP the saving to finance so much investment would not have been forthcoming.)

2. Japanese business has sought to duplicate production conditions, including the use of capital, of efficient Western firms, particularly those in the

Table 7-3. *International Comparisons of Gross Fixed Investment*
by Nonresidential Business, 1970 and 1960–71

Percentages of U.S. values

Measure	Price weights	United States	Japan	France	West Germany	United Kingdom	Italy
Gross investment during 1970	United States	100.0	90.8	119.3	114.3	53.4	59.0
per civilian employed in 1970	Other country	100.0	78.3	106.5	97.2	49.0	50.8
Gross investment from 1960	United States	100.0	64.3	103.0	102.8	54.6	57.2
through 1971 per civilian	Other country	100.0	55.5	91.9	87.5	50.1	49.3
employed in 1971							

Sources: Gross investment in 1970 prices of the United States and the other countries from Irving B. Kravis and others, *A System of International Comparisons of Gross Product and Purchasing Power*, United Nations International Comparison Project: Phase One (Johns Hopkins University Press for the World Bank, 1975), table 13 and appendix table 13 for the respective countries; gross investment in 1963 prices of the respective countries from Organisation for Economic Co-operation and Development, *National Accounts of OECD Countries, 1960–1971* (Paris: OECD, 1973), table 2; civilian employment from OECD, *Labour Force Statistics, 1961–72* (Paris: OECD, 1974), table II.

United States. The effort to raise output per worker by adopting American practices, including the amount of capital used per worker, appears to have been pursued more consciously and energetically than in other countries. The ratio of capital input to labor input in the nonresidential business sector in fact rose greatly: it was 3.61 times as high in 1971 as in 1953 (table 4-4, columns 2 and 5), which is equivalent to a growth rate of 7.4 percent.[18] The point to be stressed, however, is that the capital–labor ratio was very low in 1953 and the burst of investment has by no means brought the ratio of capital to labor into unexplored territory; other countries have higher ratios.

That this is so for fixed capital can be inferred from investment data obtained from the United Nations study by Kravis and associates.[19] The top two rows of table 7-3 compare gross fixed investment in four European countries and Japan in 1970 with gross fixed investment in the United States. The United States is compared with each of the other countries by the use of both U.S. price weights and the other country's price weights. Residential construction and construction of types performed primarily for general government and nonprofit organizations are omitted in order to approximate investment by nonresidential business (see appendix O, page 255). The comparisons in the table are based on investment per civilian worker. The gross amount invested during 1970, per employed civilian, was much less in Japan than in France or West Germany, and less also than in the United States. Moreover, it is obvious that Japan's capital stock position in any recent year

18. The change in the ratio of capital to labor used *effectively* was somewhat less because the proportion of labor misallocated to agriculture and self-employment was curtailed. But even on this basis the increase was huge.

19. Irving B. Kravis and others, *A System of International Comparisons of Gross Product and Purchasing Power*, United Nations International Comparison Project: Phase One (Johns Hopkins University Press for the World Bank, 1975).

has compared less favorably with other countries than its investment position, because capital stock depends on previous investment and investment has been rising fastest in Japan.

To secure rough international comparisons of cumulative investment during the twelve years from 1960 through 1971, the estimates of investment by each country in 1970 were multiplied by the ratio of 1960–71 investment to 1970 investment that is obtained from data for investment valued in the country's own constant prices. The results, per civilian employed in 1971, are shown in the two bottom rows of table 7-3. They give an indication of the position of the countries with respect to fixed nonresidential business capital per civilian worker at the end of 1971, even though allowance must be made for a wide margin of error if they are so interpreted.[20] When measured in U.S. prices, cumulative investment from 1960 through 1971 per civilian worker was 60 percent higher in France and West Germany than in Japan, and 56 percent higher in the United States. Japan was, however, above the United Kingdom and Italy.[21] All the countries compare less favorably with the United States when calculations are based on their prices. Cumulative investment per civilian worker was higher in the United States than in France or West Germany on this basis, and some 80 percent higher than in Japan.

To judge relative capital intensities it would be better to divide net stock, or investment, in the nonresidential business sector by employment in that sector rather than by total civilian employment. When this is done for three countries, the following indexes are obtained for 1960–71 gross fixed investment by nonresidential business per person employed in that sector in 1971.

Percentages of U.S. values

Price weights	United States	West Germany	Japan
United States	100	91	51
Other country	100	77	44

20. For the United States and West Germany perpetual inventory estimates, based on thirty-five-year service lives for construction, fifteen-year lives for equipment, and straight-line depreciation, were also prepared for comparison. They yielded an estimate that at the end of 1971 net stock per civilian worker in Germany was 100 percent of the United States figure, based on U.S. price weights, as compared with the 1960–71 gross investment ratio of 102.8 percent shown in table 7-3. Similar estimates were not attempted for Japan because the Japanese time series for constant-price investment do not separate construction from equipment.

21. The 1970 percentages for the European countries shown in table 7-3 exceed essentially similar percentages for the beginning of 1964 that are shown in Denison, *Why Growth Rates Differ* (table 12-13, p. 170) by amounts larger than are explicable by changes during the interviewing time period. The two sets of estimates therefore should not be treated as statistically comparable.

The change drops Japan relative to both the United States and West Germany, and West Germany relative to the United States. Although satisfactory data for business employment in other countries shown in table 7-3 are lacking, we think it probable that the percentage of civilian employment allocated to the business sector is smallest in the United States and biggest in Japan. If so, use of business employment would lower Japanese investment per worker relative to all the other countries, and investment per worker in all the other countries relative to the United States.

In any case, it is evident even from table 7-3 that at the end of 1971 Japan was far from a world leader in business capital per worker.

3. Labor was becoming much more expensive relative to capital in Japan. Hence the incentive to increase the use of capital was great. In the nonresidential business sector current-price earnings of labor, per unit of labor input, were 6.3 times as large in 1971 as in 1953 while the comparable ratio for capital was 2.6.[22] Prices of capital goods themselves rose little. Whereas the price of GNP was 2.08 times as high in 1971 as in 1953, the price of private nonresidential fixed investment (which determines depreciation costs) was only 1.44 times as high, and for goods held in private inventories the 1971 price was only 1.14 times the 1953 price.[23]

4. General economic conditions and the political system were favorable, or at least not unfavorable, to investment. Stabilization policy was generally successful during the period considered. Prices were stable enough for efficient planning and operation, and recessions were mild and brief enough to keep production near capacity most of the time. Taxes, including those on corporate profits and upper bracket personal incomes, were not onerous and tax rates were repeatedly reduced; the absence of defense expenditures and a swiftly rising tax base helped to make this comfortable policy possible.[24] Fairly low interest rates were maintained except in brief periods of overexpansion. This was especially important for business investment, which in Japan is financed heavily by bank loans. Capital goods could be imported as freely as the nation's foreign exchange earnings allowed, and investment

22. The index of each factor's estimated total earnings in current prices (net of depreciation, in the case of capital) was divided by the index of the quantity of its input to secure these ratios. Total earnings are the yen values underlying table 4-1. The input indexes are from table 4-4. Capital earnings, as estimated, include "pure" profit, so the comparison is only an approximation.

23. Ratios quoted in this sentence are based on the Economic Planning Agency's deflators for its national product series.

24. By U.S. bookkeeping methods there may have been government deficits, but the current account budget for general government was in surplus, and this was considered the budget appropriate to tax policy.

shared with raw materials the first claim to whatever exchange was available. Relations between business and the governing Liberal Democratic party were amicable. Threats of nationalization or other punitive attacks on business that could jeopardize the safety of investment were confined to the opposition Marxist parties, which were always in a minority position. Foreign governments restricted Japanese exports, to be sure, but on balance restrictions were not increasing and only a small percentage of the national product was affected. In short, business operated in an atmosphere of confidence in its own and the nation's future. The Economic Planning Agency as well as private organizations repeatedly issued optimistic projections, these were surpassed, and the next projections were both higher and accepted even more confidently by business.

Dwellings

In measuring the contribution made to the growth rate by increases in the services of dwellings, we seek to establish the amount contributed to the increase in the actual output measure, based on the methods of measurement actually used. In the case of Japan, this contribution to 1953–71 growth is estimated to be 0.30 percentage points. This is about the same as the contribution in Canada (1950–67) and the United States (1948–69) but much above the contributions in Europe (table 4-8).

Housing has been persistently insufficient and inadequate in Japan, so the strong demand for dwelling space, and hence for new construction, is not difficult to explain. The rise in real income was so rapid as to virtually guarantee that housing demand would rise faster than the capital stock of dwellings could be improved and increased. This would have been so even if there had been no shortage at the conclusion of World War II, which was of course far from the case. The rise in residential construction, relative even to total investment, has already been noted.

There is little doubt that the increase in national income earned in the provision of housing services was especially large in Japan, but it must be admitted that international differences in the contribution made by this component to the growth of output as actually measured depend almost as much on estimating methods in different countries as on changes in the stock of housing. In most countries there is little correspondence between changes in gross rents of dwellings (the starting point for estimates of national income originating in this sector) and changes in the gross stock of dwellings, both expressed in constant prices. Japan is no exception; the annual rent on dwellings, measured as a component of personal consumption expenditures in 1965 prices, rose 7.6 percent a year from 1953 to 1971 and 8.3 percent from 1961 to 1971. This is far more than estimates of the gross capital stock of dwellings, also measured in 1965 prices. Estimates for the United States display a similar differential.

International Assets

The net inflow of property income from abroad has remained just slightly negative at all dates. (Table 3-3, column 6, shows the constant-price estimates.) The contribution to growth has consequently been approximately zero. This is partly because net foreign investment has not usually been large (table 7-2) and partly because it took the form mainly of changes in international financial assets yielding no, or little, return. However, some direct investment has been undertaken.

In the other ten countries the contribution of international assets ranged from −0.12 points in Canada (1950–67) to 0.10 in the Netherlands (1950–62).

Land

Land is scarce and expensive in Japan, and during the postwar years its price has increased many times over. Availability and ownership of land obviously condition the composition and distribution of output. But in the absence of changes in the quantity of land available for use in production, the contribution of land to the growth rate of total output is necessarily zero. This is the case in all countries.

CHAPTER EIGHT

Advances in Knowledge

IN THIS BOOK estimates of the contribution that advances in knowledge have made to growth refer to improvements in the techniques of production, distribution, and business organization that are *adopted* in a particular period, not to the contribution that new knowledge developed in that period would permit. Thus they include what can be regarded conceptually as two separate growth sources: the contribution made possible by newly developed knowledge—which is to say the increase in productivity that would be obtained from new knowledge by a country in which average practice was continually at the world's production frontier—and the positive or negative contribution which is secured if average practice moves closer to or further from that frontier.

The concept of "knowledge" is comprehensive in that it includes managerial and organizational as well as technological knowledge, so long as it is pertinent to the nation's production. However, the scope of the estimates is limited in two important respects by the way output is measured. First, incorporation of new knowledge into the productive process can raise output per unit of input, as it is actually measured, only in nonresidential business. Second, even within this sector a contribution to measured growth is made only by those advances that reduce the labor, capital, and land used to produce a unit of final product of existing types, as distinguished from advances that result in the introduction of new or improved final products (that is, in "unmeasured" or "noneconomic" quality change).[1]

The contribution made by the incorporation of new knowledge into pro-

---

1. Growth rates in nonresidential business and the contribution of advances in knowledge do reflect reductions in the unit costs of obtaining final products that result from improvements in capital goods. Hence, the contribution of advances in knowledge includes what is sometimes called technical progress "embodied" in capital.

duction can be estimated only as a residual, secured by eliminating from the growth rate of national income the contributions of all other growth sources which are considered significant and reasonably ascertainable. Consequently, it is combined with the effects of miscellaneous determinants that are not estimated.[2] (It also includes the net error in the total contribution of series that are estimated.)

A résumé of estimates for other countries is required to permit interpretation of results for Japan. The growth rate of the residual index for the contribution of advances in knowledge and miscellaneous determinants to growth of output in the U.S. nonresidential business sector was 1.43 percent a year from 1948 to 1969. Aside from a small dip of dubious significance during the middle years, this rate was stable throughout the period. It was judged that the miscellaneous determinants were probably of little importance so that 1.43 percentage points approximated the contribution of the incorporation of advances of knowledge into production. Moreover, it seems unlikely that in the U.S. economy, the most productive and largest in the world, the rate at which advances were incorporated departed much from the worldwide rate of new advances; that is to say, it is not likely that average practice moved closer to or further from the frontier of best practice enough to affect the growth rate very much.[3] The rate of 1.43 percent in 1948–69 was almost double the rate of 0.72 percent in 1929–48. Although comparable data are not available for prior years, it is highly unlikely that the postwar rate was matched in any earlier period.[4]

The contribution to the growth rate of U.S. national income in the whole economy, including sectors where no contribution was made to measured growth, was of course lower: 1.19 percentage points in 1948–69 (and 0.62 points in 1929–48).[5] We have similar estimates of the contributions of advances in knowledge and miscellaneous determinants to growth in eight European countries during each of two rather short time periods. The estimates from 1955 to 1962 for Belgium, Denmark, West Germany, the

2. Miscellaneous determinants included in the U.S. estimates are listed and discussed in Denison, *Accounting for Growth,* pp. 76–79, and citations provided there. They (the "n.e.c." portion of "advances in knowledge and n.e.c.") are the same in the Japanese estimates.

3. Edward F. Denison, *The Sources of Economic Growth in the United States and the Alternatives Before Us,* Supplementary Paper 13 (Committee for Economic Development, 1962 [reprinted 1973]), pp. 234–37, 254–55; "The Unimportance of the Embodied Question," *American Economic Review,* vol. 54 (March 1964), pp. 90–93; and *Why Growth Rates Differ,* pp. 144–50, 282.

4. *Accounting for Growth,* pp. 79–83.

5. Ibid., p. 127.

Netherlands, Norway, and the United Kingdom were all in the narrow range of 0.75 to 0.96 percentage points; for Italy the estimate was 1.30 points and for France 1.51 points. Belgium, France, Norway, and the United Kingdom had rates in 1950–55 that were close to their 1955–62 rates. Three of the other European countries (West Germany, 2.55 percentage points, Italy, 2.12, the Netherlands, 1.79) had particularly high residual rates in 1950–55 and one (Denmark, 0.05 points) a low one. These four residuals were considered likely to have resulted either from the elimination of immediate postwar imbalances or from errors of estimate. With both periods considered, only the data for France suggested any significant "catching-up" with the United States in technique, and even the difference between France and the United States was moderate.[6] Finally, the estimate of the contribution in Canada is 0.66 percentage points during the 1950–67 period.[7] The statistical discrepancy between two series for Canadian output is rather large, and an alternative procedure would yield a residual of nearly 1.0 percentage point.

These previous investigations suggest two conclusions. First, it is hardly likely that—with the ratio of actual to best practice held constant—the postwar advance of the world's knowledge has been sufficient to raise output per unit of input in the nonresidential business sector of advanced economies much, if any, faster than the 1.43 percent annual rate observed in the United States from 1948 to 1969. This implies a rate for whole economies which is lower by an amount that depends on the weight of other sectors in a particular country and period. Second, although one might expect it to be easy for modern economies like those of Western Europe and Canada to slash the efficiency gap between themselves and the most advanced country, the United States, such evidence as we have indicates that they usually have not done so.[8]

Against this background the Japanese performance is impressive. Within nonresidential business the index of the contribution of the adoption of advances in knowledge and miscellaneous determinants (table 4-5) grew at an annual rate of 2.30 percent from 1953 to 1971 as compared with 1.43 percent in the United States from 1948 to 1969. If the U.S. rate measures the rate of advance in new knowledge, this leaves 0.87 points in Japan for narrowing of the gap between actual and best practice. Moreover, the Japa-

6. Data for Europe are from *Why Growth Rates Differ*, pp. 283–84. When that study was made, the estimate for the United States was 0.76 percentage points in 1950–62 (and in both subperiods). It was subsequently revised upward to 1.15 points, which strengthens the original conclusion that there was little catch-up in Europe. See *Accounting for Growth*, p. 345.

7. See table 4-8, above.

8. We do not have estimates for Europe after 1962. A detailed investigation would be required to test whether the situation there has changed.

nese rate was higher in the latter part of the period.[9] We estimate that it was 1.76 percent until the end of 1962 and 2.91 percent thereafter. Difficulties of eliminating cyclical influences make it hard to be sure just when to date the acceleration, and a later date would also be tenable. Its use would yield an even higher growth rate for the later period.

The contribution to the growth rate of national income in the entire economy made by the incorporation of knowledge into production, together with miscellaneous determinants, was 1.97 percentage points in 1953–71. This exceeded the contributions to growth of standardized national income in all of the other ten countries—by amounts ranging from 0.46 percentage points in the case of France (1950–62) to as much as 1.07 to 1.31 points in the cases of Norway, West Germany, Belgium, the United Kingdom, Denmark, the Netherlands (all 1950–62), and Canada (1950–67). The contribution to Japanese growth was even higher in 1961–71, 2.43 percentage points.

The gap between the United States and Japan in output per worker, shown for 1970 in table 2-1, is big—sufficiently so to leave no doubt that Japan was also decidedly below the United States in output per unit of input, even after eliminating effects of all determinants that are measured separately in our growth analysis (labor, capital, and land input per worker, irregular factors, resource allocation, and economies of scale). Comparisons of this type showed that in 1960 what was termed "residual efficiency" was 28 percent lower in Northwest Europe than in the United States when output was measured in U.S. prices. Residual efficiency in individual countries ranged from 23 percent lower in France to 34 percent lower in the United Kingdom in 1960.[10] Crude estimates prepared in this study show that on a comparable basis Japan was 30 percent below the United States in 1970.[11]

The study from which the European estimates are drawn put residual efficiency in Western Europe in 1960 much below that in the United States in 1925. It expressed the opinion that the difference in residual efficiency between the United States in 1925 and the United States in 1960 is ascribable to new knowledge developed in the interim but that the larger difference

9. In a way this is surprising. Kazushi Ohkawa and Henry Rosovsky (*Japanese Economic Growth: Trend Acceleration in the Twentieth Century* [Stanford University Press, 1973], pp. 91–95) point, plausibly, to two factors especially favorable to technological progress in the earlier years: the previous widening of the gap between average practice and the world's best practice in the period of Japanese isolation during the 1930s and World War II, and the "spillover" of experience gained in wartime production to production of civilian products after the war.

10. *Why Growth Rates Differ*, table 20-2, column 1, p. 289.

11. Appendix table O-1, column 1.

between Western Europe in 1960 and the United States in 1960 could not reasonably be laid to differences in the knowledge available to the two areas.[12] Knowledge is a worldwide commodity. Lags in its availability are at most a few years, not several decades. Especially is this so when the leading country is the United States, where nearly all knowledge circulates freely and where productivity teams sent from other countries for the express purpose of observing American practices have been not only welcomed but sponsored. What applies to the gap between the United States and Europe applies also to the gap between the United States and Japan.[13]

One would like to know what the determinants of international differences in residual productivity are, how they arise, and, most of all, how it is possible for them to persist for long periods. Only then could one hope to explore successfully why Japan was better able to cut into the gap in residual efficiency than were other countries in the periods for which we have estimates. For Japan's success is less surprising than the inability of other countries to do as well.

Attitudes and practices that *may* have helped Japan can be suggested. The Japanese people are reputed to be unusually attracted by and receptive to new and foreign ideas. The search for useful information from abroad, and its application in Japan, has been favored and supported by the Japanese government since the Meiji restoration. When Japanese accept practices found effective in America or elsewhere, they seem more willing than Europeans to adopt them without incurring more than a minimum of delay and expense in an effort to improve upon them before adoption. (This, of course, implies no lack of interest in improvement of a practice once established.) Workers' resistance to the introduction of labor-saving procedures seems rarer than in some if not all Western countries; with management determined to reduce costs by innovation, this can be an important advantage. This advantage is a perhaps inseparable part of a labor relations package that includes guaranteed employment to the age of fifty-five or so for permanent employees of large firms, differentials in individuals' compensation based more on seniority and education and less on duties and performance than is customary elsewhere, paying employees much of their compensation as semiannual bonuses that may vary with a firm's success, an unusual degree of paternalism and of employee identification with the enterprise, and unions that are organized on a

12. *Why Growth Rates Differ*, p. 335.

13. Japan's payments for foreign (mostly American) technology do not qualify this discussion materially. They were largely confined to late developments in high-technology manufacturing industries, for the most part were required only because foreign firms were barred from direct entry to Japan, and at their peak scarcely exceeded one-fourth of 1 percent of the Japanese national income.

company- rather than a craft- or industry-wide basis. Some of these conditions, viewed separately, seem more likely to reduce than to raise efficiency, although they may not affect the growth rate unless they change in strength.

Management is a key element in efficiency. Our measures of labor input include proprietors and hired managers, as well as all other workers, but we found no way to bring into the measures the special talents of management people, procedures for selecting them, or the effects of competition or its absence on managerial performance. Changes in managerial performance necessarily are reflected largely in the residual. A characteristic feature of management in large Japanese firms is decisionmaking by consensus. Whether this leads to better decisions we cannot judge. Although it may delay decisions, good or bad, it is said to facilitate wholehearted implementation by all concerned.

Other possibly pertinent conditions may be mentioned. Competition among Japanese firms and, in international markets, from foreign firms may have become stronger and intensified pressure to reduce costs, but we do not know whether this has been of real importance. We have no reason to quarrel with the judgment of Trezise and Suzuki that government planning and detailed governmental intervention in business were not major positive factors, but we attempt no independent appraisal of their impact.[14] We note that the largest residuals appear for two countries, Japan and France, with developed systems of indicative planning, but suspect that it is a coincidence. We also note the curious fact that the Japanese record was achieved despite the exclusion of foreign firms, usually primary carriers of technology, and despite requirements to secure government approval of licensing and other arrangements for introduction and use of foreign technology. Evidently the strategy of securing the most valuable technology while avoiding foreign control and minimizing foreign exchange costs succeeded.

One cannot be sure how closely the high rate for the residual in Japan corresponds to the effects of incorporating new knowledge into production as distinguished from the effects of miscellaneous unmeasured determinants or, consequently, just how much of a catching-up with best knowledge is implied. But the large residual is certainly consistent with the common belief that Japan has been closing the gap with the United States, and we believe this to be the case.

14. See Philip Trezise with the collaboration of Yukio Suzuki, "Politics, Government, and Economic Growth in Japan," in Hugh Patrick and Henry Rosovsky, eds., *Asia's New Giant: How the Japanese Economy Works* (Brookings Institution, 1976).

CHAPTER NINE

Reallocation of Resources

FOR AN ADVANCED country, Japan allocates an unusually large percentage of employment to agriculture. Within nonagricultural employment, the percentage of self-employed and unpaid family workers is high. Both percentages are well above those that would maximize national income. They are also well above those in Western countries, except Italy. In 1970 the employment distribution, like output per worker, was about the same in Japan and Italy.

From 1953 to 1971 both agricultural employment and nonfarm self-employment declined substantially relative to total employment. The adverse effects on total output of declines in these employment categories were small relative to the increments added by the labor released to nonagricultural wage and salary employment. We estimate that these shifts of labor contributed some 0.94 percentage points to the growth rate of national income. Relaxation of international trade barriers brought to 0.95 points the total contribution of improved resource allocation—or, more precisely, of the aspects of resource allocation that we attempt to estimate. This chapter, supplemented by appendix J, explains these estimates.

Agriculture

Some 35.6 percent of all employed persons were primarily engaged in agriculture in 1953. This may have been a little above a "trend" percentage; immediately after the war farm employment was swollen by disruption of the nonfarm economy and the repatriation of Japanese from abroad, and in absolute numbers it did not clearly recede until after 1955. The percentage, however, dropped every year from at least 1952, touching 26.1 percent in 1961 and 14.6 percent in 1971.[1]

1. These percentages, computed from table 3-4, are based on the new agricultural employment series from the Labor Force Survey. This is much smaller than the agri-

A decline of nearly three-fifths in eighteen years in the agricultural percentage is not really exceptional; it is only a bit above the average of the advanced countries examined. Moreover, the decline in the agricultural percentage in Japan was facilitated by a particularly large increase in total employment. The actual reduction in agricultural employment was 46 percent, from 14,035,000 in 1953 to 7,509,000 in 1971.

What is unusual about the Japanese situation is that agriculture was so important that the decline in the agricultural percentage represented an especially large proportion (21 percent) of the total labor force. The Japanese situation was matched only in Italy, though the employment shift was also big in some other countries, including France and West Germany.

To estimate gains from reallocation we relate agriculture to totals for nonresidential business rather than for the whole economy.[2] Agriculture's percentages of key nonresidential business aggregates in the boundary years of our periods are as follows:[3]

	1953	1961	1971
Employment	38.66	28.11	15.92
Labor input	32.64	22.85	12.51
National income in 1965 prices	20.33	14.14	4.82

With technical progress and mechanization there was a steady decline in the proportions of employment and labor input whose allocation to agriculture would have maximized national income. The actual proportions, though also falling, were always much above the optimum for the same date. Our estimates of the gains from reallocation are based on the percentages of labor input rather than of employment. The labor input percentages are lower

---

cultural employment used in earlier appraisals of gains from reallocation. (See appendix J, page 225, for some employment comparisons.) Also, forestry and fisheries, important industries in Japan, have sometimes been combined with agriculture in reallocation studies. We have not done this because earnings in these industries do not appear to be low enough to give any clear indication of misallocation in the distribution of employment by industry. (The self-employed in these industries, however, are counted in estimating gains from the reduction in importance of nonagricultural self-employment.)

2. Our estimates of the proportion of labor devoted to agriculture are considerably smaller than those used by most earlier analysts because we use labor input instead of employment, our agricultural employment estimates themselves are lower, and we exclude forestry and fisheries. This lowers estimates of the reduction in misallocation, and hence of the contribution to growth. However, in comparisons of estimates it must be stressed that ours include the gain from raising productivity within agriculture by eliminating excess labor while some others do not.

3. Appendix table J-1 provides estimates for all years from 1952 through 1971. Labor input percentages shown in this text table were obtained by linking overlapping series to improve comparability; see table J-1, footnote a.

because agriculture has a bigger percentage of part-time workers than non-agricultural industries, fewer males, and a less educated labor force.[4]

The percentage by which national income in constant prices originating in the nonresidential business sector would have been raised each year if labor input had been distributed in the following year's proportion is calculated on the basis of two estimates. The first is that if labor input had been 1 percent smaller in farming in any year, agricultural national income would have been smaller by one-fourth as much, or 0.25 percent. The ratio of one-quarter is placed much below the labor share of agricultural national income (two-thirds to three-fourths) because the farm employment eliminated, which was mainly excess labor on small farms, was that with the least output.[5] This ratio is not firmly based, but it could be changed considerably without altering our final estimates much because national income per unit of input is much smaller in agriculture than in nonagricultural industries.[6] The second estimate is that in nonagricultural nonresidential business if labor input had been 1 percent larger output would have been larger by a fraction of 1 percent equal to the labor share in that subsector (0.72 to 0.82 percent, depending on the year). A chain index of annual percentage gains (table 4-5, column 2) is used to calculate contributions to the growth rate of nonresidential business output (table 4-6, columns 1 to 3); these are reduced appropriately to arrive at contributions to the growth rate of total national income (table 4-6, columns 4 to 6). The amount is 0.64 percentage points in 1953–71.

The contribution, it should be noted, is affected not only by the amount of labor diverted from agriculture and the relationships between percentage changes in labor input and output in farm and nonfarm business, but also by the ratio of national income in 1965 prices per unit of labor input in agricul-

---

4. The distribution by age in agriculture is often presumed to be adverse too, but on the basis of our weighting structure this is not so; a paucity of teenagers offsets an above-average proportion of elderly people. Differences between agriculture and nonagriculture in hours of full-time workers of the same sex are not considered a difference in labor input.

5. There were no really large farms. Even in 1940 there were few large farms and land reform under the occupation limited farm size to three hectares (twelve in Hokkaido). Land reform also nearly eliminated tenancy. As there are hardly any hired farm workers, farm labor consists almost entirely of farm owners and members of their families.

6. Our assumption lies between assumptions implicit in procedures that handle reallocation gains as gains from shifts in industry weights and those often implied by two-sector models that divide an economy into a growing modern sector and a dwindling traditional sector. The former procedures assume that agricultural output is reduced by the same proportion as agricultural employment (or by the product of this percentage and the labor share), whereas two-sector models often imply that agricultural output is not reduced at all if employment is cut.

ture to the corresponding figure in nonagricultural industries. In 1953 and 1965 the ratio was 0.53; it dropped to 0.35 in 1971. The lower the ratio, the greater is the gain in constant price national income from the transfer of labor. Substantial government support for agriculture, especially rice, helped to make the output ratios expressed in 1965 prices higher than they would otherwise have been and hence to minimize the gain in constant price national income from labor reallocation.[7] Partly because this ratio was higher in Japan, the contribution to Japanese growth from 1953 to 1971 was 0.40 percentage points less than the contribution to growth in Italy from 1950 to 1962, and less by much smaller amounts than the contribution to French and West German growth from 1950 to 1962. (It probably was not smaller than in France or West Germany in 1953–71.) The Japanese advantage over the United States (1948–69) and over Belgium, the Netherlands, and the United Kingdom (all 1950–62) was a sizable 0.41 to 0.58 percentage points.

Nonagricultural Self-Employment

In Japan and Italy an extraordinarily large proportion of civilian nonagricultural employment has consisted of self-employed and unpaid family workers. In 1964, for example, the proportion in these countries was 24 to 25 percent as compared with 12 to 16 percent in the other continental European countries listed in table 4-9, 11 percent in the United States, and 7 percent in the United Kingdom. In all these countries the percentage has been declining. In all, too, are independent professionals and proprietors of large establishments whose labor is in no sense misallocated, but also many own-account and family workers who operate firms too small to occupy their time fully or to permit efficient operation. With no cash payroll, or almost none, to meet, they can continue in business despite low earnings. Among this group are many who could earn more in paid employment but stick stubbornly to the independence of self-employment, often until death or retirement arrives and their children decide not to take their places.

We believe the decline in the percentage of self-employed and unpaid family workers is concentrated among those least efficiently utilized—usually

7. It may also be noted that the use of 1965 prices yields higher ratios throughout the 1952–71 period than would the use of prices of any earlier year in the period, and lower ratios than would the use of prices of any later year in the period. This is implied by the fact that within nonresidential business the ratio of national income originating in agriculture to national income originating in nonagricultural industries is higher in current prices (table 3-2) than in constant prices (table 3-3) in all years before 1965 and lower in all subsequent years.

in businesses with no paid employees—and with the lowest value of output. The effect of their disappearance on output could be made good by an increase in the output of the remaining self-employed or family workers or by a much smaller increase in wage-salary employment. Specifically, we assume that to perform the same work an increase of only one nonagricultural wage and salary worker—or, more exactly, of one unit of labor input—was required to offset the loss of four units of labor previously performed by self-employed and unpaid family workers.[8]

Expressed as a percentage of total nonagricultural employment in nonresidential business, self-employed and unpaid family workers dropped from 39.8 in 1953 to 29.9 in 1961 and 24.4 in 1971. The corresponding percentages for labor input were 34.6, 25.7, and 21.3.[9] These are sharp declines. They were achieved not by an absolute drop in the number of self-employed but by a huge increase in the number of wage and salary workers. The percentage gain in output per unit of input in nonresidential business from the reduction in misallocation is the same either way, of course, but the general increase in employment made it much easier to achieve.

Reduction of the overallocation of labor to self-employment is estimated to have contributed 0.30 percentage points to growth of the total national income in 1953–71. This exceeds the contributions in all of the other countries. The Japanese advantage was greatest (0.20 to 0.26 points) over Canada, the United States, and the United Kingdom.

Together, the reallocations of labor from agriculture and from nonfarm self-employment are estimated to have contributed 0.94 percentage points to the 1953–71 growth rate of output in the economy as a whole, more than in any of the other countries examined except Italy.[10] Because of the emphasis many writers have rightly placed upon the dual labor market as a factor in Japanese growth, some readers may have expected an even higher figure. Comments on this expectation are in appendix J, part 3.

8. See Denison, *Why Growth Rates Differ,* chap. 16, for Western data and further discussion.

9. Appendix table J-2 shows employment and labor input percentages annually from 1952 through 1971. Labor input percentages cited above were obtained by linking overlapping series to improve comparability; see table J-2, footnote a.

10. The division of this estimate between its two components has an arbitrary element in that the calculation implies that the reduction in the agricultural share of business employment is initially offset by proportional increases in self-employment and wage-salary employment in nonagricultural business, and that the decline in self-employment as a percentage of nonagricultural business employment is then offset by an increase in wage-salary employment in nonagricultural business. Alternative conventions could be used, though not easily.

It is possible that the distribution of wage and salary workers among enterprises of different sizes approached the optimal distribution more closely or diverged further from it. We have attempted no estimate of the contribution, positive or negative, of such a change but believe it cannot be large relative to the effects of reallocation from agriculture and self-employment.

Reduction in International Trade Barriers

Artificial barriers to international trade prevent the most efficient international division of labor and restrict the size of markets and hence economies of scale. Reduction of barriers to both imports and exports contributed appreciably to the growth of some European countries. This was not so in Japan, where there was little change in trade barriers. Throughout the period we examine, imports of both raw materials and machinery were unrestricted or restrained only by the availability of foreign exchange. The market for rice was consistently reserved for domestic farmers. Imports of manufactured consumer products were forbidden or subjected to prohibitive tariffs throughout the period. Restrictions on Japanese exports also seem, on balance, to have changed little relative to the size of the Japanese economy.

These statements must be modified to note that some slight easing of restraints on both sides, including increased access to the Japanese market for foods other than rice, is observable in the 1960s, especially after 1968, but this easing had little effect on trade until after the period we consider. Estimates by Kiyoshi Kojima credit Japanese import liberalization with only 2.7 percent of the growth of Japanese imports and foreign import liberalization with only 6.2 percent of the growth of Japanese exports even from 1961 to 1971.[11] These increases amount to 0.36 percent and 0.58 percent, respectively, of Japanese GNP in 1971.

To give quantitative expression to our qualitative impression of how trade barriers may have affected the growth rate of output per unit of input, we introduced the index in table 4-5, column 4. We held the index constant until 1962, then raised it by 0.01 percent a year until 1968, and by 0.03 percent a year thereafter. This pattern implies that, in nonresidential business, output,

11. Kiyoshi Kojima, *Taiheiyō Keizaiken to Nippon* [Japan and the Pacific Free Trade Area] (Kunimoto Shobō, 1969), quoted by Lawrence B. Krause and Sueo Sekiguchi, "Japan and the World Economy," in Hugh Patrick and Henry Rosovsky, *Asia's New Giant: How the Japanese Economy Works* (Brookings Institution, 1976). The percentages cited are from Krause and Sekiguchi, pp. 423, 427.

and hence output per unit of input, was 0.15 percent bigger in 1971 than it would have been if there had been no change in trade barriers. This in turn implies the gain was almost one-sixth of the total induced increase in trade turnover (exports plus imports).

The implied contribution to growth of total national income from 1953 to 1971 comes to only 0.01 percentage points. In other countries amounts ranged from nothing in the United States and Canada up to 0.16 points during 1950–62 in Belgium, Italy, and the Netherlands.

CHAPTER TEN

Economies of Scale

GROWTH OF AN ECONOMY automatically means growth in the average size of the local, regional, and national markets that business serves. Growth of markets brings opportunities for greater specialization—both among and within industries, firms, and establishments—and opportunities for establishments and firms to become larger without impairing the competitive pressure that stimulates efficiency. Longer production runs for individual products become possible, as, in almost all industries including wholesale and retail trade, do larger transactions in buying, selling, and shipping. Expanded regional and local markets permit greater geographic specialization and less transporting of products. The opportunities for greater specialization, bigger units, longer runs, and larger transactions provide clear reason to expect increasing returns in the production and distribution of many products, and examples of increasing returns are plentiful.

In our judgment, gains from economies of scale are important in all modern economies. Moreover, as markets and output grow, knowledge of technology and business organization develops about, and adapts to, the new situation resulting from enlarged markets, and opportunities for scale economies are constantly replenished. We classify gains from economies of scale as a separate source of growth. They magnify substantially the difference that would have existed between growth rates in Japan and elsewhere if constant returns to scale had prevailed.

Derivation of Estimates

To estimate the size of the gains from this source we followed procedures very similar to those used previously for European countries.[1] The estimates were made in two parts.

1. See Denison, *Why Growth Rates Differ*, chap. 17. The chief modification is that the estimates "in U.S. prices" were derived by reference to growth in the nonresidential

1. In the appraisal of U.S. growth it was estimated that each increase of 1 percent in total input in the nonresidential business sector, or gains from advances in knowledge, reallocation of resources, or any other change that would have raised national income by 1 percent under constant returns to scale, actually raised the output of the sector by 15 percent more than this, or by 1.15 percent.[2] (No such gains occur in other sectors.) In the appraisal of European growth it was argued that this percentage would be only a little higher in smaller (but still large) nations like France, West Germany, and the United Kingdom if price relationships among commodities and the composition of output had been the same as in the United States.[3] The same reasoning (which stresses that most output consists of products with markets of a size either smaller or bigger than the nation, and that countries tend not to impose protection when its cost is excessive) applies to Japan, and 16 percent was used to correspond to 15 percent in the United States. This implies that when output is valued in U.S. prices 13.79 percent (16/116) of the growth rate of Japanese output in nonresidential business is due to economies of scale. To secure an index of Japanese output in U.S. prices, the index of nonresidential business national income valued in 1965 Japanese prices (table 4-4, column 1) was divided by the index of gains from economies of scale associated with income elasticities (table 4-5, column 9), the series to be described next. The resulting estimates are identified as economies of scale with output "measured in U.S. prices."[4]

2. Actually neither price relationships among individual consumer goods and services nor the distribution of consumption among individual goods and services were the same in Europe or Japan as in the United States, and the differences were systematic.

Differences in consumption patterns between eight European countries and the United States reflect chiefly differences in levels of per capita income and consumption. Although per capita consumption of nearly every product was lower in Europe than in the United States in 1950 (the year for which data are most abundant), the gap was wider the greater the income elasticity of demand for the product. Also, chiefly because of economies of scale, the

---

business sector (as in Denison, *Accounting for Growth*, pp. 71–76 and 314–17) rather than to growth in the whole economy.

2. The estimate was based on correlation analysis described in *Accounting for Growth*, pp. 71–76 and 314–17.

3. *Why Growth Rates Differ*, pp. 228–33.

4. Estimates shown here for the European countries and Canada include a small allowance for independent growth of local markets brought about by population shifts and increased automobile use. The estimates for the United States and Japan are assumed to include this item.

higher the income elasticity and the lower the consumption of a commodity in a European country relative to the United States, the higher was the ratio of the European to the American price. Consequently, the lower the level of per capita consumption in a European country, the more consumption patterns and relative prices diverged from those in the United States.

Where per capita consumption in Europe has risen markedly toward the U.S. level during the postwar period, the increase in consumption has been heavily concentrated in products for which demand is income-elastic and European prices are high. In France, for example, per capita consumption of product groups for which the ratio of French to U.S. prices was above average by more than half increased by 74 or 79 percent (depending on the weights applied) from 1950 to 1962. These groups were fats and oils; sugar; footwear; clothing and household textiles; fuel, light, and water; household goods; purchases of transportation equipment; operation of transportation equipment; and books, newspapers, and magazines. In contrast, there was only a 19 percent increase in product groups for which the ratio of French to U.S. prices was below average by more than half. They were cereal and cereal products; alcoholic beverages; housing services; domestic service; education; and miscellaneous. The former groups include products such as consumer durables and utilities that offered especially large possibilities to secure gains from economies of scale by adopting methods and techniques that were already in use in the United States but could not have been used in Europe until a sufficiently large market came into existence. They are given a much higher weight, and the latter groups—which appear poor prospects for gains from economies of scale—a much lower weight, when French price weights are used to measure changes in consumption than when U.S. price weights are used. European experience indicates that the greater is the rise in per capita consumption in a country and the lower its initial level, the larger is the amount by which the rise in consumption in each country measured in its own constant prices exceeds the rise measured in U.S. constant prices.

The difference between the growth rate of national product when the components of consumption are weighted by U.S. prices and the rate when they are weighted by national prices reflects the concentration of consumption increases in products where potential gains from economies of scale are particularly large. For this reason it is classified as a gain from economies of scale, labeled as "associated with income elasticities."

As explained in appendix L, the procedure actually used to measure this series for European countries was indirect.[5] It rested on the systematic re-

5. Also see *Why Growth Rates Differ*, pp. 235–51.

lationship between the ratios of European to U.S. per capita consumption by the alternative sets of price weights. The regression line expressing this relationship, together with time series for each country that were based on its own prices, permitted estimation of the change in per capita consumption that use of U.S. price weights would yield in European countries, and hence calculation of the difference between series based on U.S. and on national price weights. The situation in Japan paralleled that in Europe. When the ratio of Japanese to U.S. per capita consumption in 1967 was calculated in both U.S. and Japanese prices, the relationship between the two fell close to the regression line established from European data. (See appendix L.) The same procedure was therefore followed to secure estimates for Japan.

Importance in Growth

Both components of economies of scale made large contributions to growth. Together they contributed 1.94 percentage points to the growth rate of total national income in 1953–71 (1.90 points in 1953–61 and 1.96 in 1961–71). They raised the 1953–71 growth rate of standardized national income 28 percent above what it would have been without scale economies.

Gains from economies of scale were greater than in any other country and much greater than in most; the differential ranged from 0.33 to 1.58 percentage points. The chief reason is that both markets in general and per capita consumption were expanding faster in Japan; the separate significance of per capita consumption is that, starting from a very low level, its fast advance caused a particularly great shift in consumption patterns.[6]

6. The statement about consumption patterns cannot be confirmed directly because the Japanese national accounts show little detail for consumption. It is, however, supported by production data.

The contribution of economies of scale associated with income elasticities is smaller than would otherwise be the case because the ratio of consumption to output has been both low and falling in Japan, and because the base year for deflation in Japan (1965) is later than in the output series used for the other countries (1954 or 1958). The contribution in most European countries was probably smaller after 1962 than in the period covered.

CHAPTER ELEVEN

Sources of Differences in Level of Output per Person Employed

WE OBSERVED EARLIER that in 1970 gross domestic product per person employed was 55.2 percent as big in Japan as in the United States if U.S. prices are used in the output comparison (table 2-1). It was 44.3 percent as big if Japanese prices are used. Suppose, reasonably, that the ratio was the same for domestic national income as for gross domestic product. Then the percentages for total national income were a little lower—54.8 percent based on U.S. prices and 44.0 based on Japanese prices—because the United States was a net recipient of property income from abroad while Japan was a net payer.

Why was output per person employed lower in Japan than in the United States? The reasons can be explored by the same techniques that were applied to examine temporal changes within a country. This chapter reports such an investigation. The analysis is confined to national income in the whole economy, based on *U.S.* prices. This shows national income per worker to have been 54.8 percent as big in Japan as in the United States (expressed in table 11-1 as a "shortfall" of 45.2 percent), but we repeat that the comparison based on Japanese prices, which yields a much bigger difference between the two countries, is equally valid.

The use of U.S. price weights enables us to set results for Japan against those for nine other countries which have been similarly compared with the United States, though for 1960 rather than 1970. Table 11-1 shows all these

Table 11-1. Contributions to Shortfalls from the United States in National Income per Person Employed, 1970 or 1960[a]
Percentage of U.S. national income per person employed

Sources of difference	Japan	North-west Europe[b]	Belgium	Denmark	France	West Germany	Nether-lands	Norway	United Kingdom	Italy	Canada
Total difference	**45.2**	**41.0**	**39.0**	**42.0**	**41.0**	**41.0**	**35.0**	**41.0**	**41.0**	**60.0**	**18.3**
Total factor input	**10.6**	**11.3**	**8.5**	**11.0**	**11.0**	**14.0**	**2.8**	**5.3**	**11.0**	**18.7**	**0.7**
Labor	1.0	1.1	1.0	2.8	1.0	2.5	-4.7	-0.4	-0.6	4.4	0.0
Hours of work	-3.9	-3.9	-3.2	-3.5	-4.1	-3.9	-5.9	-3.4	-3.1	-4.9	-2.8
Age-sex composition	2.3	1.2	0.1	2.2	1.1	2.3	-0.9	0.1	0.7	0.8	-1.6
Education	2.6	3.8	4.1	4.1	4.0	4.1	2.1	2.9	3.0	8.5	4.4
Capital	8.4	9.7	6.9	7.7	9.6	11.0	7.0	5.2	9.9	13.8	1.3
Dwellings	2.9	1.9	2.1	1.8	2.1	1.9	1.9	2.1	1.6	3.2	0.2
International assets	0.6	0.4	0.3	0.5	0.5	0.7	0.2	1.0	0.0	0.6	2.0
Nonresidential structures and equipment	3.6	6.6	3.5	4.8	6.1	7.4	4.8	1.5	7.5	8.7	-0.7
Inventories	1.3	0.8	1.0	0.6	0.9	1.0	0.1	0.6	0.8	1.3	-0.2
Land	1.2	0.5	0.6	0.5	0.4	0.5	0.5	0.5	0.5	0.5	-0.6

Output per unit of input	**34.6**	**29.7**	**30.5**	**31.0**	**30.0**	**27.0**	**32.2**	**35.7**	**30.0**	**41.3**	**17.6**
Overallocation to agriculture	6.0	2.3	0.2	3.1	5.8	3.7	-0.2	6.1	-1.1	12.3	1.5
Overallocation to nonagricultural self-employment	3.3	0.3	2.7	1.5	1.9	0.4	1.1	2.1	-1.7	4.6	-0.6
Use of shift work	0.2	0.1	0.1	0.1	0.1	0.1	0.2	0.2	0.2	0.0	n.a.
Economies of scale[c]	3.5	4.9	5.9	5.7	4.8	4.7	5.9	6.2	4.6	4.5	5.2
Labor disputes	-0.1	n.a.	n.a.	n.a.	n.a.	n.a.	n.a.	n.a.	n.a.	n.a.	n.a.
Irregularity in pressure of demand	-4.3	-1.6	-1.8	-1.8	-1.7	-1.7	-1.8	-1.8	-1.3	-1.4	1.4
Irregularity in agricultural output	0.0	0.0	0.0	0.0	0.0	0.0	-0.5	0.0	0.0	0.0	0.0
Lag in the application of knowledge, general efficiency, and errors and omissions	26.0	23.7	23.4	22.4	19.1	19.8	27.5	22.9	29.3	21.3	10.1

Sources: Japan, appendix table O-1; European countries, Denison, *Why Growth Rates Differ*, p. 332; Canada, Dorothy Walters, *Canadian Income Levels and Growth, An International Perspective*, 1968.

n.a. Not available.

a. Data for Japan are for 1970. Those for all other countries refer to 1960. All data are based on comparisons in U.S. prices of the year compared.

b. Includes Belgium, Denmark, France, West Germany, the Netherlands, Norway, and the United Kingdom.

c. Includes size of local markets and national markets, and effects of barriers to international trade.

estimates. Initially, however, attention will be directed only to the first column, in which the difference between output per worker in Japan and the United States is allocated among sources. This chapter summarizes the approach and the main results. The estimates are described more fully in appendix O.

One important source of Japanese growth, economies of scale associated with income elasticities, has no counterpart in the explanation of the difference between American and Japanese national income measured in U.S. prices. This determinant helps, instead, to explain why the shortfall of Japanese national income per worker is even bigger when Japanese prices are used.

The use of American prices to combine output components has another implication: it suggests that U.S. rather than Japanese weights should also be used to combine inputs—not only labor, capital, and land but also types of each of these inputs—and this has been done.[1]

A final methodological point concerns the elimination of the statistical interaction term. To understand the problem, suppose that there were only two output determinants, one of which would, by itself, make output 15 percent lower in Japan than in the United States and the other 25 percent lower. Actual output would be lower not by 40 percent but by only 36.25 percent: $1 - (1 - 0.15)(1 - 0.25)$. The difference of 3.75 percentage points is the interaction term. To obtain results comparable to those for growth (pages 35–39) we adopted a procedure to allocate the interaction term that may be described as based on pseudo growth rates. For the purpose of this calculation we suppose that at some imaginary future date—assumed to be 1990—Japan would be at the 1970 position of the United States with respect to the level of national income per person employed, of each of the input factors per person employed, and of each component of output per unit of input. The contribution that each source would make to the growth rate from 1970 to 1990 if this were to happen was then computed in the same way as was done for actual periods in analyzing the sources of past growth. The 1970 gap was then allocated in proportion to these contributions.[2] In the illustration, 13.06 points of the 36.25 percent shortfall would be allocated to the first factor and

---

1. For further discussion of the choice of U.S. weights, as well as of the treatment of the interaction term which is discussed in the following paragraph, see *Why Growth Rates Differ*, pp. 196–99.

2. See appendix O for further discussion of the procedure. Indexes from which estimates without allowance for interaction may be obtained are shown in table O-1, column 1, and these estimates are also cited in the text of this chapter.

23.19 points to the second. As explained below (page 105, note 16), a modification to the procedure was made for dwellings and international assets.

We turn now to a brief discussion of each determinant.

Determinants Favorable to Japan: Hours of Work and Irregular Factors

Aside from irregular factors only one determinant was more favorable to high output per worker in Japan than in the United States.[3] This is the length of working hours.

Average hours worked in the business sector per person employed in that sector were 22 percent longer in Japan than in the United States. However, we appraise the Japanese advantage in labor input per worker in the sector at only a little over 7 percent because—as explained in discussion of the time series data—we judge that very long hours add little or, above a certain point, nothing to output. Details of the calculation are provided in appendix O.

We must also recognize that the measurement of output *assumes* that differences between countries in hours worked by government employees do not affect their output; in computing the real value of government purchases, Kravis and his associates assumed that output per worker, not per hour, is the same in the two countries. Consequently, no part of the difference in total output per worker can be ascribed to differences in hours of government workers.

However, after allowance for this special characteristic of measurement, labor input per worker in the whole economy is still estimated to be just about 7 percent bigger in Japan as a result of differences in hours. Part of this amount reflects the smaller proportion of part-time workers in Japan but most results from the difference in full-time hours in the business sector.

The weight of labor in total input in the whole U.S. economy is 79.62 percent, so the difference in total input per worker due to the difference in working hours is 5.6 percent (79.62 percent of 7 percent). This percentage drops to 3.9 (the figure shown in table 11-1) when the gap is expressed as a percentage of U.S. output per worker and the interaction with other determinants is handled by the pseudo growth rate procedure.

One figure that emerges from the international comparison is so striking that we cannot forbear reporting it even though it has no direct bearing on

3. This statement obviously is true only within the confines of the classification of determinants that is utilized. A more detailed classification would doubtless yield others.

the problem under investigation. Although Japanese were only one-half as numerous as Americans, the total number of hours worked in the business sector (including agriculture) was over 91 percent as large in Japan as in the United States. This is the result of having a much larger percentage of the population in the labor force, a lower unemployment rate, a smaller percentage of employed persons working in general government, households, and institutions, and far longer average hours.

A comparison of national income per man-hour worked in 1970 is also of interest. Based on our estimate that in the economy as a whole average hours worked were 25 percent longer in Japan, national income per hour worked was only 44 percent as large in Japan as it was in the United States when U.S. price weights are used to compare output and 35 percent as large when Japanese price weights are used. These percentages compare with 55 percent and 44 percent, respectively, for national income per person employed.

The big difference between average hours in Japan and the United States causes estimates of the sources of difference in the level of output per worker to be more sensitive than we should like to variations in assumptions concerning the effects of hours upon output.[4] These assumptions are much less important in the analysis of Japanese growth because hours did not change much.

The United States was in a recession in 1970 while Japan was in a boom. We have estimated that the intensity of utilization of employed resources, as affected by intensity of demand, was more favorable to high output per unit of input in Japan and less favorable in the United States in 1970 than in any other year from 1952 through 1971. This happenstance made the difference between the two countries in income per worker smaller than would otherwise have been the case. We take the 1961–70 average as a standard for intensity of utilization in both countries.[5] As shown in table 11-1, divergence of 1970 from this standard narrowed the gap in national income per worker by 4.3 percent of the U.S. figure (6.2 percent before allowance for interaction).

Time lost as a result of labor disputes was especially big in the United States in 1970, chiefly because of a strike by automobile workers at the General Motors Corporation, and the adverse effect on productivity narrowed the gap by another 0.1 percentage points as compared with a typical year.

4. If we underestimate the amount by which shorter hours curtail output (that is, if the efficiency offset is smaller than we suppose), the gap between the two countries in output per unit of input is even bigger than we calculate. If we overestimate the impact of shorter hours, we also overestimate the gap.

5. In the United States the 1961–70 average for this index was close to the value estimated to be consistent with a 4 percent unemployment rate under average conditions.

Age-Sex Composition of Hours Worked

All other output determinants favored higher output per person employed in the United States than in Japan. We consider first the composition of hours worked, classified by the age and sex of workers.

Some 40.5 percent of all hours worked in the business sector in the United States were provided by men thirty-five to sixty-four years of age whereas in Japan this percentage was only 31.9. As is shown in table 11-2, the U.S. percentage was also larger for teenage males but the Japanese percentage was bigger for males in the three remaining age brackets (including the over-sixty-five group despite the convention of early "retirement") and for females in all five age brackets.

Table 11-2 also shows U.S. hourly earnings weights. Men thirty-five to sixty-four years old receive the highest weight by far—as is also the case in Japan and other countries. When the distributions in the two countries are weighted by U.S. hourly earnings, the average value of an hour's work is 4.4 percent less in Japan than in the United States, and we use this difference to compare this aspect of labor input in nonresidential business. In the whole economy it is reduced to 4.0 percent by allowance for the assumption in the output measure that there is no international difference in output per worker

Table 11-2. *Distributions of Total Hours Worked in Nonresidential Business among Age-Sex Groups, United States and Japan, 1970*

		Percentage distribution of business hours	
Sex and age	*U.S. weight*	*United States*[a]	*Japan*[b]
Males			
14–19	36	4.04	2.74[c]
20–24	77	7.09	8.60
25–34	114	16.32	17.47
35–64	128	40.46	31.91
65 and over	88	2.43	2.73
Females			
14–19	49	2.36	2.89[c]
20–24	59	4.74	6.99
25–34	68	5.30	7.19
35–64	68	16.43	18.37
65 and over	54	0.81	1.11

Source: See appendix O.
a. Data for 1969.
b. Includes entire economy.
c. Excludes fourteen-year-olds.

in general government, households, and institutions. Multiplication by the share of labor earnings and allowance for interaction yields 2.3 percent of U.S. output per worker as the amount of the Japanese shortfall to be ascribed to age-sex composition.

Education of Employed Persons

Table 11-3 shows for the United States and Japan percentage distributions of persons employed in 1970 by highest school grade completed. Distributions of full-time equivalent persons employed in nonresidential business in the United States were obtained from Denison, *Accounting for Growth*. U.S. earnings weights, also shown in table 11-3, were obtained from the same source.[6] Distributions for Japan were obtained from table 6-1 above, and adjusted to conform to the class intervals in the U.S. distributions.[7] The U.S. distributions obviously are higher pitched.

Based on the U.S. earnings weights, the weighted average of the Japanese distribution for males is 91.6 percent of the weighted average of the U.S. distribution for males, while the corresponding percentage for females is 89.2. These percentages would provide an appropriate comparison of the educational component of labor input in nonresidential business in the two countries if employed persons who had completed the same school grade were considered to have received an equivalent education. We prefer the assumption that recent students who had completed the same grade had received the same amount of education.[8] Because the procedures used in the time series imply that in the United States, but not in Japan, recent students have received more education than students who completed the same grade earlier

6. The data are from appendix tables I-15 and I-13, respectively.

7. These data are not on a full-time equivalent basis. They exclude employed persons still in school, regardless of age, whereas the U.S. data exclude employed persons under eighteen, regardless of whether or not they are in school. Only persons employed in business should be counted but the actual Japanese data also include persons employed outside business. Their number is relatively small and the calculations assume that their omission would not change an index calculated from the distribution.

The U.S. advantage in level of education is a little greater for all employment than for business employment as measured here. U.S. percentages in the two highest education groups would be considerably bigger if persons outside the business sector were included.

8. In comparisons of the United States with European countries the results of this assumption were averaged with those of another: that recent students who left school at the same age had received the same amount of education. That procedure probably would not change a comparison of the United States and Japan much because children enter school at about the same age.

Table 11-3. *Distributions of Persons Employed in Nonresidential Business, by Years of School Completed, United States and Japan, 1970*

		Percentage distribution of employed persons[a]			
		Males		Females	
Years of school completed	U.S. weight	United States	Japan	United States	Japan
0	75	0.46	0.24	0.21	0.55
1–4	89	2.46	1.16	1.00	1.06
5–7	97	7.07	10.21	4.19	19.26
8	100	10.82	20.06	8.14	13.70
9–11	111	17.91	33.09	18.16	38.66
12	124	36.77	21.41	50.60	21.37
13–15	147	12.67	8.50	12.70	5.00
16	189	7.27	4.00	3.49	0.35
17 or more	219	4.62	1.33	1.52	0.05
Total	...	100.00	100.00	100.00	100.00

Source: See text.
a. See p. 102 for coverage.

and were still at work in 1970, an adjustment to the U.S. distributions is required which raises the Japanese percentage for males from 91.6 percent of the United States to 95.8 and that for females from 89.2 to 93.1. These two percentages were weighted by labor input weights from appendix table G-2 to secure 95.2. This is the index (United States = 100) appropriate for the education component of Japanese labor input in a comparison of output per person employed in nonresidential business. It was averaged with an index of 100 in general government, households, and institutions (for the same reason that this was done for other labor input components) to secure 95.6 as the percentage for the economy as a whole.[9]

This difference of 4.4 percent implies that total input, and hence output, per worker was 3.5 percent less in Japan than it would have been if Japanese workers had held the same education as American workers, or 2.6 percent (table 11-1) after allowance for the interaction term.

To compare the education of employed persons on the basis of highest school grade completed is undoubtedly an oversimplification even where, as in the present case, there are important similarities between education in the

9. The adjustment from 95.2 to 95.6 is something of an overcorrection because the output comparison does take account of education in some occupations. See Irving B. Kravis and others, *A System of International Comparisons of Gross Product and Purchasing Power,* United Nations International Comparison Project: Phase One (Johns Hopkins University Press for the World Bank, 1975), p. 162.

countries compared.[10] It is necessary to assume that the education received was equally appropriate to future participation in economic life, and that the quality of education was similar.[11] Education outside the regular school systems or their equivalent is omitted from the comparisons.[12]

Despite these qualifications, we have little doubt that the implication of our estimates is correct: the difference in education can account for only a small part of the difference in output per worker, and such difference as exists favors the United States.

Total Labor Input

The more favorable distributions of labor among age-sex and education groups in the United States somewhat more than offset the effects of longer full-time hours and fewer part-time workers in Japan.[13] On balance, labor input per person employed was 1.8 percent smaller in Japan. With labor's weight nearly 80 percent of total input, and Japan's income much lower than America's, this translates to a contribution of only 1.0 percentage point to the difference between Japanese and American national income per worker. Thus only 2 percent of that difference is attributable to labor itself.

Capital Input

Capital input accounts for an important part of the international difference in national income per person employed in 1970. Our estimate is that the

10. Education starts at approximately the same age. Since 1947 the structure of the educational system has been the same. Neither system is highly selective: at least until the high school graduation level approaches, few students fail of promotion except for absenteeism, and admission to college has provided the main academic hurdle for a student striving to continue his education. In the United States appreciable numbers have been eliminated just before high school graduation, and elimination from college for poor performance after admission has been common only in the United States.

11. Resources devoted to education, other than the student's own efforts, are greater per student in the United States. The general belief is that Japanese students study harder at the elementary and secondary levels and less hard at the higher education level. Japanese students from thirteen years of age to the last year of high school have performed exceptionally well, and American students poorly, on international mathematics tests. Torsten Husen, ed., *International Study of Achievement in Mathematics,* International Project for the Evaluation of Educational Achievement (Wiley, 1967).

12. See *Why Growth Rates Differ,* chap. 8 and appendix F, for discussion of the general problems of international comparisons of education.

13. The "unallocated" labor input component is omitted because of lack of detailed data. But it is clear that the size of its contribution is very close to zero.

smaller stock of capital in Japan was responsible for 8.4 percentage points, or nearly one-fifth, of the 45.2 percent gap in national income per person employed. This estimate is obtained as the sum of four components.

Relative to the United States, much the greatest shortage of capital in Japan is in the housing stock. In comparing total output in their study for the United Nations, Kravis and his associates estimated the per capita quantity of housing services (i.e., the value of the services provided by dwellings, excluding fuel and power but including upkeep) to be 39.1 percent as large in Japan as in the United States.[14] This per capita figure translates to only 31.7 percent per person employed. Kravis and his associates use the comparison to measure gross rents, a component of consumer expenditures in the national product, but it is equally applicable to a comparison of the stock of dwellings, including sites. Comparisons of dwelling units which differ as much as those in Japan and the United States are difficult, of course, but the methods used and the result seem reasonable and we cannot improve upon them. In any case, this is the estimate that enters into the output comparison we seek to explain.

We now assume that purchases from other industries (maintenance, etc.) plus depreciation absorb about the same percentage of gross rent in the two countries when measurement is in U.S. prices (as is, indeed, the case in each country's own prices). This assumption implies that net output originating in the services of dwellings sector, when divided by total employment, is 31.7 percent as big in Japan as in the United States—the same percentage as gross rent.[15] It is, therefore, 68.3 percent less.

In the United States, national income originating in the dwelling sector (the counterpart of the Japanese figures provided in column 3 of table 3-2, above) amounted to 4.25 percent of the national income. Therefore, the difference in housing per person employed was responsible for a difference in national income per person employed equal to 2.9 percent of U.S. national income per person employed (68.3 percent of 4.25).[16]

The second capital component is net property income received from abroad, the contribution of international assets to the national income. The

14. *A System of International Comparisons*, p. 176.
15. The comparison is necessarily the same at factor cost as at market prices.
16. Expressed as a percentage of Japanese national income measured in U.S. prices the effect of the housing gap is much bigger, 5.3 percent. Note that for this determinant and for international assets we have computed the effect directly as a percentage of the U.S. output figure. Because housing and income from abroad are separate, one-factor sectors in which output per unit of input is the same in different countries, we do not regard them as entering into the general interaction among output determinants.

United States is a major creditor nation and in 1970 net property income from abroad amounted to $4,566 million.[17] This is 0.6 percent of the national income and equal to $55 per person employed. In Japan, net property income from abroad was slightly negative, −¥75 billion (table 3-2). When converted at the exchange rate (360 yen to the dollar in 1970) as is customary for this component in international comparisons, this amounts to −$208 million or −$4 per person employed.[18] Per person employed, it was 107.4 percent less in Japan than in the United States. It contributes 0.6 percent of the U.S. figure (107.4 percent of 0.6) to the international difference in output per worker.

The third component is nonresidential structures and equipment. Per person employed in the whole economy the Japanese stock measured in U.S. prices was estimated to be 41.0 percent smaller than the U.S. stock. This crude estimate was based on the comparison of accumulated investment in table 7-3 and an adjustment to date the comparison at 1970. Appendix O provides a full explanation. Nonresidential structures and equipment constituted 9.37 percent of inputs in the United States, so, based on that weight, total input was 3.8 percent (9.37 percent of 41.0 percent) smaller with the Japanese than with the U.S. stock per person employed. The usual procedure assigns 3.6 percentage points of the difference between U.S. and Japanese national income per worker to nonresidential structures and equipment.

The relative quantity of inventories in the two countries is hard to ascertain. We compromised between two estimates, one based on a direct comparison of estimated inventory values, the other on the assumption that the ratio of inventories to the output of the nonresidential business sector is the same in the two countries. (See appendix O). This yields an estimate that private inventories per person employed in the whole economy were 46 percent smaller in Japan than in the United States. Their weight in total U.S. input was only 3.04 percent, so national income is estimated to have been 1.4 percent lower than it would have been with U.S. stocks per worker. This results in the assignment to inventories of 1.3 percentage points of the international difference in output per worker.

Japanese stocks of structures and equipment and of inventories were rising much faster than American stocks. Consequently, the ratio of Japanese stocks of these assets, per worker, to American stocks were rising sharply, and the

17. *Survey of Current Business* (July 1974), table 1.13, p. 17.
18. The Kravis study for the United Nations omits this component because only domestic product is measured, but it uses the exchange rate as the purchasing power parity for net exports, in which net property income from abroad is ordinarily included. Kravis and others, *A System of International Comparisons*, p. 159.

percentage differences, even if accurate for 1970, are representative only of that year, not of a longer period.

Land and Natural Resources

Japan has only 6.4 percent as much land area per person employed as the United States, a smaller percentage of Japanese land is suitable for agriculture, and Japan's mineral resources are scant. Nevertheless, we ascribe to nonresidential land only a small part—1.2 percentage points, or 2.9 percent —of the international gap in national income per person employed.[19] The main reason for this low estimate is that land is not a very big input in a modern economy; we assign to nonresidential land only 3.2 percent of the total weight of inputs in the United States.

Most of even this amount, 1.8 percentage points, attaches to sites for nonresidential business structures and other business uses (outside agriculture and mining). The quantity of such sites is assumed to be the same, per person employed, in both countries and therefore it is not calculated to be responsible for any of the difference in national income per person employed. The main rationale for this assumption is that such sites require only a small fraction of the total land area even in Japan, generally represent a superior use so that whatever amount is needed will be preempted, and for the most part require no special physical characteristics that are not readily available.

Agricultural land receives 1.1 percent of the total weight of inputs in the United States and mineral land less than 0.3 percent. To compare land input in agriculture we have counted the area of arable land plus one-third of permanent meadows and pastures. On this basis, Japan had only 3.7 percent as much agricultural land input per worker in the whole economy as the United States. (It had only 1.0 percent as much per farm worker.) Mineral input too was estimated to be 3.7 percent as large as in America per person employed in the whole economy. This is based on a comparison of mineral production, and may even overstate Japan's relative position because poorer mineral sources are worked. (Coal is the biggest Japanese mineral resource.) Since agricultural and mineral lands represent only 1.4 percent of total input, even the enormous difference between the two countries in these inputs was not a major source of difference in output per worker. Appendix O describes the land estimates in detail.

19. To be precise, the estimate for land refers to the situation that would exist in the absence of greater overallocation of labor to agriculture in Japan than in the United States. The cost of greater misallocation is separately estimated.

Overallocation to Agriculture

We have previously stressed the large amount of agricultural employment in Japan, and have just pointed out how restricted is the land base for a big agricultural labor force. In 1970 Japan had 2.3 times as many people employed in farming as did the United States.[20] It had 0.032 times as much arable land and 0.015 times as much agricultural land area (which includes permanent meadows and pastures as well as arable land).

We assume that if overallocation to farming were equally costly in the two countries the ratio of output per unit of input in Japan to the corresponding American figure would have been as high in all industries combined (including agriculture) as it was in all nonagricultural industries combined, when the services of dwellings and property income from abroad are excluded in both cases. As explained in appendix O, we estimate that actual output per unit of input (and, therefore, per worker) in the whole economy was 8 percent lower in Japan than it would have been if this condition had been met. With allowance for interaction, this amounts to 6.0 percentage points out of the total difference between the countries of 45.2 percent of U.S. national income per worker.

Overallocation to Nonfarm Self-Employment

Self-employed and family workers constituted over 25 percent of employment in nonagricultural business in Japan as against 11.5 percent in the United States.[21] It seems likely that the industrial structure is more favorable to small family enterprises in Japan, and we assume that a Japanese percentage of 15 would be as favorable to efficiency as 11.5 in America. On the assumptions used in the time series analysis, Japanese national income was 4.5 percent smaller than it would have been if the self-employed percentage had been reduced from 25 to 15 by transferring 10 percent of workers in nonagricultural business to wage and salary work. With the usual interaction allowance, this becomes 3.3 points of the international difference in national income per person employed.

20. Japan had as many people employed in agriculture in 1970 as all seven countries classified here as Northwest Europe (Belgium, Denmark, France, West Germany, the Netherlands, Norway, and the United Kingdom) plus Ireland, Sweden, Switzerland, Austria, and Canada.

21. An alternative estimate for the United States is still lower. See *Accounting for Growth,* pp. 172–74.

Use of Shift Work

The use of fixed capital can be extended by working two or more shifts. Shift work is used relatively little in Japan. Only perhaps 7 percent of plant workers in manufacturing industries worked on other than the first shift, as compared with about 10 percent in the Northwest European countries, 16 percent in Italy, and 23 percent in the United States. Shift work is less common in nonmanufacturing industries. In Japan the percentage on other than the first shift in an aggregate covering a wide range of nonmanufacturing industries is under 5. Comparable data for the United States are lacking; we assume the percentage to be the same as in Japan.

Suppose fixed capital that is used two shifts in one country contributes twice as much to output as identical capital used one shift in another country; that the international difference between the United States and Japan in use of shift work in manufacturing is confined to production or plant workers; that the difference between the countries in use of shift work in manufacturing is not due to differences in the industrial composition of manufacturing or other differences in the composition of the capital stock but is due to differences in the same industries and for the same types of capital; and that manufacturing production workers use one-fifth of the total stock of structures and equipment in nonresidential business. On these assumptions Japanese national income was 0.3 percent smaller than it would have been if shift work were as frequent as in the United States, and accounts for 0.2 percentage points of the gap in national income per person employed.[22]

Economies of Scale

The Japanese economy was 34 percent as large as the American economy in 1970 if output is valued in U.S. prices. Foreign trade was moderately larger relative to output, though not because of policy but because Japan was heavily dependent on imports for raw materials and fuels and had to export to pay for them. Domestic production and consumers were concentrated in a far smaller geographic area in Japan, but relative scarcity of cars and home

22. See appendix O for sources of data and details of calculation. Shift work was omitted from the tables referring to sources of growth over time because of its unimportance, the apparent absence of appreciable changes, and the impossibility of satisfactorily eliminating from changes in aggregate percentages for shift work the effects of changes in the "mix" of the capital stock. See Edward F. Denison, "Some Major Issues in Productivity Analysis: An Examination of Estimates by Jorgenson and Griliches," *Survey of Current Business* (May 1969), pp. 19–21.

storage space, including refrigeration, made for more frequent marketing at retail and for less extended retail markets.

In *Why Growth Rates Differ*, economies of scale related to the size of the national market were estimated to have made 1960 national income in U.S. prices 4 percent lower in France, West Germany, and the United Kingdom than it would have been with markets of American size. Economies of scale related to the size of local markets (which we have combined with the size of national markets in time series analysis of Japan) were estimated to have made a difference of 2.5 percent.[23]

The Japanese economy was nearer the size of the United States in 1970 than were the large European economies in 1960, but markets were extended much less by foreign trade while automobile ownership, important to the size of local markets, was less prevalent. We assume that the total effect of markets smaller than those of the United States was three-fourths as large for Japan in 1970 as for the big European countries in 1960. This implies that Japanese national income per worker was 4.8 percent smaller than it would have been with markets the size of those of the United States. With allowance for interaction, the contribution to the difference in output per worker is 3.5 percentage points.[24]

Lag in the Application of Knowledge, General Efficiency, and Errors and Omissions

Output per unit of input was 30.2 percent lower in Japan than in the United States for reasons not separately identified and measured.[25] Included are the effects of the lag in the application of knowledge and of other determinants not separately measured (including services provided by government labor and capital that affect private productivity); the net error in other estimates; and differences in efficiency that may be present for no ascertainable reason. This result, that the index for "residual efficiency" in Japan was 69.8 percent of that for the United States, was obtained by dividing the index for output per unit of input, 61.9, by the product of the indexes for its other components, 88.7. After allowance for the interaction between this determinant and others, it is estimated that some 26.0 percentage points of the difference between the countries in national income per person employed is due to this factor.

23. *Why Growth Rates Differ*, pp. 234–35 and 254–55.

24. As stated earlier, economies of scale associated with income elasticities do not contribute to the difference in output valued in U.S. prices. See *Why Growth Rates Differ*, p. 251.

25. The difference between Japan and the United States would be even bigger if the sectors (all but nonresidential business) in which the method of measuring output precludes any difference were omitted.

This difference between the two countries is remarkably big and the fact that such a result is not novel should not be permitted to obscure its impact. To say that residual efficiency is 30.2 percent lower in Japan than in the United States is equivalent to saying that it is 43.3 percent higher in the United States than in Japan. This is almost exactly the increase in residual productivity which occurred in the United States in the forty-year period from 1929 to 1969, so it appears that in 1970 Japan had reached the efficiency attained by the United States about four decades earlier.[26] Moreover, the gap in residual efficiency is so big that it will take a long time to close even at the rate of progress Japan has achieved in its best period. If Japan continues to receive an annual contribution from the residual of the size that it did in 1961–71, a very favorable period, and the United States continues to receive the annual contribution that it did in 1948–69, it will not be until 2002 that the gap between the two countries in residual efficiency is eliminated. If, instead, the future annual contribution in Japan averages the same as in 1953–71, still a high figure by international standards, the date will be delayed until nearly 2020.[27] These calculations are presented not as forecasts but to stress how big was the gap in efficiency in 1970 that remains after allowance is made for all determinants whose effects we have ventured to estimate directly. We reiterate our belief that, although new knowledge was responsible for the growth of the residual in the United States, availability of knowledge cannot explain so big a gap between countries. We shall not speculate further about the conditions that *are* responsible.

The General Pattern

Some 23 percent of the total difference between Japan and the United States in national income per worker in 1970 can be ascribed to differences in input per worker—not only capital and land but also characteristics of the labor force and the hours it worked. This leaves 77 percent for differences in output per unit of input. The share of inputs would have been smaller if 1970 had been a more normal year. When the negative contributions of irregular factors are eliminated from the international difference in output per worker, inputs accounted for only 21 percent.

26. The calculation is based on table 9-4 in *Accounting for Growth,* p. 127.

27. These results are obtained by giving separate treatment to the nonresidential business sector. (See p. 117 below.) Otherwise the years are 1999 and 2016. Contributions used in the latter calculations are 1.19 percentage points for the United States in 1948–69 (from *Accounting for Growth,* table 9-4, p. 127) and 2.43 and 1.97 points, respectively, for Japan in 1961–71 and 1953–71 (from table 4-6 above). It is, of course, the differences between the Japanese and American rates used in the calculations (1.24 and 0.78 percentage points) that govern the results of the calculations.

The 45.2 percent by which Japanese output per worker fell short of that in the United States is the net of 53.5 percentage points contributed by determinants that were less favorable in Japan and 8.3 points contributed by determinants that were more favorable. Nearly half—49 percent, or 26.0 percentage points—of the total contribution by adverse determinants was contributed by the residual, what we term in table 11-1 the "lag in the application of knowledge, general efficiency, and errors and omissions." Almost one fifth—19 percent—stemmed from greater overallocation of labor to farming and to nonfarm self-employment than was present in the United States. Less capital was responsible for nearly one-sixth—16 percent, of which 9 percent resulted from less enterprise capital in the form of nonresidential structures and equipment and inventories. One-eleventh was due to characteristics of labor: less education of the labor force (responsible for 5 percent) and less concentration of labor in the age-sex groups whose earnings are highest (responsible for 4 percent). The remainder was divided among economies of scale (7 percent), land (2 percent), and less use of shift work (under 1 percent). On the same basis (i.e., with the total contribution of factors unfavorable to Japan taken as 100 percent) the contribution of the length of working hours, the only determinant that has been persistently favorable to high Japanese output, contributed −7 percent to the gap and irregular factors −8 percent.

Table 11-1 also allocates among determinants the 1960 difference between national income per worker in the United States and ten Western areas: Northwest Europe, its seven component countries, Italy, and Canada.

One of the largest differences between the columns for Japan and Northwest Europe has no lasting significance. In 1960 Europe was in a stronger position than the United States with respect to the business cycle, but the difference was less than that between Japan and the United States in 1970. Hence the negative contribution of "irregularity in pressure of demand" is bigger in the Japanese column than in that for Northwest Europe.

If the contributions of irregular factors are eliminated, the pattern for Japan in 1970 is almost startlingly similar to the pattern for Northwest Europe in 1960. Not only the total difference from the United States in output per worker but also the contributions of most of the individual determinants were within a couple of percentage points of one another.[28] The Japanese figure is almost always within or barely outside the range encompassed by the individual Northwest European nations.

28. The difference in years must be stressed. It can be readily inferred from table 2-1 that in 1970 Japan fell much further below the United States in output per worker than did Northwest Europe in 1970.

The contributions of labor and its hours component were almost the same in the columns for Japan and Northwest Europe, and the contributions of age-sex composition and education differed by only 1.1 and 1.2 perentage points, respectively. The contributions of capital and land, together, were only 0.6 points apart, although individual components differed more. The shortfall from the United States in output per worker due to the overallocation of labor to agriculture was considerably—3.7 percentage points—bigger for Japan in 1970 than for the Northwest European countries as a whole in 1960 but no bigger than for one of these countries, Norway. The shortfall from the over-allocation of labor to nonagricultural self-employment was also considerably bigger—by 3.0 percentage points—for Japan than for Northwest Europe but bigger by only 0.6 points than in one of these countries, Belgium. Contributions of economies of scale differed by 1.4 points. Although the contributions of the residual were 2.3 points apart, this is a difference of less than one-tenth. The Japanese column for 1970 could be fitted into the block of figures for the Northwest European countries in 1960 without appearing remarkable in any way.

Various points of similarity between Italy and Japan have been noted in previous chapters. Output per worker was higher in Italy than in Japan by a moderate amount in 1970, according to table 2-1. It was higher by a larger amount in 1960. We cannot compare determinants of their output levels in the same year but table 11-1 compares the sources of the gap between the United States and Japan in output per worker in 1970 with the much bigger gap between Italy and the United States in 1960. The difference in the size of the gap was equal to 15 percent of U.S. output per worker, or 12 percent if the contribution of irregular factors is eliminated. Three determinants were mainly responsible: greater costs of misallocation of labor to agriculture in 1960 in Italy (6 percentage points), less education of labor (also 6 points), and less capital (5 points). Differences in other determinants, including residual efficiency, were relatively small and mostly offsetting. The differences between the entries for Japan and Italy in the rows for misallocation and capital chiefly reflect the difference in dates. This is not true of education. The Japanese labor force was much more educated than the Italian labor force in 1960 and, by a probably diminished margin, in 1970.

Table 11-1 brings out one point strongly. There is nothing unique about the reasons that output per worker in Japan falls below the United States. If the label were removed from the Japanese column for 1970 and it were placed among the columns for the Western European countries in 1960, its numbers would convey no hint to the reader that it referred to a nation half a world away.

CHAPTER TWELVE

Can the Growth Rate
Be Sustained?

IN THE 1950s Japanese frequently credited fast growth to highly temporary factors, especially recovery from disruptions caused by war and defeat. Many regarded much slower growth as imminent. By late 1960 confidence had so increased that the government announced its plan to double national income in ten years. But even this target required a growth rate of only 7.2 percent, a large drop from the rate then prevailing. By 1970 popular projections extended the growth rate of real gross national product in the 1960s, which exceeded 11 percent by Japanese deflation procedures, into the indefinite future. Japan was expected to lead the world in output per person by the late 1980s and in total output not so very much later. In 1971 even the careful Japan Economic Research Center, in analyzing the future, was assuming a 10 percent growth rate in real GNP from 1970 to 1985. Achievement of this rate, which took into account expected costs of controlling pollution, would make GNP 4.2 times as large in 1985 as in 1970.

By 1973 growth anticipations were receding. Premier Kakuei Tanaka was promising a new initiative sacrificing growth for other welfare purposes, especially dispersion of population and industry. The yen had been revalued upward, making it more difficult to export—although actual experience was not alarming. In 1974 expectations were further dampened in some quarters by the high price of oil, almost all imported, and by a recession—brought on by credit tightening to check the 1972–73 inflation as well as by recession abroad—which, unlike earlier recessions, brought an absolute drop in output in Japan in 1974. By the end of 1974 anticipations were diverse.

Insofar as there is continuity between the past and the future, examination

Table 12-1. *Sustainable and Transitional Contributions to the Standardized Growth Rate of National Income, 1961–71, and Year Transitional Contribution Expires*

Rate or source	Total (1)	Sustainable (2)	Transitional (3)	Year transitional contribution expires[a] (4)
	Contribution in percentage points, 1961–71			
Standardized growth rate	9.56	3.24	6.32	...
Labor	1.78	0.68	1.10	...
Employment	1.09	0.33	0.76	1973
Hours	0.11	−0.15	0.26	1974
Age-sex composition	0.19	0.11	0.08	1977
Education	0.35	0.35	0.00	...
Unallocated	0.04	0.04	0.00	...
Capital	2.57	0.86	1.71	...
Inventories	0.86	0.21	0.65	1976
Nonresidential structures and equipment	1.44	0.38	1.06	1976
Dwellings	0.27	0.27	0.00	...
International assets	0.00	0.00	0.00	...
Land	0.00	0.00	0.00	...
Advances in knowledge and n.e.c.[b]	2.43	1.28	1.15	2002
Contraction of agricultural inputs	0.62	0.00	0.62	1982
Contraction of nonagricultural self-employment	0.19	0.00	0.19	1990
Reduction in international trade barriers	0.01	0.00	0.01	2002
Economies of scale				
Measured in U.S. prices	1.14	0.42	0.72	c
Income elasticities	0.82	0.00	0.82	1995

Source: Column 1, table 4-6, column 6.
a. Assumes contribution continues at 1961–71 size until expiration.
b. Not elsewhere classified.
c. The distribution among years follows: 1973, 0.10 points; 1974, 0.03; 1976, 0.22; 1977, 0.01; 1982, 0.08; 1990, 0.02; 1995, 0.11; 2002, 0.15.

of the postwar sources of growth can bring perspective to the outlook and that is our purpose here. We do not discuss the special events of 1973 and 1974.

We first divide the contribution made by each determinant to the 1961–71 growth rate into two parts (see table 12-1, columns 1–3). One part, which we call the "transitional" component, is the amount that was possible only because Japan was a latecomer to economic development or, closely related, was eliminating a cause of chronic inefficiency. Some random developments which could not continue may also be included. The remainder of the contribution is the "sustainable" portion. The sustainable components will not necessarily contribute the same amounts in the future as in the past but there is no apparent reason they cannot do so, and changes are unlikely to be big.

The 1961–71 standardized growth rate of national income, based on U.S. deflation procedures, was 9.56 percent a year. Of this amount, it is estimated, sustainable sources contributed 3.24 percentage points and transitional sources, 6.32 points. We hasten to stress that the purpose of this chapter is not to arrive at this result; anyone familiar with long-term growth in a number of countries could probably guess that a figure in the neighborhood of 3 percent or so would be arrived at in such an examination of any advanced nation. Rather, the purpose is to identify transitional growth sources, quantify their separate importance, and appraise the prospects for continuing their contributions. In each case, we ask, how much of a backlog remains? To put the estimates in a common framework, column 4 of table 12-1 shows the last year in which the transitional component of the contribution of each growth source would be obtained if the possibilities for gains were used up fast enough to maintain the contribution at its 1961–71 size. We would not actually expect so abrupt a cessation in most cases; it is more likely that the contribution would start to decline before the specified year and a reduced contribution would be obtained for a time thereafter.

The transitional component of the Japanese growth rate is exceptionally big, but it should be understood that probably all countries have a transitional component. The United States, for example, secured a contribution to its 1948–69 growth rate from the contraction of agricultural employment and nonfarm self-employment that is estimated at 0.30 percentage points, and a small contribution from increasing labor force participation by students and adult women.

The glitter is in no way removed from the Japanese achievement by the finding that it was made possible only by initial economic backwardness. The existence of possibilities to secure rapid growth from transitional sources, which we shall now detail, by no means ensured that they would be seized and rapid growth actually attained.

We shall now review the individual growth sources. It facilitates explanation to examine most components of output per unit of input before considering the input components. As stated, our base is the period from 1961 to 1971 and we refer to standardized national income.

Advances in Knowledge and Miscellaneous Determinants

In Japan the 1961–71 growth rate of the nonresidential business sector index for the incorporation of new knowledge into production, together with the effects of miscellaneous determinants, was 2.71. We suggested earlier that, on the basis of American and other Western experience, the worldwide advance of knowledge has been sufficient to raise national income originating in nonresidential business by about 1.43 percent a year, or 52.8 percent as much. It thus appears that of the contribution of 2.43 percentage points made by advances in knowledge and n.e.c. to the growth rate of national income in the *whole* economy only 52.8 percent or 1.28 percentage points represented the contribution that would have been made if new knowledge had been incorporated at the rate at which it appeared. The remaining 1.15 points resulted from narrowing the gap between average Japanese practice and best practice. Only the portion associated with the appearance of new knowledge can continue indefinitely.[1]

We estimated that after the effects of all measurable sources of difference in output are eliminated residual efficiency was 30 percent lower in Japan than in the United States in 1970. The reasons for this gap are not known, but, as stated earlier, it is not likely that simple ignorance of U.S. practice can account for most of it. The gap of 30 percent implies that a contribution of the 1961–71 size could be obtained from this source through 2001—or 2002 if allowance is made for a probable increase in the weight of nonresidential business—before average practice in Japan was as near to best practice as it was in the United States in 1970. This seems a realistic criterion for our estimate of the exhaustion of transitional gains even though Japan conceivably could approach the technological frontier still more closely.

Reallocation of Labor from Agriculture

From 1961 to 1971 agricultural employment dropped from 26.1 percent of total employment to 14.6 percent, or by 1.15 percentage points a year, and this shift in the use of labor contributed 0.62 percentage points, all classified as transitional, to the growth rate. Suppose productivity gains continue until the agricultural percentage drops another 10.6 points, to 4.0. It seems unlikely to go lower, or even this low, although it has already done so in the

1. Obviously, the rate at which new knowledge appears and becomes available to all countries may be higher or lower in the future than in the past.

United States and the United Kingdom. As a first approximation, one might calculate that a contribution of 0.62 points could be secured for nine years (10.6 divided by 1.15) after 1971. Provided the base year for deflation remains 1965, this can be stretched a little, because it is likely that the ratio of farm to nonfarm national income measured in 1965 prices will be lower than it was in 1961–71 and that the labor share will be bigger. We use 1982 as the date by which continuation of a contribution of the previous size would exhaust this source. Of course, we expect a more gradual decline.[2]

Reallocation of Labor from Nonagricultural Self-Employment

As a percentage of nonagricultural business employment, nonagricultural self-employment (including unpaid family workers) declined from 29.9 percent in 1961 to 24.4 percent in 1971, which was still much higher than 1971 percentages in Western countries except Italy. The drop of 0.55 points a year in this percentage was responsible for a contribution of 0.19 percentage points, all transitional in character, to the growth rate of national income in the whole economy.

The percentage that would eliminate misallocation may be higher than in the West because cramped living quarters and custom encourage eating out and (though decreasingly so) purchases of commercial amusements and personal services, activities adapted to small enterprises. Estimates that labor and capital earn only moderately less in noncorporate firms as a group, outside agriculture, than in corporate firms reinforce this suspicion. But even if, as in the previous chapter, we consider the percentage required for efficiency to be as high as 15, which is much above present percentages in major Western countries except Italy, a contribution to the growth rate of non-agricultural nonresidential business as large as in 1961–71 could continue for seventeen years after 1971. Because of the probability that the weight of this sector in national income and the labor share will both be higher, the period can be extended through 1990.

2. Continuation of a drop of 1.15 percentage points a year in the agricultural share of employment would require that the decline in farm employment each year be bigger in the future than in 1961–71 in absolute terms (because total employment will increase less) and far bigger in percentage terms (because farm employment will be smaller). Even so, the agricultural percentage may drop quite rapidly. The Japan Economic Research Center projection called for only 8 percent of employment in all primary industries in 1985, which implies only about 6 percent in agriculture. Japan Economic Research Center, "Japan's Economy in 1985: The Outlook for a Trillion Dollar Economy" (abridged translation, processed; 1971), p. 3.

The annual gain from this source in the near future could easily surpass 0.19 points, and the total remaining potential gain may be greater than we imply because the 15 percent figure we selected may be too big.

Reduction in International Trade Barriers

The contribution from this source could surely continue at the 1961–71 amount of 0.01 percentage points until at least 2002, the last year obtained for any other determinant. This is so if Japanese and foreign trade barriers reduce national income by as little as 0.3 percent in 1971. In view of the small size of the contribution, greater precision is unnecessary.

Economies of Scale Associated with Income Elasticities

Like gains from improved resource allocation, economies of scale associated with income elasticities are entirely transitional. When and if per capita consumption reaches the U.S. level, it will be found to do so whether Japanese or U.S. price weights are used in the comparison, because consumption patterns and price ratios will converge in the two countries; at least, this is the implication of our estimates. This source will then disappear. The gap between Japanese and American per capita consumption, and hence the amount by which the size of the gap differs when different price weights are used, is still big. A contribution of 0.82 percentage points, the 1961–71 amount, could continue through 1995 before the growth possibilities are exhausted.

Employment

The annual growth rate of 1.07 percent in total population from 1961 to 1971 was made up of rates of −0.95 percent for people less than fifteen years old, 1.84 for those fifteen to sixty-four, and 2.52 for those sixty-five and over. The fast growth of the population of working age resulted from the earlier era, continuing into World War II, during which birthrates were at or near their peak, combined with the long and continuing decline in death rates. Unless augmented by immigration, such fast growth of the working-age population was rare in advanced Western nations during the 1960s and will be rarer in the future. Japan's own rate already has dropped abruptly.

Table 12-2. *Population and Labor Input, Selected Growth Rates*

Item	Estimates from this study		Estimates from Japan Economic Research Center			
	1961–71 (1)	1960–70 (2)	1960–70 (3)	1970–75[a] (4)	1975–80[a] (5)	1980–85[a] (6)
Population						
Total	1.07	1.05	1.06	1.19	1.11	0.87
Aged 15–64	1.84	1.81	1.81	0.85	0.75	0.85
Employment	1.42	1.49	1.46[b]	0.76[b]	0.46[b]	0.39[b]
Hours	0.18[c,d]	0.30[c,d]	n.a.	n.a.	n.a.	n.a.
Average hours	−0.41[c]	−0.37[c]	−0.55	−1.0	−0.7	−0.4
Efficiency offset	0.58[c]	0.59[c]	n.a.	n.a.	n.a.	n.a.
Intergroup shift offset	0.01[c]	0.08[c]	n.a.	n.a.	n.a.	n.a.
Age-sex composition	0.29[c]	0.26[c]	0.3	0.3	0.2	0.1
Education	0.53[c]	0.53[c]	0.3	0.4	0.3	0.3

Sources: Columns 1 and 2 computed from tables 3-4 and 4-3, except that population figures were obtained from the Bureau of Statistics, Office of the Prime Minister. Other columns from (or computed from) Japan Economic Research Center, "Japan's Economy in 1985: The Outlook for a Trillion Dollar Economy" (abridged translation, processed; 1971), pp. 2, 20, 24.
n.a. Not available.
a. Projections.
b. Labor force.
c. Estimates refer to the nonresidential business sector.
d. Refers to the product of the three component indexes.

Labor force and employment grew 1.40 and 1.42 percent a year, respectively, from 1961 to 1971—less than the working-age population because the age of leaving school rose and the decline of agriculture reduced the labor force participation rate of females. These influences, of which the second and perhaps both should be considered transitional, offset part of the employment increase from population change.

Projections to 1985 by the Japan Economic Research Center help us to appraise future changes in labor input. In table 12-2 the projections by five-year periods are shown, as are the Center's estimates of actual changes from 1960 to 1970 and the most nearly corresponding estimates from our own study for 1961–71 and (to provide an overlap) 1960–70.

From 1970 to 1985 the population fifteen to sixty-four years old will grow at a rate about one full percentage point less than in 1961–71, and employment will do so after 1975. The projected rates for the working-age population are above the median for Western Europe in recent years but not greatly so. The employment projection assumes that, unlike the United States in the 1960s but like a majority of Western countries, Japan will not experience a substantial increase in the labor force participation rate of women outside agriculture (which already is high).[3]

We shall suppose that in the absence of transitional factors the 1961–71 growth rate of employment would have been 0.42 percent instead of 1.42 percent. Of the contribution of employment to the growth rate, which was 1.09 percentage points, we first calculate that only 0.32 points (1.09 times 0.42 divided by 1.42) were sustainable. Although we judge that the share of labor in national income would have been greater if Japan had not been in a transitional state, our adjustment raises the figure only to 0.33, leaving 0.76 points as the transitional component of the employment contribution. Table 12-1 implies that the transitional component is about exhausted. To secure an employment contribution at the 1961–71 rate after 1971 would have used up the margin in the projected 1970–75 growth rate of employment by 1973, and after 1975 there is no margin. Numbers for the actual labor force after 1970 show only small increases.

Hours

Two circumstances introduced a large transitional element into the contribution of hours in 1961–71. The less important was the last phase of the absorption into full-time employment of persons who had been able to secure only part-time work during the previous period of labor surplus. The more important was that hours of full-time workers were so long that their reduction, we estimate, had almost no effect on the work done in a week or year. If part-time employment had not diminished and if the reductions in full-time hours had been from the levels prevalent in the United States, changes in hours would have contributed about −0.23 percentage points to the 1961–71 growth rate of total national income on the basis of the actual labor share, or −0.24 points when the share is adjusted upward. However, a typical figure for the contribution of hours in an advanced Western country not experiencing a rising female share of employment would be perhaps −0.15 points, and we use this as the sustainable component, leaving 0.26 points as the transitional component.

Absorption of involuntary part-time employment was completed by 1971, but full-time hours still were very long. Both male and female full-time wage and salary workers in nonagricultural business worked about two more hours

3. Where such an increase has occurred, much of the employment expansion has been in part-time work. If we were to assume it would occur in Japan, the effect on the employment entries in table 12-1 would be partially offset in the entries for hours and age-sex composition.

a week in Japan in 1971 than in the United States in 1929. This means the efficiency offset to reductions in hours of such workers was still big, but it is likely to mean also that workers will demand large reductions so as to approach Western standards. "Backwardness" in the retention of long hours will become a handicap to future growth when the efficiency offset dwindles while hours are reduced rapidly. This is likely to happen in the 1980s at the latest.

Suppose that in the future the percentage of part-time employment and average part-time hours do not change; that average full-time hours in agriculture and nonagricultural self-employment either do not change or are fully offset by greater output per hour; that average full-time hours of non-agricultural wage and salary workers drop smoothly to the 1969 U.S. level by 1985; and that our assumed relationship between hours and output of those workers applies. Under these conditions, and with a small allowance for a probable increase in the share of nonresidential business labor, the contribution of hours to the 1970–85 growth rate would be −0.26 percentage points (as against 0.11 points in 1961–71). The contribution, which fell to zero in 1970 and turned to a slight negative in 1971, would continue to decline—that is, to become a larger negative. It would hit −0.15 percentage points, the sustainable rate, about 1975 and thereafter fall below it. After 1975 the transitional component would be negative because of the fast drop in full-time hours that we have assumed. Even in 1971–75 the transitional component is less than in 1961–71, so under our assumptions the former contribution could not be maintained until 1975. We enter 1974 in table 12-1.

Age-Sex Composition of Hours Worked

A reduction in young workers as young people remain in school longer is normal for an advanced society. But a declining female component of the labor force is not; in Japan it is the consequence of dwindling agricultural employment.[4] Two-fifths of the advance in the age-sex composition index

4. The reduction in nonagricultural self-employment also contributed. In 1973 labor force participation rates for women were 62.7 percent, 60.0 percent, and 39.1 percent in households headed, respectively, by farm owners with fifty or more ares of land, owners of nonagricultural family businesses, and employees. The labor force participation rate for women actually increased from 39.6 percent in 1960 to 44.9 percent in 1970 in densely inhabited districts while it declined from 60.2 percent in 1960 to 54.8 percent in 1970 in other districts. Data cited in this footnote are from Shunichirō Umetani, "The Japanese Women in the Labor Market," *Japan Labor Bulletin*, January 1, 1975.

from 1961 to 1971 resulted from a reduction in the percentage of hours worked by females. We therefore regard as transitional two-fifths, or 0.08 percentage points, of the 0.19 points contributed to the growth rate by changes in age-sex composition of hours worked. The sustainable contribution was then 0.11 points.

Based on the relation between estimates for past and future growth shown by the Japan Economic Research Center series (table 12-2), changes in age-sex composition will contribute about 0.20 percentage points to the growth rate of national income in 1970–75, 0.13 points in 1975–80, and 0.07 points in 1980–85. If the contribution continued at the 1961–71 level until the opportunity for a transitional contribution were exhausted, this would occur six years after 1971, or in 1977.

Education and Unallocated Labor Input

Education of the labor force in Japan is comparable to that in Western countries, it can increase at the 1961–71 rate for a long time (many decades), and we classify its entire contribution as sustainable. We do so even though education cannot continue to increase forever. If there is any transitional element in the small "unallocated" component, we disregard it.

Capital

Two transitional conditions were responsible for the big increase in investment and consequently for most of the contribution of capital to the growth of output. One was the sharp drop in the relative price of capital goods; the other, the high growth rate of real output which resulted from transitional elements in many growth sources. In addition, the current saving rate was above the average saving rate in the past, a relationship that could not continue indefinitely.

Measured as the sum of expenditures, in 1965 prices, and by Japanese deflation techniques, growth rates from 1961 to 1971 were 10.2 percent for GNP and 12.5 percent for gross private investment (business, residential, and net foreign). The difference was due to the falling relative price of investment goods; the current-price ratio of national saving or investment to GNP did not change much.[5] When judged by American price relationships, the ratio

5. In 1971 the ratio was actually a bit lower than in 1961 but, as shown in table 7-1, a little above 1960. Table 7-2 suggests some uptrend in this period.

of capital goods prices to prices of personal consumption expenditures (or of all GNP) in the 1950s apparently was high in Japan, as it was in Europe. Estimates by Kravis and associates show that even in 1970, after the long decline, relative prices of producers' durables and nonresidential structures were considerably higher in Japan than in the United States.[6] We consider the decline to be transitional—in part, especially in the case of inventories, it may have been random. We assume that in its absence gross private investment would have grown at about the same rate as GNP when both are measured in constant prices.

To estimate the sustainable portion of the growth rate of output, we must anticipate the results for components not yet estimated, including capital itself. We conclude that a little over 3 percentage points out of the 9.5 percent growth rate of adjusted national income resulted from sustainable contributions. In the absence of transitional contributions the figure for the GNP series used in the previous paragraph would have been around 3⅓ percent, and we assume that the growth rate of gross investment in constant prices would also have been 3⅓ percent. The fact that the average level of the saving rate was higher in 1961–71 than it had been earlier would have meant a growth rate of capital stock above that of investment, but the consequences of this change in the saving rate are themselves transitional. Hence we use 3⅓ percent as the sustainable growth rate of capital stock as well as of gross investment.

If inputs of nonresidential structures and equipment and of inventories had each grown only 3⅓ percent a year instead of at their actual rates, the contribution of the former would have been cut from 1.44 percentage points to 0.41 points and that of inventories from 0.86 points to 0.23 points. Allowance for the probability that the appropriate weights of these inputs would have been smaller under conditions prevalent in more advanced economies reduces our estimates of the sustainable portions of their contributions a bit further to 0.38 and 0.21 percentage points. The entire contributions of dwellings and international assets are entered as sustainable, partly because the actual figures seem only remotely related to the growth of capital stock.

How long could transitional contributions of the 1961–71 size be obtained from nonresidential fixed capital and inventories? A possible reference point for the end of transitional gains is provided by capital stock per worker in the United States. We estimate that, per person employed in the whole economy, the stock of private nonresidential business structures and equip-

6. Irving B. Kravis and others, *A System of International Comparisons of Gross Product and Purchasing Power,* United Nations International Comparison Project: Phase One (Johns Hopkins University Press for the World Bank, 1975).

ment was 69 percent greater in the United States than in Japan in 1970 and the stock of inventories was 79 percent greater.[7] To provide as large a transitional contribution to growth as in 1961–71, the stocks of nonresidential structures and equipment and of inventories would have to increase so fast that both would attain the then prevailing U.S. level per person employed soon after the end of 1976.[8]

Capital per worker in Japan may, of course, rise above the U.S. level and break new ground. If it does so, the additional growth would hardly be regarded as transitional.[9]

Economies of Scale, U.S. Prices

The contribution of this source to growth in 1961–71 was allocated between sustainable and transitional components in the same proportion as the sum of all other growth sources (except economies of scale associated with income elasticities). Of the total of 1.14 percentage points, 0.42 points result from growth of the market attributable to contributions from sustainable sources and 0.72 points from growth attributable to transitional sources. The period for which transitional gains could continue at the 1961–71 rate depends on continuation of gains from other transitional sources. Transitional gains from economies of scale, measured in U.S. prices, were therefore allocated among expiration dates like the transitional contributions from the sources that make them possible.

The Combined Estimates

When summarized, our estimates imply that sources we deemed sustainable contributed 3.24 percentage points to the 9.56 percent growth rate of standardized national income from 1961 to 1971 and sources we deemed

7. Calculated from appendix table O-1, column 1. Use of U.S. price weights is implied.

8. These results are obtained without allowance for lower capital shares of national income in the future. The effect of lower shares is offset by the absence of an allowance for the fact that the ratio of capital to labor in the whole economy can be higher than in the United States before the capital–labor ratio in nonresidential business, the relevant ratio, becomes higher.

9. We have chosen to regard no part of the contribution of dwellings as transitional but note that, if U.S. housing is used as a standard for comparison, it would in any case take a long time to eliminate the transitional element. The estimates of Kravis and his associates in *A System of International Comparisons* imply that in 1970 the quantity of housing per worker in the United States was 315 percent of the Japanese quantity. (The per capita quantity, perhaps more pertinent for this component, was 256 percent.)

transitional contributed 6.32 points. For the most part, contributions from transitional sources were possible only because Japan was a latecomer to growth, but this circumstance did not make growth at the high rate achieved inevitable, or even probable if we judge from the experience of other nations.

From table 12-1 it can be easily computed that if the transitional contribution of each source continued at its 1961–71 level until the potential for a further contribution was exhausted, if sustainable sources continued indefinitely to contribute the same amount as in 1961–71, and if no new sources appeared, the growth rate would be as follows:

Actual		*Implied*	
1961–71	9.56	1971–73	9.56
		1973–74	8.70
		1974–76	8.41
		1976–77	6.48
		1977–82	6.39
		1982–90	5.69
		1990–95	5.48
		1995–2002	4.55
		2002–	3.24

The assumptions stated are not necessarily those one would wish to introduce if he were preparing an actual projection, but they do bring past experience to bear upon the future.

All rates calculated after 1973 are down from the 1961–71 rate. The calculated 1977–82 rate is down by one-third and the 1982–90 rate by two-fifths. All transitional elements will be gone by 2002. We would, of course, expect the exhaustion of individual transitional sources to cut into the standardized growth rate less abruptly than assumed in the table above, but this pattern gives approximate timing.

The rate implied for standardized national income is 7.1 percent from 1971 to 1985, 6.5 percent from 1971 to 1995, and 6.2 percent from 1971 to 2000. Rates based on Japanese deflation procedures would be a little higher throughout.

The costs of conforming to regulations for environmental protection will adversely affect the future growth rate, but by an amount that is likely to be small. Government actions intended to shift priorities away from growth are also unlikely, in our view, to have much effect on growth. The outlook for the price of oil is too uncertain for us to venture any appraisal of its possible influence.

Irregular factors may cause actual growth rates in any period to depart widely from standardized rates. Indeed, they have already done so in the period from 1971 to 1975, which is included in the calculation above. Irregular factors whose past influence we have attempted to isolate, and especially changes in output per unit of input that result from fluctuations in intensity of utilization, can be very important quantitatively. Employment and working hours have not previously been sensitive to changes in business activity but may become more so in the future. If they do, this will provide additional scope for actual output to diverge from standardized output. Actual national income is estimated to have been 1.2 percent below standardized national income in 1971.[10] The deficiency was many times as large in the far more depressed conditions of 1974 and 1975. The low initial level will elevate rates computed with these years as a base.

For all these reasons the calculated growth rates are not forecasts of the future course of actual national income. Our intention is to confine the scope of our study to a description of past growth and the implications of this description for future growth prospects.

10. See appendix table N-1, column 8.

Appendixes

Output and Employment
in Three Special Sectors

IN TABLES 3-2, 3-3, and 3-4 the economy is divided into four sectors.[1] Estimates for the three smaller, special sectors are described here. Our objective
is to extract the output estimates which are included in the Economic
Planning Agency's national income and product aggregates and the employment estimates included in aggregate employment (our table 3-4). Some
components are not estimated separately by the Economic Planning Agency
(EPA), and it is necessary to try to approximate the series that are implied
by EPA estimates for the aggregates.

Part One: General Government, Households, Nonprofit
Institutions, and Foreign Governments

This covers all persons employed outside the business sector. The number
of such persons and the values of their output in current and constant prices
are obtained as the sum of four major components. The values of gross
national product, net national product (NNP) at market prices, and national
income at factor cost are the same because in this sector depreciation is not
included in GNP and there are no indirect taxes or subsidies. In current
prices, this value is simply the compensation of employees. Calendar year
estimates were desired, but it was sometimes necessary to adjust fiscal year
estimates to arrive at calendar year estimates. (Fiscal year 1965, for example,

---

1. In two sectors—the services of dwellings and international assets—employment
is zero by definition; hence they are omitted from table 3-4.

covers April 1, 1965, through March 31, 1966.) Descriptions of the four major components of employment and output follow.

General Government

All data for general government were obtained directly from the EPA, and are components of its series, except for employment before 1964. However, it was necessary to infer calendar year data for output before 1962 from fiscal year data. Below we provide detailed descriptions of the series.

Estimates of Current Price and Constant Price Series for Output or Compensation

For calendar and fiscal years from 1962 through 1971, compensation of general government employees in current prices and the corresponding value of output in constant 1965 prices were obtained from the Economic Planning Agency.[2] Compensation of general government employees in current prices for fiscal years 1951 through 1961 was provided by the EPA from its worksheets. We estimated compensation in each calendar year from 1952 through 1961 to be equal to compensation in the corresponding fiscal year minus one-fourth of the increase from the previous to the current fiscal year. Column 1 of table A-1 shows the complete calendar year series in current prices.

The EPA also provided from its worksheets its quarterly series of deflators for compensation of government employees. We computed an annual calendar year price series from these data; it is shown in column 7 of table A-1. The deflator, according to the EPA, is constructed as:

$$D_t = \frac{\Sigma P_t N_t}{\Sigma P_0 N_t},$$

where P_0 and P_t stand for the average compensation of full-time employees in a particular classification, based on education and length of employment, in periods 0 and t, and N_t is the number of employees in that particular classification in period t. We deflated current dollar compensation

2. *Annual Report on National Income Statistics 1973* (1973), tables 3 and 4, pp. 24–25, 28–29, 54–55, and 58–59, and the same tables of the 1972 report. The series are obtained by subtracting "gross national expenditure at market prices (excluding personnel expenditure of general government)" from "gross national expenditure at market prices." The 1962 figures were calculated from 1963 data and 1962–63 percentage changes.

Table A-1. *General Government: National Income in Current and Constant Prices, Employment, and Related Series, 1952–71*

Calendar year (1)	National income[a] (billions of yen) Current prices (1)	Constant 1965 prices[b] (2)	Employment (thousands) (3)	National income per person employed (thousands of yen) Current prices[c] (4)	Constant 1965 prices[b] (5)	Indexes of average earnings per person employed (1965 = 100) (6)	Deflator for government personnel expenditure[b] (1965 = 100) (7)
1952	376	1,368	2,047	184	668	24.6	27.4
1953	464	1,399	2,072	224	675	29.9	33.1
1954	541	1,446	2,137	253	677	33.8	37.4
1955	585	1,461	2,205	265	663	35.4	40.0
1956	618	1,449	2,207	280	657	37.4	42.6
1957	670	1,436	2,191	306	655	40.9	46.6
1958	723	1,466	2,164	334	677	44.7	49.3
1959	787	1,522	2,214	355	687	47.5	51.7
1960	911	1,559	2,278	400	684	53.5	58.4
1961	1,076	1,651	2,337	460	706	61.5	65.2
1962	1,275	1,772	2,477	515	715	68.9	71.3
1963	1,512	1,893	2,598	582	729	77.8	79.6
1964	1,797	2,005	2,725	659	736	88.1	89.4
1965	2,102	2,096	2,812	748	745	100.0	100.0
1966	2,370	2,173	2,870	826	757	110.4	108.9
1967	2,661	2,246	2,918	912	770	121.9	118.2
1968	3,034	2,310	2,964	1,024	779	136.9	131.4
1969	3,511	2,402	3,015	1,165	797	155.7	146.1
1970	4,199	2,482	3,073	1,366	808	182.6	169.0
1971	4,972	2,570	3,134	1,586	820	212.0	193.7

Sources: See text.
a. Same as compensation of employees, gross and net national product.
b. Based on Japanese deflation procedures.
c. Equal to average annual compensation of employees.

by this price series to secure calendar year estimates at constant prices, shown in table A-1, column 2.

Estimates of Employment

For the fiscal years 1964 to 1970, the EPA provided from its worksheets employment data corresponding to the compensation series. Similar data were not available for earlier years. A series was approximated by an EPA analyst (T. Tange) by use of a series for average pay of government employees; average compensation in 1964 was extrapolated back to 1951 by this series. Employment was then computed as the quotient of total compensation and estimated average compensation of government employees. This completed a fiscal year employment series for 1951 to 1970. We estimated calendar year employment from 1952 through 1970 to be equal to employment in the corresponding fiscal year minus one-fourth of the increase from the previous to the current fiscal year. Employment in 1971 was obtained by averaging the results of two assumptions: that the increase from the preceding year in employment was the same in 1971 as in 1970, and that the increase in constant price national income per person employed was the same in 1971 as in 1970.

Comparison with Other Estimates of Government Employment

The coverage of general government employment, the series just described, does not correspond to that of any series commonly published in Japanese statistics. It covers much more than "public administration" or the government "industry," for which statistics are commonly provided. These classifications exclude public education and health, as well as less important activities. On the other hand, general government covers much less than all government employment because it excludes government enterprises such as the postal and telephone service and government-owned railroads. We have compared the series in table A-1 with other data in order to check the reliability of (1) the general level in recent years and (2) the movement from 1953 to recent years.

Two rough checks on the level of the employment series provided by the EPA for recent years confirm that it corresponds to the desired concept and is generally consistent with other sources.

First, the Establishment Census for July 1, 1969, reports 1,750,000 persons engaged in local government and 1,498,000 in national government and public corporations, a total of 3,248,000. Those employed in industry divisions other than services and those in the "health and sanitary services" industry (not to be confused with "medical services") within the services division may be eliminated as almost entirely employed by government enterprises. This leaves 1,702,000 for general government (1,404,000 local and 298,000 national).[3] The Establishment Census excludes "government" as defined in the Standard Industrial Classification of Japan, so 1,702,000 covers only government employees in other industries. An estimate by Shōzō Ichino for the Center for Econometric Data Development and Research (CEDDR) puts employment in the government industry at 1,531,000 in 1968; if the percentage increase was the same as in the closely related

3. Data from Bureau of Statistics, Office of the Prime Minister, *Japan Statistical Yearbook, 1971* (1972), pp. 82–85.

EPA calendar year series for public administration, the 1969 figure would have been 1,579,000.[4] Total general government employment in 1969 would then have been 3,281,000 (1,702,000 plus 1,579,000). This compares with our estimate, obtained from the EPA, of 3,015,000 for calendar 1969.

Second, the Survey on Wages of Local Government Employees by the Local Administration Bureau, Ministry of Home Affairs, reports 2,463,296 local government employees as of April 1, 1970. The "fixed" or budgeted number of national government employees in fiscal year 1970 is reported by the Budget Bureau, Ministry of Finance, to be 1,992,793. Adding these two figures and deducting local government general administration employees classified in "public enterprises" (154,452), national government employment in the postal service (322,823), and national government "government corporations' employees" (808,107) leaves 3,171,000 as an approximation to general government employment in 1970. A similar calculation for 1971 yields 3,248,000.[5] Our estimates are 3,073,000 for calendar year 1970 and 3,134,000 for calendar year 1971.

The differences between our estimates, obtained from the EPA, and those derived as described are not disturbing. Small refinements were omitted from the latter. Also, different decisions as to whether schoolteachers are counted as employed during vacations could be responsible for discrepancies of these magnitudes. Both the Establishment Census of July 1 and the April 1 survey of local government employees include all government-employed teachers. We do not know whether or not the EPA estimate counts teachers as employed during vacation periods. If not, this would explain why it is lower on an annual-average basis than the alternatives. A difference in counting of teachers in vacation periods is the main reason that in the United States markedly lower figures for government employment are obtained from the household surveys (Current Population Survey) than from establishment sources, which count teachers as employed during vacation periods.

The employment estimates for the early years are a weak part of the general government data. Our series rises by 742,000 from fiscal year 1953, when it was 2,087,000, to fiscal 1965, when it was 2,829,000. It is not hard to obtain bigger or smaller estimates of the increase. Thus the EPA analyst cited (T. Tange) noted that the average salary series he used in deriving our employment series before 1964 rose less from 1965 to 1970 than the quotient

---

4. The EPA series for public administration is published in *Annual Report on National Income Statistics, 1973*, table 1, pp. 208–15, and the corresponding table in *Revised Report on National Income Statistics, 1951–1967* (1969).

5. Data used in this paragraph are from *Japan Statistical Yearbook, 1971*, pp. 594–95.

of EPA data for compensation and employment (although the pattern of annual movements is similar). If this experience is used to introduce a bias correction in prior years, employment in those years is lowered and the 1953–65 increase is raised from 742,000 to 896,000. On the other hand, a much smaller increase might be deduced. General government employment and compensation conceptually can be divided between public administration (for which series are published by the EPA from 1953 on in *Annual Report on National Income Statistics 1973*, table 1, pages 208–15, and the corresponding table in *Revised Report on National Income Statistics, 1951–1967*) and other industries, mainly health and education, which the EPA does not estimate separately. Subtraction of public administration from general government yields fiscal year series for compensation of government employees in other industries in 1953–71 and for employment in other industries in 1965–70. Suppose 1965 average earnings in "other" industries are extrapolated backward to 1953 by average earnings in public administration, that employee compensation is divided by average earnings to secure employment in other industries, and that the latter figure is added to public administration to secure general government employment. The result is a fiscal 1953 employment estimate of 2,345,000 and a 1953–65 increase of only 484,000, much less than our 742,000. However, it does not appear to us that the data for public administration are statistically consistent with those for general government.[6] A still different result could be obtained by substituting for the EPA employment series for public administration the series for employment in government (as defined in the Japanese Standard Industrial Classification) prepared by Shōzō Ichino for CEDDR. If the calculation described above were repeated with this substitution (but with the EPA series for total compensation retained), a 1953–65 increase in general government employment of 937,000, much more than our estimate of 732,000, would be obtained.

The employment series adopted increases by an amount which is in the middle range of possible series, and it is fairly free of erratic movements. Figures derived from its use in conjunction with the current and constant price output series, shown in columns 4 to 7 of table A-1, are not unreasonable. Conceptually, the rise in national income per person employed in constant 1965 prices (column 5) and the greater rise in the index of average earnings per person employed (column 6) than in the deflator for government personnel expenditure (column 7) must result from a rise in the ratio of full-time equivalent to total employment and/or a shift in the composition of employment toward persons with more experience and education. Changes

6. Series for "other" industries derived in the way described are erratic—even after 1965—and the series for compensation implies longer-term changes for either average compensation or employment that appear implausible.

before 1964 seem plausible in comparison with those after 1964, which are based on actual EPA employment estimates.

Private Households

Estimates for private households are shown in table A-2.

Compensation of employees of private households valued in current prices, as estimated by the EPA, was obtained from the EPA *Sourcebook*,[7] page 1079, for 1953–67 and from EPA worksheets for 1968–71. The series is not separately deflated by the EPA; it is included in a large miscellaneous group of private consumption expenditures which is deflated as a unit. Because compensation of domestic servants is not a price index component, deflation of this item is, in effect, by prices of a sample of consumer goods and services. To approximate the EPA procedure, we deflate by the all-commodity index of the consumer price index for cities, the procedure that the EPA follows in deflating expenditures of nonprofit institutions (a rather similar case).

Employment in 1950, 1955, 1960, 1965, and 1970 was obtained from Bureau of Statistics, Office of the Prime Minister, *Comparison of Employed Persons by Industry in the Population Censuses, 1920 through 1970,* table 1. Annual estimates of employment for 1953–65 were obtained from the EPA *Sourcebook,* page 1078. For 1955 and 1960 EPA employment data are the same as the Census figure. We use the EPA data annually up to 1960. The 1965 EPA employment figure is lower than the Census count, presumably differing because it was prepared before Census data became available. We interpolated the 1960 and 1965 Census figures by the EPA employment series to obtain our 1961–64 employment estimates. Employment in 1966–69 and 1971 we estimated by straight-line interpolation and extrapolation of the Census data. Employment and compensation may not be statistically comparable to one another after 1960.

Private Nonprofit Institutions

The EPA includes private nonprofit institutions in its national income, national product, and employment aggregates but does not estimate them separately. We prepared the series for nonprofit institutions shown in table A-2. These series are the sum of the estimates for three types of institutions, which are described in the following subsections; the objective was to determine the amounts implicitly included by the EPA in its aggregates.

7. *Shōwa 40-nen. Kaitei kokumin shotoku tōkei* (Suikei Shiryōshū) [Sourcebook of Revised National Income Statistics, Base Year 1965] (1970).

Table A-2. Households, Institutions, and Foreign Governments: National Income in Current and Constant Prices and Employment, 1952–71

| | National income[a] (billions of yen) | | | | | | Employment (thousands) | | |
| | Current prices | | | Constant 1965 prices[b] | | | | | |
Calendar year	House- holds (1)	Nonprofit institutions (2)	Foreign governments[c] (3)	House- holds (4)	Nonprofit institutions (5)	Foreign governments[c] (6)	House- holds (7)	Nonprofit institutions (8)	Foreign governments (9)
1952	19	70	54	31	140	55	305	456	225
1953	22	81	60	34	144	61	318	449	229
1954	24	88	56	35	143	56	330	442	211
1955	27	100	52	39	161	52	343	454	194
1956	28	114	48	41	181	47	339	461	173
1957	29	128	48	41	196	47	334	470	157
1958	30	143	38	42	216	40	330	482	102
1959	31	155	31	43	229	31	326	490	82
1960	33	172	29	45	246	29	321	501	75
1961	35	234	28	45	312	29	301	559	69
1962	38	281	29	46	344	31	278	584	68
1963	39	358	30	44	409	31	253	632	64
1964	37	435	31	40	472	32	224	691	55
1965	36	571	32	36	570	32	192	738	53
1966	31	707	35	29	671	35	184	783	52
1967	34	803	39	31	735	38	177	819	52
1968	40	954	43	35	851	46	169	857	51
1969	43	1,114	48	35	926	46	161	893	49
1970	44	1,343	52	34	1,042	47	153	917	40
1971	50	1,554	52	36	1,146	46	145	941	33

Sources: See text.
a. Same as compensation of employees, gross and net national product.
b. Based on Japanese deflation procedures.
c. Includes all net labor income received from abroad; see text.

Medical and Health Services

Employment in private nonprofit institutions in the medical and health services industries is mainly in hospitals and clinics. Our estimates are based upon Establishment Census data for persons engaged, cross-classified by form of organization and industry.[8] For 1966 and 1969 employment consists of persons engaged who were employed by corporations other than (profit-making) companies and by unincorporated associations (a minor component) in the "medical services" and "health and sanitary services" industries. Estimates for 1951, 1954, 1957, 1960, and 1963 were obtained in the same way, except that employment by companies, which had to be eliminated, was not reported separately in these censuses. It was estimated at the same percentage (6.3) of total employment in corporations and unincorporated associations in these industries as it represented in 1966.

Estimates of employment in intervening years were obtained by interpolation, with nonprofit components of employment reported in the National Survey of Medical Facilities used as the interpolating index in 1967–68 and the CEDDR series by Ichino for total medical and health employment (which is some five times as big as the private nonprofit component) used in earlier years. The series derived from the National Survey was used to extrapolate the 1969 Census figure to 1970 and 1971.

Compensation of employees (national income in current prices) is the product of employment and estimated average compensation; estimates of average compensation were pieced together from the National Survey of Medical Facilities, Establishment Census, and National Living Standard Annual Report.

To secure national income in constant prices, compensation was deflated by the medical care component of the consumer price index (CPI) for cities of 50,000 population or more. This corresponds to the EPA deflation procedure for all private medical care expenditures (of which this is a part), except that the EPA also gives some weight (corresponding to farm families medical expenditures) to the similar index for small cities.

Educational Institutions

Employment in 1951, 1954, 1957, 1960, 1963, 1966, and 1969 was derived from Establishment Census data for the education services industry by

8. Establishment Census data for 1951 are reported in *Japan Statistical Yearbook, 1954,* from the table appearing on p. 53; for 1954, in the 1958 *Yearbook,* p. 59; for 1957, in the 1960 *Yearbook,* p. 61; for 1960, in the 1964 *Yearbook,* p. 65; for 1963, in the 1966 *Yearbook,* p. 73; and for 1969, in the 1971 *Yearbook,* p. 82.

the same procedure as was followed for medical and health services. "Companies" accounted for 12.6 percent of the total for corporations and unincorporated associations in 1966, and this percentage was used to estimate company employment, which had to be eliminated, in earlier census years. Intercensal years before 1966 were estimated by use as an interpolator of the CEDDR series by Ichino for total employment in the education industry (which is five to ten times as big as the private nonprofit series). Straight-line interpolation and extrapolation were used to estimate 1967, 1968, 1970, and 1971.

Compensation of employees is estimated as the product of employment and average compensation. In 1970 and 1971 average earnings in the education industry from the Monthly Labor Survey were used. Average earnings in public administration were used to extrapolate the 1970 figure back to 1955, and the wage index for all industries to extrapolate the 1955 figure back to 1952.

To secure national income in constant prices, compensation was deflated by the education component of the CPI for cities of 50,000 population or more. This corresponds to the EPA deflation procedure for all private education expenditures, except that the EPA also gives some weight (corresponding to farm families expenditures) to the similar index for small cities.

Services of Religious Organizations and Other Nonprofit Institutions

In the terminology of the EPA national income statistics, the designation "private nonprofit institutions" excludes medical and educational services but appears to cover comprehensively the remainder of nonprofit organizations serving individuals. Compensation of employees in the years 1952–67 was obtained from the EPA *Sourcebook*, page 1070. The 1967 estimate was extrapolated to 1971 by the "expenditure of nonprofit institutions," from the *Annual Report on National Income Statistics, 1973,* table 3, pages 54–55.

To secure national income in constant prices, compensation was deflated by the EPA implicit deflator for "expenditures of nonprofit institutions," which is the same as the consumer price index (all items). Compensation of employees is the bulk of the expenditures of nonprofit institutions.

Employment was obtained as the sum of series for religious and other organizations.

For religious organizations, employment in 1954, 1960, 1963, 1966, and 1969 was obtained from the Establishment Censuses.[9] There are no "com-

9. The reported 1957 Census figure was incredibly small (less than one-tenth of 1954 or 1960) and was disregarded. The 1951 Establishment Census figure was also rejected because it implied a 50 percent employment decline from 1951 to 1954, whereas

panies" in this industry, so the sum of data for corporations and unincorporated associations was used. The CEDDR series by Ichino for religious organizations was used to extrapolate back to 1952 and to interpolate in the missing years between 1954 and 1966. The years 1967, 1968, 1970, and 1971 were estimated by straight-line interpolation and extrapolation of the 1966 and 1969 figures.

Employment in other nonprofit organizations in 1951, 1954, 1957, 1960, 1963, 1966, and 1969 was derived from Establishment Census data for persons engaged. It is the sum of the number of persons employed by corporations, except companies, and by nonprofit associations in "social insurance and welfare services," "scientific research services," and "political, economic, and cultural nonprofit organizations." (Before 1969 these industries were combined.) The procedure was the same as that for medical and health services. Estimates for 1952, 1953, 1955, and 1956 were obtained by straight-line interpolation. Estimates for 1958, 1959, 1961, and 1962 were obtained by use as an interpolating index of the employment series for nonprofit organizations prepared for CEDDR by Ichino. A combination of the CEDDR series and 1960, 1965, and 1970 Census of Population employment data for social insurance and welfare services, scientific research institutes, and political, economic, and cultural nonprofit organizations was used to obtain interpolated estimates for 1964, 1965, 1967, and 1968, and to extrapolate from 1969 to 1970. The increase from 1970 to 1971 was assumed to be the same as that from 1969 to 1970.

Foreign Governments

The estimates for national income in current and constant prices, shown in table A-2, are described in the next section (International Assets).

The number of Japanese employed by foreign governments (industry 170) in 1950, 1955, 1960, 1965, and 1970, as reported in the Census of Population, was obtained from *Comparison of Employed Persons by Industry in the Population Censuses, 1920 through 1970,* page 313. Other years shown in table A-2, except 1952 and 1954, were estimated by interpolating or extrapolating the Census figures by reported U.S. government employment of Japanese in Japan. The latter series, which is described in the following paragraph, is available for 1953–73 except 1954. It accounted for 80 to 83 percent of employment reported in the Census in 1955, 1960, and 1965 and

---

in the same period the CEDDR series by Ichino shows a 1 percent employment decline for religious organizations, and from 1950 to 1955 the Census of Population yields a 12 percent increase.

for 90 percent in 1970. Estimates for 1952 and 1954 are based on straight-line interpolation.

Nearly all U.S. government employment in Japan consists of "indirect hires" on military bases, for which the Japanese government acts as agent for the U.S. government. The series for reported U.S. government employment of Japanese in Japan is the sum of indirect hires by the U.S. Department of Defense, as reported by that agency, and direct hires by all agencies, as reported by the U.S. Civil Service Commission.[10] For 1963–71 the Department of Defense series for indirect hires is very close in level and movement to a series, which starts in 1963, that is reported by the Japanese government.[11]

Part Two: International Assets

The contribution of international assets to the national income is the net flow of investment income from abroad. The net flow of labor income from abroad, already reported in table A-2 under the heading "foreign governments," is also described in this section.

In current prices, total factor income received from abroad and total factor income paid to abroad, as defined by the EPA, are published on a calendar year basis in EPA, *Annual Report on National Income Statistics, 1973,* and *Revised Report on National Income Statistics, 1951–1967,* part 1, account 6. We divided these series among labor income, investment income, and other income, and subtracted payments from receipts to secure net receipts (table A-3).

The EPA provided from its worksheets the details of labor income received from abroad and labor income paid to abroad, both on a calendar year basis. The labor series is completely dominated by the compensation of Japanese employed on U.S. bases (¥54 million in 1952 and ¥56 million in 1971). The difference between other labor income received and all labor income paid is less than ¥1 million in all years until 1969, and never exceeds ¥4 million.

Investment income received and paid is published in the EPA sources cited above, part 2, table 17.

Other income is obtained by subtraction for calendar years. Detailed data obtained on a fiscal year basis show the series to be dominated by payments

10. The Civil Service Commission series began only in 1963. Direct hires by the Department of Defense were available throughout the period. Before 1963 they were increased by 650 each year to cover other agencies.

11. Defense Facilities Administration Agency, Labor Wage Administration Section, Labor Division, *The Report on Actual Status of Wage for USFJ Employees: Master Labor Contract, Mariner Contract, and Indirect Hire Agreement* (Government of Japan, 1964 and 1972).

Table A-3. *Net Factor Income*[a] *Received from Abroad, by Type, in Current and Constant Prices, 1952–71*

Billions of yen

	Current prices				Constant (1965) prices			
Calendar year	Total (1)	Labor income (2)	Investment income (3)	License fees, royalties, and other (4)	Total[b] (5)	Labor income[b] (6)	Investment income (7)	License fees, royalties, and other (8)
1952	46	54	−2	−6	49	55	−1	−5
1953	43	60	−8	−9	47	61	−7	−7
1954	32	56	−14	−10	35	56	−12	−9
1955	25	52	−15	−12	29	52	−12	−11
1956	18	48	−14	−16	22	47	−11	−14
1957	10	48	−18	−20	16	47	−14	−17
1958	3	38	−14	−21	7	40	−13	−20
1959	−7	31	−13	−25	−6	31	−13	−24
1960	−16	29	−12	−33	−16	29	−12	−33
1961	−37	28	−17	−48	−34	29	−16	−47
1962	−50	29	−33	−46	−49	31	−33	−47
1963	−66	30	−43	−53	−64	31	−41	−54
1964	−98	31	−70	−59	−94	32	−68	−58
1965	−99	32	−68	−63	−99	32	−68	−63
1966	−99	35	−67	−67	−96	35	−65	−66
1967	−107	39	−64	−82	−105	38	−63	−80
1968	−150	43	−91	−102	−147	46	−89	−104
1969	−169	48	−103	−114	−160	46	−98	−108
1970	−159	52	−75	−136	−149	47	−72	−124
1971	−115	52	−17	−150	−111	46	−21	−136

Sources: See text.
a. As defined by the Economic Planning Agency.
b. Based on Japanese deflation procedures.

of license fees and royalties. For fiscal year 1966, for example, the detailed values, in thousands of millions of yen, are as follows:

	Receipts	Payments	Net receipts
License fees and royalties	6.5	71.4	−64.9
Film fees	0.2	6.0	−5.8
Real estate income	0.5	0.3	0.1
Total	7.2	77.7	−70.5

These payments are presumably deducted as costs in the computation of profits of domestic businesses. They need not be deducted again when national income is derived from net domestic product at factor cost calculated as the sum of income shares.

To obtain estimates in constant prices, all receipts from abroad are deflated by the implicit deflator for "exports of goods and services and factor income received from abroad" and all payments by the implicit deflator for "imports of goods and services and factor income paid abroad." The deflators are from table 5, pages 62–63, of *Annual Report on National Income Statistics, 1973,* and the corresponding table of *Revised Report on National Income Statistics, 1951–1967.*

Part Three: Services of Dwellings

To derive national income and product series for the services of dwellings industry, three series are needed in current and constant prices. A fourth is needed in current prices only. These series and the output series derived from them are shown for calendar years in table A-4.

1. Private consumption expenditure for rent valued in current prices is from table 3, pages 24–25 and 54–55, and in constant prices from table 4, pages 28–29 and 58–59, of *Annual Report on National Income Statistics, 1973,* and corresponding tables of *Revised Report on National Income Statistics, 1951–1967.* Data for all calendar and fiscal years from 1951 to 1971 are provided.

2. Expenditures for maintenance, insurance, and miscellaneous expenses, valued in current prices, were obtained from EPA worksheets for fiscal years 1964 to 1970. The ratio of these expenses to private consumption expenditure for rent in each of these fiscal years was multiplied by private consumption expenditure for rent in the corresponding calendar year to secure a calendar year estimate for maintenance, insurance, and miscellaneous expenses. The 1964 ratio was used for all earlier years and the 1970 ratio for 1971. The same ratios were multiplied by private consumption expenditures for rent in constant prices to secure estimates of expenditures for maintenance, insurance, and miscellaneous expenses in constant prices.

3. Depreciation allowances on dwellings in current prices were obtained, separately for private and government dwellings, from the reports already cited (table 16, pages 240–41 of the 1973 *Annual Report*). To secure constant price estimates, private and government depreciation allowances were deflated by the implicit deflators for construction of private dwellings and government dwellings, respectively, obtained for calendar years from the same reports (table 5, pages 62–63 of the 1973 *Annual Report*).

4. Property taxes on dwellings were obtained from EPA worksheets for fiscal years 1964 to 1970. Calendar year estimates for 1952 to 1971 were obtained in the same way as expenditures for maintenance, insurance, and miscellaneous expenses. Constant price estimates were not needed.

National Product and Income

Output measures were derived as follows. GNP at market prices, in current and constant prices, is private consumption expenditure for rent minus expenditures for maintenance, insurance, and miscellaneous expenses. GNP at factor cost, in current prices, is GNP at market prices less property taxes. NNP at market prices, in current and constant prices, is GNP at market prices less depreciation allowances. National income at factor cost in current prices (NNP at factor cost) is NNP at market prices less property taxes. National income at factor cost in constant prices is the current price value in 1965 extrapolated to other years by NNP at constant market prices.

These estimates for dwellings, we believe, are at least approximately consistent with the all-industry aggregates to be analyzed and therefore appropriate for use in this study. We cannot fail to note, however, that relationships among series for dwellings are puzzling. One would expect consumption expenditure for rent, the gross capital stock of dwellings, and depreciation on dwellings to move similarly when all are measured in constant prices. In fact, consumption expenditures for rent rise far more than available series for the gross capital stock. Based on estimates of the gross capital stock of dwellings made by Tadashi Kusuda, the ratio of annual rent to capital stock at the beginning of the year, both measured in constant 1965 prices, rose from 0.060 in 1956 to 0.099 in 1970. Depreciation allowances rose even more than rent.[12] With both measured in constant prices, the ratio of depreciation to rent rose from 0.134 in 1956 to 0.268 in 1970. Consequently, the ratio of depreciation allowances to gross stock at the start of the year, both measured in constant prices, rose very greatly, from 0.0080 in 1955 to 0.0265 in 1970.[13] A ratio that was constant at a level somewhere between 0.02 and 0.03 would be more reasonable. If one assumes the capital stock series to be correct, then the effect on national income of the bigger rise in rent is partly offset by the still bigger rise in depreciation.[14]

12. The constant price depreciation estimates are ours, but the result is dictated by the steep rise in the current price estimates by the EPA. The EPA current price depreciation allowance series which we have deflated is estimated by an indirect procedure. See the EPA *Sourcebook,* p. 1130.

13. The Kusuda series for capital stock is available only for the beginning of the years 1956–70, but other available data indicate the rise in all the ratios was under way throughout the 1952–71 period.

14. Rent also rises much faster than capital stock in estimates for the United States, but depreciation is consistent with the capital stock because it is based on it.

Table A-4. *Services of Dwellings: Output and Related Series, 1952–71*
Billions of yen

	Current prices								Constant (1965) prices					
Calendar year	Consumption expenditure for rent (1)	Maintenance, insurance, and miscellaneous expense (2)	Property taxes (3)	Depreciation (4)	Gross national product at market prices (5)	Gross national product at factor cost (6)	Net national product at market prices (7)	National income (net national product at factor cost) (8)	Consumption expenditure for rent (9)	Maintenance, insurance, and miscellaneous expense (10)	Depreciation (11)	Gross national product at market prices (12)	Net national product at market prices (13)	National income (net national product at factor cost) (14)
1952	195	18	9	50	177	169	127	119	853	77	96	776	680	636
1953	261	24	12	64	237	225	173	161	905	82	105	823	718	672
1954	309	28	14	69	281	268	212	199	962	87	106	875	769	720
1955	363	33	16	70	330	314	260	244	997	90	114	907	793	742
1956	425	38	19	90	387	368	297	278	1,046	94	140	952	812	760
1957	494	45	22	104	449	427	345	323	1,105	100	150	1,005	855	801
1958	568	51	25	120	517	492	398	372	1,223	110	175	1,113	938	879
1959	694	63	31	130	631	600	501	471	1,350	122	179	1,228	1,049	982

1960	832	75	37	167	757	720	590	553	1,441	130	219	1,311	1,092	1,023
1961	980	88	43	208	891	848	683	640	1,582	143	237	1,439	1,202	1,125
1962	1,146	104	51	249	1,043	992	794	744	1,664	150	272	1,514	1,242	1,163
1963	1,324	120	59	283	1,204	1,146	921	862	1,729	156	300	1,573	1,273	1,192
1964	1,635	148	72	341	1,488	1,415	1,146	1,074	1,833	165	349	1,668	1,319	1,235
1965	1,970	180	88	402	1,790	1,702	1,388	1,300	1,969	180	401	1,789	1,388	1,300
1966	2,335	213	110	492	2,122	2,012	1,630	1,520	2,117	193	464	1,924	1,460	1,367
1967	2,708	248	128	606	2,460	2,333	1,855	1,727	2,283	209	525	2,074	1,549	1,451
1968	3,143	289	149	749	2,854	2,706	2,106	1,957	2,527	232	613	2,295	1,682	1,575
1969	3,647	334	172	906	3,314	3,142	2,408	2,236	2,735	250	698	2,485	1,787	1,674
1970	4,286	391	202	1,102	3,896	3,694	2,794	2,592	2,955	270	790	2,685	1,895	1,774
1971	5,042	460	237	1,261	4,583	4,346	3,321	3,084	3,213	293	863	2,920	2,057	1,926

Sources: Columns 1, 4, and 9, from Economic Planning Agency; columns 2, 3, 10, and 11, see text for derivation; column 5, column 1 minus column 2; column 6, column 5 minus column 3; column 7, column 5 minus column 4; column 8, column 6 minus column 4; column 12, column 9 minus column 10; column 13, column 12 minus column 11; column 14, 1965 from column 8, other years extrapolated by column 13.

National Income in Current Prices, by Sector and Industrial Branch

THIS APPENDIX describes the derivation of the series shown in table 3-2, which refers to national income measured in current prices.

Total national income (column 1) is the sum of net domestic product at factor cost, measured from the income side of the accounts, and net labor and investment income from abroad.[1] Net domestic product at factor cost is from table 1, pages 212–15, of Economic Planning Agency, *Annual Report on National Income Statistics, 1973,* and the corresponding table of *Revised Report on National Income Statistics, 1951–1967.* Net labor and investment income from abroad are from table A-3, columns 2 and 3.

Estimates of national income originating in the three special sectors (columns 2, 3, and 4 in table 3-2) were described in appendix A.

National income originating in agriculture is the sum of (1) "net national product before stock valuation at factor cost" originating in agriculture, and (2) the stock valuation adjustment in agriculture, forestry, and fishing. For 1964–71 the first is from *Annual Report on National Income Statistics, 1973,* table 2, page 217, while the second is derived by subtracting the data for agriculture, forestry, and fishing in that table from net national product at factor cost originating in agriculture, forestry, and fishing as shown in table 1, pages 48–49. Data for earlier years were obtained from the corresponding

1. It differs from the national income series published by the Economic Planning Agency only by the value of net receipts from abroad of "license fees, royalties, and other," as shown in appendix table A-3, column 4.

tables of *Revised Report on National Income Statistics, 1951–1967*. The procedure assumes the stock valuation adjustment to be small in forestry and fishing.

Series for income originating in nonresidential business and in nonagricultural nonresidential business were obtained by subtraction.

National Product and Income in Constant Prices, by Sector and Industrial Branch

THE SERIES shown in table 3-3, which refers to national income measured in constant (1965) prices, are discussed in this appendix. Three sets of estimates needed for its derivation will be described before we turn to that table as such.

The last section of this appendix will describe the estimates based on U.S. deflation procedures. Up to that point the discussion will be concerned only with the estimates based on Japanese deflation procedures.

Gross National Product at Market Prices

The only constant price series actually published in the Japanese national income reports is gross national product at market prices, obtained as the sum of expenditure series and classified only by type of expenditures. This series is shown in table C-1, column 1. We believe estimates obtained from the income side of the accounts are more consistent statistically with employment data and hence more appropriate for use in the study of productivity. To secure constant price GNP from the income side, which is shown in column 2, column 1 was multiplied by the ratio of current price GNP measured from the income side to current price GNP measured from the product side; this is equivalent to deflating current price GNP measured from the income side by EPA's GNP deflator.[1]

1. Account 1, pp. 36–37, of Economic Planning Agency, *Annual Report on National Income Statistics, 1973,* and the corresponding account in *Revised Report on National*

Table C-1. *Gross National Product at Market Prices Valued in Constant (1965) Prices, Selected Series, 1952–71*[a]

Billions of yen

| | Measured from expenditure side— | Measured from income side | | | | |
| | | Total, all sectors[b] | | Nonresidential business | | |
Calendar year	total, all sectors (1)	(2)	Dwellings (3)	Total (4)	Agriculture (5)	Nonagricultural industries (6)
1952	10,506	10,056	776	7,687	1,408	6,279
1953	11,101	11,003	823	8,549	1,520	7,029
1954	11,783	11,920	875	9,377	1,768	7,609
1955	12,859	12,893	907	10,285	2,192	8,093
1956	13,888	13,691	952	11,032	2,004	9,028
1957	14,997	15,097	1,005	12,386	2,058	10,328
1958	15,801	15,981	1,113	13,117	2,147	10,970
1959	17,258	17,361	1,228	14,321	2,358	11,963
1960	19,699	19,935	1,311	16,757	2,280	14,477
1961	22,766	22,273	1,439	18,813	2,255	16,558
1962	24,228	24,447	1,514	20,773	2,294	18,479
1963	26,785	26,907	1,573	22,998	2,202	20,796
1964	30,466	29,839	1,668	25,690	2,264	23,426
1965	31,879	31,692	1,789	27,237	2,304	24,933
1966	35,133	34,888	1,924	30,121	2,387	27,734
1967	39,878	39,575	2,074	34,514	2,698	31,816
1968	45,558	45,368	2,295	39,945	2,775	37,170
1969	51,059	50,778	2,485	44,982	2,703	42,279
1970	56,329	56,620	2,685	50,402	2,600	47,802
1971	59,841	60,224	2,920	53,527	2,413	51,114

Sources: Column 1, from Economic Planning Agency; columns 2 and 5, see text for derivation; column 3, table A-4, column 12; column 4, column 2 minus the sum of column 3 and table A-1, column 2, table A-2, columns 4, 5, and 6, and table A-3, column 7; column 6, column 4 minus column 5.

a. Based on Japanese deflation procedures.

b. Includes "general government, households, institutions, and foreign governments" and "international assets"; see table 3-3 for data.

GNP at constant market prices originating in nonresidential business, shown in table C-1, column 4, was derived from this series by deducting the estimates for the three special sectors.

Income Statistics. 1951–1967, provide GNP at market prices measured from the expenditure side. They also provide the items (provisions for the consumption of fixed capital and indirect taxes) which must be added to national income (as shown in table 3-2 above) or subtracted from it (current subsidies) to secure GNP at market prices measured from the income side.

Table C-2. *Capital Consumption Allowances in Current and Constant Prices, 1952–71*

Billions of yen

Calendar year	Current prices					Constant (1965) prices				
			Nonresidential business					Nonresidential business		
	Total (1)	Dwellings (2)	Total (3)	Agriculture (4)	Nonagricultural industries (5)	Total (6)	Dwellings (7)	Total (8)	Agriculture (9)	Nonagricultural industries (10)
1952	434	50	384	50	334	608	96	512	66	446
1953	553	64	489	67	422	735	105	630	85	545
1954	702	69	633	98	535	910	106	804	124	680
1955	790	70	720	104	616	1,025	114	911	131	780
1956	934	90	844	109	735	1,103	140	963	123	840
1957	1,044	104	940	111	829	1,145	150	995	116	879
1958	1,129	120	1,009	109	900	1,278	175	1,103	117	986
1959	1,300	130	1,170	118	1,052	1,448	179	1,269	127	1,142
1960	1,590	167	1,423	125	1,298	1,722	219	1,503	131	1,372
1961	2,037	208	1,829	135	1,694	2,107	237	1,870	137	1,733
1962	2,413	249	2,164	174	1,990	2,476	272	2,204	177	2,027
1963	2,855	283	2,572	223	2,349	2,925	300	2,625	226	2,399
1964	3,512	341	3,171	246	2,925	3,554	349	3,205	249	2,956
1965	4,024	402	3,622	276	3,346	4,024	401	3,623	276	3,347
1966	4,760	492	4,268	301	3,967	4,604	464	4,140	293	3,847
1967	5,506	606	4,900	363	4,537	5,162	525	4,637	345	4,292
1968	6,670	749	5,921	399	5,523	6,182	613	5,569	377	5,192
1969	8,098	906	7,192	462	6,730	7,297	698	6,599	426	6,173
1970	9,571	1,102	8,469	533	7,936	8,285	790	7,495	475	7,020
1971	10,642	1,261	9,381	571	8,809	9,144	863	8,281	508	7,773

Sources: Columns 1–5, from Economic Planning Agency, as described in text; column 6, column 7 plus column 8; column 7, table A-4; column 8, column 9 plus column 10; columns 9 and 10, see text for derivation.

GNP originating in agriculture at constant market prices, shown in column 5, was estimated as follows. First, the ratio of GNP at market prices to the value of domestic output, with both measured in current prices, was calculated for agriculture each year. GNP in current prices is equal to gross domestic product at market prices in agriculture, without elimination of imputed service charges and stock valuation adjustment, from table 2, pages 282–83, of Economic Planning Agency, *Annual Report on National Income Statistics, 1973,* minus imputed service charges in agriculture, from table 4, page 311, minus the stock valuation adjustment in agriculture, forestry, and fishing (described in appendix B). The value of domestic output of agriculture in current prices is from table 1, pages 280–81, of the same report. Data for years not given in the 1973 report are from corresponding tables of *Revised Report on National Income Statistics, 1951–1967.* Second, the ratio of GNP to domestic output in agriculture in current prices was multiplied by the value of agricultural domestic output in constant 1965 prices to secure estimated agricultural GNP in constant prices. The constant-price domestic output series for agriculture was estimated within the EPA as part of an interindustry study.[2]

GNP in constant prices originating in nonagricultural nonresidential business, shown in table C-1, column 6, was obtained by subtraction.

Capital Consumption Allowances

Capital consumption allowances in current and constant prices are shown in table C-2.

The current price series are all derived from *Annual Report on National Income Statistics, 1973* and *Revised Report on National Income Statistics, 1951–1967.* The total is from Account 1 (pages 36–37 of the 1973 *Annual Report*), the entry for dwellings is from table 16 (pages 240–41 of the same report), and capital consumption in agriculture is the excess of gross domestic product of agriculture from table 2 over net domestic product of agriculture from table 3 (pages 282–85 of the same report). Nonresidential business and nonagricultural nonresidential business were obtained by subtraction. Data from table 16 permitted the division, not shown here, of capital consumption between private and government enterprises for use in deflation.[3]

2. The series covers 1953–70. The Japanese index of agricultural output was used to extend the series to 1952 and 1971.

3. All nonagricultural "damage of fixed capital by accidents" is included in the private portion of nonagricultural nonresidential business.

The constant price series for dwellings is from table A-4. The government enterprise portion of constant price capital consumption in nonagricultural nonresidential business was obtained by deflating the current price series by the EPA's implicit deflator for "gross domestic fixed capital formation by government, other than dwellings" while the current price series for private capital consumption in nonresidential business and the agricultural component were both deflated by the implicit deflator for gross domestic fixed capital formation by private enterprises other than dwellings.[4] Implicit deflators are from the same EPA reports, table 5 (pages 62–63 of the 1973 *Annual Report*). Other series were obtained by addition of components.

We noted in appendix A that residential depreciation rises more than appears to be consistent with the stock of dwellings. Constant price capital consumption in nonresidential business also rises more than appears likely to be consistent with changes in the capital stock, even if allowance is made for a shift in the composition of the stock toward short-lived assets.

Net National Product at Market Prices

Net national product at market prices, valued in constant (1965) prices, is shown in table C-3. The estimates are obtained by deducting capital consumption allowances (table C-2) from gross national product, estimated from the income side (table C-1).

National Income at Factor Cost, Based on Japanese Deflation Practices

This section describes the derivation of table 3-3, except columns 2 and 4. Total national income in constant prices based on Japanese deflation procedures (column 1) is the sum of series for the four sectors. The sectors, it will be noted, are combined here by their factor cost weights whereas table C-3 uses market price weights. The series for the three special sectors (columns 3, 5, and 6) were described in appendix A. The series for nonresidential business remains to be described.

---

4. Use of aggregated price series for gross investment to deflate capital consumption is by no means ideal because the mix of types of capital may differ in the two series. However, the objection is not nearly so serious as would be the use of the same price series to deflate capital stock because types of capital goods that have short service lives receive a heavy weight (compared to their weight in the capital stock) in both gross investment and capital consumption.

Table C-3. *Net National Product at Market Prices Valued in Constant (1965) Prices, Selected Series, 1952–71*[a]

Billions of yen

Calendar year	Total, all sectors[b] (1)	Dwellings (2)	Nonresidential business		
			Total (3)	Agriculture (4)	Nonagricultural industries (5)
1952	9,448	680	7,175	1,342	5,833
1953	10,268	718	7,919	1,435	6,484
1954	11,010	769	8,573	1,644	6,929
1955	11,868	793	9,374	2,061	7,313
1956	12,588	812	10,069	1,881	8,188
1957	13,952	855	11,391	1,942	9,449
1958	14,703	938	12,014	2,030	9,984
1959	15,913	1,049	13,052	2,231	10,821
1960	18,213	1,092	15,253	2,149	13,104
1961	20,166	1,202	16,943	2,118	14,825
1962	21,971	1,242	18,569	2,117	16,452
1963	23,982	1,273	20,373	1,976	18,397
1964	26,285	1,319	22,485	2,015	20,470
1965	27,668	1,388	23,614	2,028	21,586
1966	30,284	1,460	25,981	2,094	23,887
1967	34,413	1,549	29,877	2,353	27,524
1968	39,186	1,682	34,376	2,398	31,978
1969	43,481	1,787	38,383	2,277	36,106
1970	48,335	1,895	42,907	2,125	40,782
1971	51,080	2,057	45,246	1,905	43,341

Source: GNP from income side (table C-1, columns 2–6) minus capital consumption allowances (table C-2, columns 6–10).

a. Measured from income side. Based on Japanese deflation procedures.

b. Includes "general government, households, institutions, and foreign governments" and "international assets"; see table 3-3, columns 3 and 6, for data.

If it had been possible, constant price national income originating in nonresidential business would have been derived by (1) dividing current price net product at both market prices and factor cost in 1965, the base year, among detailed expenditure components; (2) extrapolating the 1965 factor cost value of each component by a constant price series at market prices for that component; and (3) summing the resulting series. This procedure would have retained the market price movement for each component but replaced 1965 market prices with 1965 factor costs as the weights by which components are combined. The data needed to implement this procedure were not available, and within nonresidential business it was possible to reweight only net output of agriculture and of nonagricultural industries as a group.

National income originating in agriculture in 1965, from table 3-2, was extrapolated to other years by net product at constant market prices originating in agriculture, from table C-3. The series for nonagricultural industries is similarly derived. National income originating in nonresidential business is the sum of the two components. It rises less than the net national product of nonresidential business (from 1952 to 1971, by 517 percent as against 531 percent) because agriculture is more heavily weighted at factor cost than at market prices, and its output rises less than that of nonagricultural industries.

National Income at Factor Cost, Based on U.S. Deflation Procedures

This series, shown in column 2 of table 3-3, differs from the corresponding series based on Japanese deflation procedures only in one sector: general government, households, institutions, and foreign governments. To obtain the series for that sector, 1965 national income originating in each of six activities, in current prices, was extrapolated by employment in that activity, and the components were summed.[5] All necessary data are provided in tables A-1 and A-2. The six components and estimated 1965 national income and employment are:

Component	National income (billions of yen)	Employment (thousands)
General government	2,096	2,812
Private households	36	192
Nonprofit institutions		
Medical and health	96	215
Education	154	223
Religious and other	320	300
Foreign governments	32	53

5. For the trifling item of labor income paid to foreigners, the Japanese deflation procedure was retained.

Estimates of Employment

THIS APPENDIX describes the derivation of the employment estimates contained in table 3-4.

Data from Labor Force Survey

It was first necessary to assemble data based on the Labor Force Survey (LFS) that were as nearly comparable over time as could be obtained. Series were compiled, by sex, for total employment, for employment in agriculture and forestry, and for employment in other industries further divided among wage and salary workers, the self-employed, and unpaid family workers. Changes in survey questions and methods introduced in 1953 and 1967 affected comparability of the originally reported LFS data, and necessitated adjustments.[1]

All of these series were available for the years 1955–71 with data for years before 1967 adjusted by the Ministry of Labor to make them comparable with those for later years. The source is *Report on the Labor Force Survey, 1972* edition.[2]

1. See Bureau of Statistics, Office of the Prime Minister, *Rōdōryōku chōsa hōkoku* [Report on the Labor Force Survey (annual)] (1967 edition), pp. 110–13, for the detail of the 1967 change and its effect on comparability with previous years. For explanation of the 1953 revision, see Bureau of Statistics, Office of the Prime Minister, *Rōdōryōku chōsa hōkoku* [Monthly Report on the Labor Force Survey] (December 1952), p. 1, and details in Bureau of Statistics, Office of the Prime Minister, *Rōdōryōku chōsa kaisan kekka hōkoku* [Report on the Revised Figures of the Labor Force Survey for the Period January 1953 to September 1961] (1963), pp. 1, 166–67.

2. Because of rounding and truncating, detail does not necessarily add to the total in these published employment figures; we adjusted the detailed figures proportionally to make them do so (after correcting a misprint in the data for 1961).

Total 1953 and 1954 employment similarly adjusted for comparability with later years, but not employment detail, was obtained from the Ministry of Labor, *Shōwa 44-nen rōdō keizai no bunseki* [An Economic Study of the 1969 Labor Market] (1970), Statistical Appendix, page 8. We used the same methodology as the ministry applied in later years to adjust the originally reported detailed figures for 1953 and 1954 to render them comparable with the adjusted 1955 estimates.[3] This methodology is described in *Report on the Labor Force Survey,* 1970 edition, pages 134–35. Because of the 1953 revision, the 1952 original data, before they could be adjusted for the 1967 change, had first to be revised to render them comparable with the following years. We computed the adjusted 1952 numbers by applying the ratio of the revised to the original 1953 numbers to the original 1952 data. We have little confidence in the employment changes we show from 1952 to 1953.

We also required series, adjusted prior to 1967 for comparability with later years, for total employment and wage and salary employment in forestry and in fisheries. (Given these series, employment of self-employed and unpaid family workers, combined, could be obtained by subtraction.) From published reports of the Bureau of Statistics of the Office of the Prime Minister, such data were available for the following time periods: total employment in forestry, 1962–71; total employment in fisheries, 1955–71; wage-salary employment in forestry, 1967–71; wage-salary employment in fisheries, 1955–71.

To estimate comparable figures for earlier years the following procedures were used. Total employment in forestry in 1952–61 was assumed to exceed the forestry employment series prepared by Shōzō Ichino for the Center for Econometric Data Development and Research (CEDDR) by an amount equal to the average absolute difference between this series and the adjusted Labor Force Survey series in the years 1962–64. Total employment in fisheries was extrapolated from 1955 to 1952–54 by the originally reported LFS data for such employment. Wage and salary employment in forestry in 1962–66 was assumed to be the same percentage of total employment in forestry as it was in 1967. In 1952–61 it was assumed to fall short of the Ichino-CEDDR series for wage and salary employment in forestry by an amount equal to the average absolute difference in 1962–64 between this series and the estimates just described. Wage-salary employment in fisheries was extrapolated from 1955 to 1952–54 by the originally reported LFS data for such employment.

3. Data are from *Report on the Revised Figures of the Labor Force Survey from January 1953 to September 1961,* 1963 edition. Obvious errors in the published estimates for 1953 cross-classifying nonagricultural employment by class of worker and sex were corrected.

Data from Economic Planning Agency

The Economic Planning Agency (EPA) estimates of employment which correspond to its data for compensation of employees, excluding compensation in agriculture, forestry, and fisheries and net factor income from abroad, are taken from *Annual Report on National Income Statistics, 1973* (1973), pages 212–15, and *Revised Report on National Income Statistics, 1951–1967* (1969), pages 226–31.[4]

Derivation of Table 3-4

Table 3-4 is derived from the two sets of data described above and the employment estimates developed in appendix A.

Total employment (column 1) is the sum of the estimates for the two sectors having employment (columns 2 and 3).

Employment in general government, households, institutions, and foreign governments (column 2) is the sum of the estimates shown in table A-1, column 3, and table A-2, columns 7, 8, and 9.

Employment in nonresidential business (column 3) is the sum of the agricultural and nonagricultural components (columns 4 and 5).

Employment in agriculture (column 4) is the adjusted LFS series for total employment in agriculture and forestry minus the adjusted LFS series for total employment in forestry.

Employment in nonagricultural industries in nonresidential business (column 5) is the sum of the estimates for the classes of worker (columns 6 and 7).

The number of wage and salary workers in nonagricultural nonresidential business (column 6) is total nonagricultural wage and salary employment (column 8) minus employment in general government, households, institutions, and foreign governments (column 2).

The number of self-employed and unpaid family workers in nonagricultural nonresidential business (column 7) is the sum of adjusted LFS series for the numbers of self-employed and unpaid family workers in industries other than agriculture and forestry plus the numbers of self-employed and unpaid family workers in forestry.

The total number of nonagricultural wage and salary workers (column 8) is the sum of the EPA employment series, the LFS series for wage and salary

4. An obvious transcription error for 1965 employment in "banking, insurance, and real estate," which appears in the 1973 report and carries into the total, was corrected.

Table D-1. *Comparison of Employment Series Adopted and Adjusted Estimates from Labor Force Survey, 1952–71*

Thousands of persons

Calendar year	Total employment			Wage and salary workers in nonagricultural business		
	Series adopted (1)	Labor Force Survey (2)	Ratio of columns 2 to 1 (3)	Series adopted (4)	Labor Force Survey (5)	Ratio of columns 5 to 4 (6)
1952	37,199	36,921	0.9925	12,739	12,461	0.9782
1953	39,376	39,092	0.9928	13,411	13,127	0.9788
1954	39,862	39,609	0.9937	13,798	13,545	0.9817
1955	41,047	40,900	0.9964	14,392	14,245	0.9898
1956	41,715	41,710	0.9999	15,553	15,548	0.9997
1957	42,778	42,810	1.0007	16,925	16,957	1.0019
1958	43,000	42,980	0.9995	18,059	18,039	0.9989
1959	43,273	43,350	1.0018	18,947	19,024	1.0041
1960	44,345	44,360	1.0003	20,053	20,068	1.0007
1961	44,640	44,980	1.0076	20,848	21,188	1.0163
1962	45,381	45,560	1.0039	22,035	22,214	1.0081
1963	45,824	45,950	1.0027	22,808	22,934	1.0055
1964	46,517	46,550	1.0007	23,669	23,702	1.0014
1965	47,453	47,300	0.9968	24,883	24,730	0.9939
1966	48,528	48,270	0.9947	26,101	25,843	0.9901
1967	49,545	49,200	0.9930	26,889	26,544	0.9872
1968	50,365	50,020	0.9932	27,639	27,294	0.9875
1969	50,757	50,400	0.9930	28,104	27,747	0.9873
1970	51,289	50,940	0.9932	29,121	28,772	0.9880
1971	51,421	51,140	0.9945	29,998	29,717	0.9906

Source: See text.

employment in forestry and in fisheries, and the series for foreign governments shown in table A-2, column 9.

Alternative Employment Series

The principal alternative to the series adopted is the LFS series, with earlier years adjusted to comparability with the 1967–71 data. Table D-1 compares the two employment series, in total and for wage and salary workers in nonagricultural nonresidential business. (Estimates of agricultural employment and the nonagricultural self-employed and unpaid family workers are the same.) The LFS series rise more from 1952 to 1961, less from 1961 to

1967, and more from 1967 to 1971, but the differences are sufficient to affect the sources of growth estimates only moderately.

A series prepared by Ohkawa and Rosovsky, which they describe as based on the Census of Population with interpolations by LFS data, rises more than ours over the whole period and fluctuates relative to it, but again differences are not great.[5] The ratio of their series to ours is 0.9968 in 1952 and 0.9998 in 1953, rises gradually to 1.0114 in 1961, recedes to 0.9999 in 1965, and rises again to 1.0144 in 1970, its last year.

On the other hand, employment from the Censuses of Population, reported by the Bureau of Statistics of the Office of the Prime Minister (in *Comparison of Employed Persons by Industry in the Population Censuses, 1920 through 1970* [1973], page 7), rises much more than our series. The ratio of employment from that source to our estimates is 0.9565 in 1955, 0.9859 in 1960, 1.0038 in 1965, and 1.0160 in 1970.

Our series and the series for total employment prepared by Ichino for CEDDR display considerably different movements. Also, the Ichino series, like employment from the Census of Population, rises much more than ours over the full period for which it is available. The ratio of this series to ours is 0.9286 in 1952 and 0.9172 in 1953, falls to 0.9033 in 1958, rises to 0.9724 in 1963, falls to 0.9556 in 1966, and rises to 0.9734 in 1968, when the Ichino series ends.

Broadly speaking, the choice lies between a set of three series, including ours, which move similarly and would all yield about the same contribution of employment to the growth rate, and a pair of series which rise more and would yield appreciably larger contributions.

The various series cited differ not only in the movement of total employment, but also in the composition of employment and in the size of compositional changes reported.

5. Kazushi Ohkawa and Henry Rosovsky, *Japanese Economic Growth: Trend Acceleration in the Twentieth Century* (Stanford University Press, 1973), p. 311.

Income Share Weights
for Inputs
in Nonresidential Business

THIS APPENDIX describes the allocation of earnings in the nonresidential business sector among labor, two types of capital, and land (table 4-1) and the derivation from these earnings of the weights (shown below in table E-2) which are used to combine various inputs in the construction of a series for total factor input (table 4-4). Various kinds of problems are encountered.

First, the incidence of taxes must be known or assumed. Our assumptions are the same as those adopted by both the Economic Planning Agency of Japan and the U.S. Department of Commerce in their measurements of national income at factor cost. As stated in the description of similar earnings distributions for the United States, our

... use of these data implies that the following statement is correct.

Given the quantity of each type of input actually used in the nonresidential business sector and its distribution among farms, nonfarm corporations, and other business:

1. The personal income tax and other personal taxes do not alter the percentage distribution among inputs of earnings measured inclusive of such taxes;

2. indirect business taxes do not alter the percentage distribution of earnings measured exclusive of such taxes;

3. the corporation income tax does not alter the distribution of earnings measured before deduction of these taxes from corporate profits; and

4. payroll taxes, whether nominally levied on employers or employees, do not alter the distribution of earnings when these taxes are included in employee compensation.[1]

1. Denison, *Accounting for Growth*, p. 268. Ibid., appendix J, discusses taxes further and also takes up a number of additional conceptual points.

Second, much of the national income accrues in the form of mixed shares so not all of the information needed to obtain the earnings of the factors can be collected; estimation (or imputation) is also necessary. Thus, proprietors' income, which is large in Japan, must be divided between labor and property earnings. Earnings from property—both the property portion of proprietors' income and relatively pure property income shares such as interest, rental income, and corporate profits—must be allocated among the earnings of nonresidential structures and equipment, inventories, and land. In actuality, they also include "pure" profit, but we have not attempted to isolate it.

Third, many of the pertinent data that do exist have either not been collected or, if collected, have not been tabulated or assembled in the way most appropriate for our needs.

National Income by Legal Form of Organization and Type of Income, 1970

To estimate the functional distribution of national income the best starting point is a cross-classification of national income by legal form of organization and type of earnings (compensation of employees, net income of businesses, and interest and rental income). The Japanese national income statistics unfortunately do not provide data by legal form (except for the net income of businesses), but much of the raw material needed is available. We therefore undertook to construct such estimates, in the first instance for calendar year 1970.

Table E-1 provides our estimates for nonresidential business.[2] Corporate transfers to households and private nonprofit institutions, which consist of write-offs of household bad debts to corporations, cash thefts from corporations, and corporate gifts to nonprofit organizations, are included in the Japanese national income but are eliminated here on the ground that they are not properly earnings of any factor.[3] (In the United States they are omitted from the official national income series.)

In table E-1, national income originating in nonresidential business is first divided between agricultural and nonagricultural industries. With insignifi-

2. Estimates for national income originating outside nonresidential business are in effect provided by table 3-2. All income originating in general government, households, institutions, and foreign governments consists of compensation of employees, and all income originating in the services of dwellings and international assets sectors consists of property income.

3. Data are from Economic Planning Agency, *Annual Report on National Income Statistics, 1973,* p. 39.

Table E-1. *National Income Originating in Nonresidential Business, by Legal Form of Organization and Type of Income, 1970*
Billions of yen

Item	Amount
Income originating in nonresidential business, total	49,365
Less corporate transfers to households and nonprofit institutions	102
Income originating in nonresidential business, adjusted, total	**49,263**
Agricultural proprietorships	**3,293**
Compensation of employees	97
Income from unincorporated enterprises	2,991
Interest and rental income	205
Nonagricultural industries	**45,970**
Corporations organized for profit	33,707
Compensation of employees	22,287
Income from private corporations	9,101
Interest and rental income	2,319
Proprietorships	10,167
Compensation of employees	1,114
Income from unincorporated enterprises	8,486
Interest and rental income	567
Other private business	644
Compensation of employees	644
Government enterprises	1,452
Compensation of employees	1,361
Profit from government enterprises	91

Sources: Total income from table 3-2. For other rows, see text.

cant exceptions agriculture consists entirely of proprietorships, so no further division by legal form is necessary. Nonagricultural industries are classified among four legal form categories. Allocations among them were made for each type of income, and national income totals for each legal form category within nonagricultural industries were obtained by addition of income types. A description of the derivation of the nonresidential business total for each income type, and its allocation by legal form, follow.

Compensation of Employees

Our national income estimates for general government, households, institutions, and foreign governments (table 3-2) were deducted from the EPA estimates of compensation of employees (*Annual Report on National Income Statistics, 1973,* page 214) to obtain compensation in the business sector, by industry division. Agriculture was assigned the same small percentage of compensation in agriculture, forestry, and fishing as it received in the 1965 input-output table (*Japan Statistical Yearbook, 1971,* page 496); the rest was assigned to nonagricultural business.

Compensation in corporations organized for profit, except financial corporations, is from the Corporation Enterprise Survey for fiscal year 1970 (*Japan Statistical Yearbook, 1971,* page 318), adjusted to a calendar year basis.[4] The sum of "payrolls to directors" and "payrolls to employees, including welfare expenses" was used.

Government enterprise employment on July 1, 1969, was taken as equal to government employment ("local government" plus "national government and public corporations") in the following industries: wholesale and retail trade, finance and insurance, real estate, transportation and communication, and electricity, gas, and water. Data are from the Establishment Census (*Japan Statistical Yearbook, 1971,* pages 82–85). Government enterprise employment in each industry was adjusted to secure the 1970 level and multiplied by average compensation of employees in the industry in 1970 to secure estimated total compensation of government employees in the industry. The industries were then summed.

The distribution of the remaining compensation of employees in industries other than finance and insurance between proprietorships and "other private business," and the distribution of all compensation in finance and insurance, except that in government enterprises, among corporations organized for profit, proprietorships, and "other private business," were based on distributions of July 1, 1969, employment, adjusted to a 1970 basis; 1969 employment is from the Establishment Census (*Japan Statistical Yearbook, 1971,* pages 82–85). For employment in "other private business" from this source, it should be noted, we use employment in "corporations" minus employment in "companies" in industries other than those in lines 82 through 88. (Employment of "corporations" other than "companies" in these excluded industries is classified in the nonprofit institutions sector rather than in business.) The industry "business association services n.e.c.," covering nonprofit organizations serving businesses, accounts for over one-half of total employment in other private business.

Bonuses to corporate managers, calculated from EPA, *Annual Report on National Income Statistics, 1973,* page 51, were added to compensation of employees in corporations organized for profit and to totals including this component.

4. None was assigned to agriculture because it was clear that corporate agriculture was trivial or zero.

Income from Private Corporations

Income from private corporations is equal to the total for that component in "net domestic product at factor cost," from *Annual Report on National Income Statistics, 1973,* page 214, minus "corporate transfers to households and private nonprofit institutions" and bonuses to corporate managers; the first is reported in, and the second calculated from, data reported in the 1973 *Annual Report,* page 51. The entire share is assigned to nonagricultural corporations organized for profit.

Profit from Government Enterprises

Profit from government enterprises, obtained from the 1973 *Annual Report,* page 51, is entirely assigned to government enterprises.

Income from Unincorporated Enterprises

Income from unincorporated enterprises is obtained, by industry division, from the 1973 *Annual Report,* page 214. The amount assigned to agriculture equals national income originating in agriculture (from our table 3-2) less compensation of agricultural employees (from table E-1 and already described) and interest and rental income in agriculture (from table E-1 and described below); it represents 84 percent of income from unincorporated enterprises in agriculture, forestry, and fisheries as reported in the 1973 *Annual Report,* page 214. The remaining 16 percent, representing forestry and fisheries, is assigned to proprietorships in nonagricultural industries.

Allocation of Interest and Rental Income, 1970

We describe the estimates of interest and rental income in table E-1 in a separate section because they require more space than the other types of income. This is mainly because an industrial distribution was a prerequisite for the estimates by legal form of organization.

The EPA presents (in the 1973 *Annual Report,* page 214) data by industrial division for net domestic product at factor cost other than compensation of employees, income from private corporations, and income from unincorporated enterprises. To secure interest and rental income in nonresidential business by industrial division, two deductions were made from this "other" income component: profits from government enterprises (taken from table

E-1 and already described) were deducted in the "electricity, gas, water supply, transportation, and communication" division; and national income originating in the services of dwellings sector (from table 3-2) was deducted in the real estate component of "finance, insurance, and real estate."[5] The rest of "other income" in the net domestic product totaled ¥3,091 billion in all industries, including agriculture. To allocate it by legal form of organization it was treated as if it were entirely interest.[6] So, initially, was ¥38 billion in the real estate industry which represents the difference between property income from dwellings (table 3-2) and (personal) "income from property: rent" from *Annual Report on National Income Statistics, 1973,* page 51, and which was later deducted entirely from the allocation to proprietorships.

Conceptually, net interest in each industry is equal to (1) monetary interest paid by business, plus (2) imputed interest paid by business (all of it by finance and insurance), minus (3) monetary interest received by corporations, minus (4) imputed interest received by business (which does not appear in finance or life insurance so that there is only a small amount in "finance and insurance"). However, the Japanese estimates are not constructed in this way statistically, and only items 2 and 4 are available separately by industry division (from *Annual Report on National Income Statistics, 1973,* page 311). Because the EPA allocates imputed interest received by Japanese business among industries in proportion to loans and discounts (rather than by deposits, as is done in the United States), the allocation (outside of finance and insurance) is similar to that of monetary interest paid. Hence there would be no advantage in separate allocations of monetary and imputed interest among legal forms of organization.

The allocation procedure which was used in each industry division to secure net interest originating in corporations organized for profit (which are the equivalent of "companies" in the employee compensation data that enter into the procedure) is described below. All interest except corporate interest was assigned to proprietorships.

The chief components are shown in billions of yen in the following table.[7] The derivation of the first column, except detail under "Agriculture, forestry,

---

5. This source uses "banking" instead of "finance" in the English titles but the Japanese is the same as that translated as "finance" in other statistical sources, and it is clear that the coverage is equally comprehensive.

6. This appears to be nearly correct but the correspondence is not exact. The problem is that income originating in the "services of dwellings" sector cannot be divided between interest and rental income.

7. The table is shown *only* to aid the reader to follow the derivation of the aggregates. The detailed figures are subject to wide margins of error.

and fisheries" and "Finance, insurance, and real estate," has already been described.[8]

	Net interest	
	Total	Corporations organized for profit
Agriculture, forestry, and fisheries	283	58
Agriculture	205	6
Forestry and fisheries	78	52
Wholesale and retail trade	875	707
Finance, insurance, and real estate	432	283
Finance and insurance	299	150
Real estate	133	133
Services	249	116
All other	1,290	1,162
Total	3,129	2,325

Agriculture, Forestry, and Fisheries

The ratio (0.204) of (1) interest and discount payable by corporations organized for profit in this division during fiscal year 1970, from the Corporation Enterprise Survey (*Japan Statistical Yearbook, 1971,* page 319), reduced to a calendar year basis, to (2) gross monetary interest paid in the industry division, approximated as the sum of net interest paid and imputed interest received, was multiplied by net interest in the division to obtain estimated corporate net interest. Fisheries accounted for 75 percent of corporate interest and discount payable; to secure the agricultural estimate, the remaining 25 percent was assumed to divide 10 percent in agriculture and 15 percent in forestry.

Total net interest in forestry and fisheries was assumed to be one and one-half times as large as corporate net interest in these industries. Total net interest in agriculture was obtained by subtraction.

Wholesale and Retail Trade

The ratio of corporate to total net interest was assumed to be the same (0.808) as the ratio of corporate inventories to the sum of corporate and

---

8. Figures in column 1, fifth, seventh, and tenth rows, exceed net interest and rental income by ¥38 billion, the difference between property income from dwellings and net rental income of persons.

proprietorship inventories in wholesale and retail trade, as reported in the Census of Commerce in 1968 (*Japan Statistical Yearbook, 1971,* page 288).

Finance, Insurance, and Real Estate

Net interest paid in real estate was estimated to be equal to interest and discount payable by real estate corporations, from the Corporation Enterprise Survey, plus a token allowance for noncorporate real estate firms, minus imputed interest received by the real estate industry; the remainder of the division total was assigned to finance and insurance. All of the estimate for real estate and half of the estimate for finance and insurance was assigned to corporations. It should be recalled that housing is not in this sector.

All Other Industries, except Services[9]

The ratio of corporate interest to total interest in all these industries combined was assumed to be the same (0.901) as the ratio of the payrolls of directors and employees of corporations organized for profit in these industries in fiscal year 1970, from the Corporation Enterprise Survey (*Japan Statistical Yearbook, 1971,* page 219), to compensation of employees in these industries in fiscal year 1970, from EPA, *Annual Report on National Income Statistics, 1973,* page 210.

Services

The ratio of corporate to total net interest was assumed to be the same (0.467) as the ratio of corporation interest and discount payable in fiscal 1971, from the Corporation Enterprise Survey, adjusted to a calendar year basis, to the sum of net interest paid and imputed interest received in the services division (i.e., of interest paid less monetary interest received; the latter is presumed to be small).

National Income by Legal Form of Organization and Type of Income, Other Years

Estimates for years other than 1970 were made in less detail and by use of short-cut procedures.

9. Industry divisions included are mining; manufacturing; construction; electricity, gas, and water; and transportation and communications.

Agriculture

Total agricultural national income is from our table 3-2. Compensation of agricultural employees was assumed to be the same small percentage of compensation of employees in agriculture, forestry, and fisheries (as reported by the EPA on pages 212–15 of the 1973 *Annual Report* and pages 226–29 of the earlier report) in other years as in 1970. Income from unincorporated enterprises in agriculture was assumed to be the same large percentage of income from unincorporated enterprises in agriculture, forestry, and fisheries (as reported by EPA on pages 52–53 of the 1973 *Annual Report* and pages 74–75 of the earlier report) in other years as in 1970. Interest and rental income was then obtained by subtracting compensation of employees and income from unincorporated enterprises from agricultural national income.

Nonagricultural Corporations Organized for Profit

Tsutomu Noda had prepared estimates of corporate GNP at factor cost, by type of income, covering the years 1952 through 1964 for the Social Science Research Council growth project conducted by Ohkawa and Rosovsky. The estimates were consistent with the Economic Planning Agency's national income estimates before the general revision which appeared in 1968. The Noda estimates of the corporate percentage of total compensation of employees appeared to be reasonably consistent with ours for 1970, and we applied these percentages to the new EPA estimates of employee compensation (as revised in *Annual Report on National Income Statistics, 1973*) to secure our 1952–64 estimates of corporate employee compensation. To secure estimates for the remaining years, 1965–69 and 1971, compensation of corporate employees in 1964 and 1970 was interpolated or extrapolated by total compensation of business employees, calculated as total compensation of employees including bonuses to managers (as reported by the EPA) minus national income originating in general government, households, institutions, and foreign governments (table 3-2).

To obtain the income of private corporations, comparable to the 1970 figure in table E-1, EPA data for bonuses to managers and corporate transfers to households and private nonprofit institutions were deducted from "income from private corporations" which is included in net domestic product. Data were obtained from *Annual Report on National Income Statistics, 1973*, pages 50–51 and 212–15, and corresponding tables in *Revised Report on National Income Statistics, 1951–1967*.

Corporate net interest was assumed to be the same large proportion in other years as in 1970 of a series obtained by deducting "profit from government enterprises" (from pages 50–51 of *Annual Report on National Income Statistics, 1973*, and the corresponding table of the 1951–67 *Revised Report*) and national income originating in dwellings (from our table 3-2) from "other" national income in net domestic product at factor cost (from pages 212–15 of the 1973 *Annual Report* and the corresponding table of the earlier report).

Nonagricultural Proprietorships, Other Private Business, and Government Enterprises

Only combined totals for the remaining three types of nonagricultural business organizations were estimated in years other than 1970. National income originating in these types of organizations is equal to national income originating in nonagricultural nonresidential business, from table 3-2, minus its corporate component, as described above, and minus corporate transfers to households and private nonprofit institutions. Compensation of employees is equal to the EPA series for total compensation (including bonuses to managers) minus our estimates for general government, households, institutions, and foreign governments, for agriculture, and for nonagricultural corporations. Income of unincorporated enterprises is equal to the EPA all-industry total minus our series for agriculture. Profit from government enterprises is the EPA series. Interest was obtained by deducting the other types of income from national income originating in nonagricultural proprietorships, other private business, and government enterprises.

Income Shares

The estimates of national income by legal form of organization and type of income were used to estimate the earnings of the factors of production. Estimates were made for each legal form of organization and added to secure totals for nonresidential business.

Corporations Organized for Profit, All Years

In corporations organized for profit labor earnings are presumed to be the same as compensation of employees.

The remaining earnings, equal to the sum of corporate profits and interest and rental income, were allocated to nonresidential structures and equipment, inventories, and land in proportion to the net value of these assets. Except for finance and insurance, asset values for 1960 and each year from 1965 through 1970 are from the Corporation Enterprise Survey (*Japan Statistical Yearbook, 1971,* pages 316–17). Data used are those reported as the values of "tangible fixed assets," "inventory assets," and "land." In 1970 data for large incorporated enterprises in finance and insurance (*Japan Statistical Yearbook, 1971,* pages 324–25) were added; the effect of the addition on the percentages was assumed to be the same in the other years as in 1970.

The values for the nonresidential structures and equipment and for the inventories held by corporations in 1960 are nearly the same as those reported for profit corporations in the National Wealth Survey (*Japan Statistical Yearbook, 1971,* pages 502–03). (The National Wealth Survey did not provide a value for land.) This is reassuring with respect to the pricing of assets. It is also somewhat reassuring with respect to the possibility that the net stock of structures and equipment may be undervalued as a result of the use of too rapid a depreciation formula. The 1955 and 1960 National Wealth Survey estimates may be assumed to be comparable to one another. The Economic Planning Agency has estimated that the net–gross ratio for incorporated enterprises in 1955 that is consistent with the capital stock estimates for that year is 0.51.[10] This ratio does not seem much too low for a date so soon after World War II and the subsequent reconversion.

Within nonlabor earnings the percentage share of structures and equipment was assumed to be the same in 1956 and 1957 as in 1960; remaining nonlabor earnings were distributed between inventories and land in proportion to asset values from the Corporation Enterprise Survey (*Japan Statistical Yearbook, 1958,* pages 270–73), adjusted to allow for the omission of finance and insurance from the survey. Percentages of nonlabor earnings in 1957, 1960, and 1965 were interpolated to secure estimates for intervening years, percentages for 1956 were used for 1952–55, and 1970 percentages were used for 1971.

Estimates for 1970, except for Corporations

For the year 1970, separate estimates for agricultural proprietorships and nonagricultural proprietorships were prepared in the following steps. First, the compensation of employees (from table E-1) was assigned to labor in-

10. Economic Planning Agency, Economic Research Institute, *Estimation of Gross Fixed Capital Stock of Private Enterprises, 1952–1964,* pp. 1–2 and 10.

come. Second, the remainder of national income, consisting of proprietors' income and interest and rental income (and also from table E-1), was allocated among labor, nonresidential structures and equipment, inventories, and land in proportion to the values these shares would have taken if (a) the earnings of self-employed and unpaid family workers of each sex were equal to the average compensation of wage and salary workers of the same sex employed in nonagricultural nonresidential business, and (b) the ratio of the earnings of each of the three types of tangible asset to its asset value were the same as in corporations.

The earnings allocated in the second step fell short of the sum of the values used to allocate them among the four shares by 68.2 percent in agricultural proprietorships but by only 4.1 percent in nonagricultural proprietorships.

Both agricultural and nonagricultural proprietorships had much lower ratios of capital earnings to labor earnings than corporations, according to our estimates.

Estimated percentage distributions of national income in 1970 are shown by legal form of organization, including the types not yet described, in the following table:

	Labor	Nonresidential structures and equipment	Inventories	Land
Nonagricultural corporations	66.1	18.5	11.2	4.1
Nonagricultural proprietorships	85.4	7.9	4.9	1.8
Agricultural proprietorships	65.0	6.0	1.3	27.7
Other private business	100.0	0.0	0.0	0.0
Government enterprises	93.7	4.8	0.5	1.0

The asset values used in deriving the proprietorship estimates will now be described.

The net values of structures and equipment in agricultural and nonagricultural proprietorships were estimated by multiplying the corporate net values in 1970 by ratios of noncorporate gross values to corporate gross values at the end of 1964 (valued in 1960 prices). These 1964 gross stock values, divided by industry division between corporate and unincorporated enterprises, were obtained from EPA, *Estimation of Gross Fixed Capital Stock of Private Enterprises, 1952–1964,* pages 7, 9. Agriculture was assumed to represent nine-tenths of the stock in agriculture, forestry, and fisheries.

The Economic Planning Agency provided the December 31, 1965, value of private inventories, classified by legal form of organization, separately for agriculture, forestry, and fisheries and for other industries. EPA data on the value of the increase in stocks and the inventory valuation adjustment were used to derive 1970 estimates. A rough estimate of inventories in forestry and fisheries was made in order to divide inventories of unincorporated enterprises between agriculture and nonagricultural industries.

The ratio of the value of land to the value of nonresidential structures and equipment was assumed to be the same for nonagricultural proprietorships as for nonagricultural corporations in 1970. The 1970 value of agricultural land was estimated by multiplying the areas of paddy fields and ordinary fields, as reported by the Ministry of Agriculture and Forestry, by the average values per ten ares of such fields outside Tokyo, Kanagawa, and Osaka prefectures, as reported by the Japan Real Estate Institute. Data are from the *Japan Statistical Yearbook, 1971,* pages 104 and 125.

Two small types of organization remain to be discussed. National income originating in "other private business" consists only of employee compensation and was allocated entirely to labor. Employee compensation in government enterprises was also allocated to labor. Profit of government corporations was allocated among the other shares in proportion to estimated 1960 asset values, derived from National Wealth Survey data for the two capital components and the assumption that the ratio of land to fixed capital was the same as in private corporations.

Estimates for Years Other Than 1970, except for Corporations

The four noncorporate groupings were consolidated into two in the derivation of estimates for other years. Agriculture was handled separately but nonagricultural proprietorships, government enterprises, and "other private business" were combined.

In both cases, employee compensation was assigned to labor earnings, while interest and rental income and (in the case of nonagricultural organizations) profits of government enterprises were assigned to nonlabor earnings. The 1970 estimates implied that 68.34 percent of the income of unincorporated agricultural enterprises and 89.17 percent of the income in unincorporated nonagricultural enterprises were ascribable to labor. The same percentages were used in other years. In both cases, nonlabor earnings (interest, profit of government enterprises, and the nonlabor portion of the income of unincorporated enterprises) were allocated among structures and equipment, inventories, and land in the same proportions as in 1970.

Table E-2. *Weights Applied to Factor Inputs in Nonresidential Business,*
1953–71

Two-year period ending	Total (1)	Labor (2)	Nonresidential structures and equipment (3)	Inventories (4)	Land (5)
1953	100.00	78.99	10.33	5.58	5.10
1954	100.00	79.01	10.33	5.58	5.08
1955	100.00	78.60	10.70	5.80	4.90
1956	100.00	77.86	11.22	6.10	4.82
1957	100.00	77.34	11.57	6.26	4.83
1958	100.00	76.42	12.29	6.63	4.66
1959	100.00	74.92	13.42	7.20	4.46
1960	100.00	73.97	14.13	7.50	4.40
1961	100.00	73.56	14.46	7.58	4.40
1962	100.00	73.20	14.76	7.66	4.38
1963	100.00	73.46	14.64	7.50	4.40
1964	100.00	74.29	14.08	7.16	4.47
1965	100.00	74.78	13.64	6.98	4.60
1966	100.00	74.69	13.52	7.04	4.75
1967	100.00	74.27	13.59	7.24	4.90
1968	100.00	73.54	13.83	7.62	5.01
1969	100.00	72.79	14.12	8.04	5.05
1970	100.00	72.38	14.31	8.30	5.01
1971	100.00	72.21	14.40	8.45	4.94

Source: See text.

Adjustment of Income Shares for Use as Weights

To minimize the effects on the earnings distributions in table 4-1 of fluctuations in the intensity of business activity and of erratic factors, five-year moving averages were substituted for the actual data for each year.[11] The resulting percentages for each two adjacent years were then averaged to secure the weights for calculation of the change in factor input from the first year to the second. These weights are shown in table E-2.

To secure the year-to-year percentage change in total input in the sector, the percentage change in each of the four inputs was multiplied by its weight in that pair of years and the products were summed. The annual percentage changes were then linked to secure the index of total factor input shown in table 4-4, column 7. Hypothetical indexes were also computed of what total

11. The 1952 percentages were used for 1950–51 in computing averages for the earliest years, and the average of the 1970 and 1971 percentages for 1972–73 in computations for the latest years.

factor input would have been if each one of the inputs had not changed while the others changed as they actually did, and weights were the same as in table E-2. The differences between the actual growth rates and the four hypothetical rates were used in table 4-6, columns 1 to 3, to allocate the contribution of total factor input among the four inputs.

Nonresidential Business: Employment and Hours by Sex and Full-Time or Part-Time Status of Workers

THIS APPENDIX presents estimates of employment, total hours worked, and average hours worked for twelve groups of workers in the business sector, as well as for all such workers combined.

Table 3-4 provided estimates of employment for three categories in the business sector: (1) wage and salary workers in nonagricultural business, (2) nonagricultural self-employed and unpaid family workers, and (3) agricultural workers. Tables F-1, F-2, and F-3 divide each of these categories into four groups: males working full time, males working part time, females working full time, and females working part time. To secure these estimates, employment in the three main categories was allocated among the four groups in proportion to the numbers of employed persons in the groups as reported in the Labor Force Survey (LFS).[1] LFS data used as allocators for the three categories refer, respectively, to (1) wage and salary workers other than

---

1. Note that forestry is classified as a nonagricultural industry in the control data from table 3-4 but with agriculture in the LFS data used as allocators, and that the LFS data used to distribute wage and salary workers in nonagricultural business inappropriately include employees of households, nonprofit organizations, and foreign governments. Persons in the government industry were excluded from the LFS data used, but it should be noted that the definition of the government industry is narrower than that of general government.

those employed in agriculture, forestry, and government; (2) self-employed and unpaid family workers outside agriculture and forestry; and (3) persons employed in agriculture and forestry. Data for average hours shown in tables F-1, F-2, and F-3 are derived from the LFS and are based upon the same classification.

To secure LFS data for the employment and average hours of each of the twelve detailed groups the following calculation was made, separately for persons of each sex in each of the three main categories, based on annual averages.[2] The number of persons at work (which is smaller than employment because persons with a job but not at work are excluded) was multiplied by the average hours of persons at work to secure total hours worked. The numbers of persons at work 1–14 hours and 15–34 hours, respectively, were multiplied by the estimated average hours for each of these class intervals.[3] The two products were then summed to secure the total hours worked by persons at work less than 35 hours; this sum is total part-time hours. The number of persons at work 35 hours or more is reported in the LFS, and the total hours they worked were obtained by subtracting total hours worked by persons at work less than 35 hours from total hours worked by all persons at work; the remainder is total full-time hours.[4] Employed persons working no hours (i.e., having a job but not at work during a survey week) are a small group in Japan (much smaller than in the United States). They were divided between full-time workers and part-time workers in proportion to the numbers at work 1–34 hours and 35 or more hours.[5] The estimated number of part-time workers working zero hours was added to the number of persons at work 1–34 hours to secure part-time employment, and a similar calculation yielded full-time employment. For each group, average hours of employed persons were obtained by division of total hours by employment (not persons at work).

The employment estimates in tables F-1, F-2, and F-3 are those of table

2. For nonagricultural wage and salary workers, it was necessary first to make all calculations with government workers included and then for government workers. Aggregates excluding government workers were obtained by subtraction.

3. The averages in the 1–14 interval (usually 9.3 to 11.1) were estimated by use of 1972 data which subdivided the 1–14-hour class into three smaller groups. For the 15–34-hour classes, 24.5 hours were used. Before 1955 data were divided between 1–19-hour and 20–34-hour classes, and the averages for each class were adjusted accordingly.

4. Any likely error in the estimate of part-time hours is too small to introduce an appreciable error in the estimates obtained for average full-time hours.

5. In the case of nonagricultural wage and salary workers, persons working no hours had also to be allocated between government and other workers in proportion to numbers at work.

3-4 allocated in proportion to the estimates derived from the Labor Force Survey. The average-hour figures are those calculated from the LFS data, while the total hours are the product of employment and average hours.

Labor Force Survey data for hours for 1952–55 are from Bureau of Statistics, Office of the Prime Minister, *Rōdōryōku chōsa kaisan kekka hōkoku* [Report on the Revised Figures of the Labor Force Survey], published November 1957. Data for 1955–70 are from the same bureau, *Rōdōryōku chōsa hōkoku* [Report on the Labor Force Survey], 1970 edition. Most detail on hours for 1971 was not available and was estimated by interpolation between 1970 and 1972. Data for 1972 (not shown in the tables) are from the 1972 edition of the same publication. Some details were secured from editions of other years. Annual averages of the numbers of persons at work and some of the averages for hours worked had to be calculated from monthly LFS data.

The following points of definition and detail should be noted.

1. Average hours are conceptually a little shorter than those published in the Labor Force Survey for persons at work because the LFS data exclude persons working zero hours.

2. Persons who usually work 35 hours or more but actually work 1–34 hours in a given week for noneconomic reasons (vacations, holidays, illness, a miscellany of personal reasons, bad weather, and industrial disputes) are classified in that week as part-time workers. In the United States (both in Bureau of Labor Statistics data and in Denison, *Accounting for Growth*), they are counted as full-time workers. The U.S. classification procedure would yield shorter hours for full-time workers than those shown in tables F-1, F-2, and F-3.[6] However, we believe the difference in classification has much less effect on full-time hours in Japan than in the United States.

3. Changes in the Labor Force Survey affect both employment and hours data. In working up the LFS data used in the derivation of tables F-1, F-2, and F-3, we constructed overlapping estimates for certain years in which changes took place (1957, and 1954 or 1955) rather than attempting to link data to secure continuous series over the whole period. Total employ-

6. Two other points may be pertinent to a comparison of the estimates here with those presented in *Accounting for Growth*. First, with full-time hours as long as they are in Japan, use of more than 35 hours as the dividing point between full-time and part-time employment might be appropriate. This would lengthen Japanese full-time hours. Second, in the U.S. estimates a control total, based on establishment data, was used for hours. This had the effect of lengthening average full-time hours obtained from the Current Population Survey—which is similar to the Japanese Labor Force Survey (see *Accounting for Growth*, table 4-3, p. 37).

Table F-1. *Wage and Salary Workers in Nonagricultural Business: Employment and Hours by Sex and Full-Time or Part-Time Status, 1952–71*

| | Employment (thousands) | | | | Total weekly hours (millions) | | | | Average weekly hours | | | |
| | Males | | Females | | Males | | Females | | Males | | Females | |
Calendar year	Full-time (1)	Part-time (2)	Full-time (3)	Part-time (4)	Full-time (5)	Part-time (6)	Full-time (7)	Part-time (8)	Full-time (9)	Part-time (10)	Full-time (11)	Part-time (12)
1952	8,219	742	3,348	430	435.28	16.09	174.63	9.30	53.0	21.7	52.2	21.6
1953	8,684	783	3,495	449	466.42	16.97	185.38	9.71	53.7	21.7	53.0	21.6
1954a	8,901	802	3,629	466	478.07	17.39	190.85	10.08	53.7	21.7	52.6	21.6
1954b	9,057	742	3,541	458	483.82	15.97	186.19	9.88	53.4	21.5	52.6	21.6
1955	9,234	833	3,770	555	495.31	18.07	200.38	11.98	53.6	21.7	53.2	21.6
1956	10,047	784	4,199	523	545.65	17.04	226.20	11.26	54.3	21.7	53.9	21.5
1957	10,917	820	4,616	572	593.12	17.96	247.56	12.36	54.3	21.9	53.6	21.6
1958	11,576	780	5,133	570	623.60	17.06	274.72	12.36	53.9	21.9	53.5	21.7
1959	12,303	848	5,262	534	660.55	18.50	279.73	11.53	53.7	21.8	53.2	21.6

1960	12,993	781	5,695	584	699.54	17.06	299.44	12.60	53.8	21.8	52.6	21.6
1961	13,375	793	6,050	630	714.63	17.39	314.96	13.63	53.4	21.9	52.1	21.6
1962	14,158	733	6,503	641	742.73	15.86	331.26	13.77	52.5	21.6	50.9	21.5
1963	14,588	812	6,708	700	759.01	17.85	337.82	15.17	52.0	22.0	50.4	21.7
1964	15,255	790	6,906	718	790.67	17.36	345.58	15.61	51.8	22.0	50.0	21.7
1965	15,999	852	7,233	799	822.99	18.86	359.05	17.43	51.4	22.1	49.6	21.8
1966	16,654	860	7,689	898	860.68	19.00	379.30	19.52	51.7	22.1	49.3	21.7
1967[a]	17,056	882	7,993	958	879.75	19.36	392.78	20.99	51.6	22.0	49.1	21.9
1967[b]	17,044	808	7,935	1,102	892.94	17.43	387.15	23.32	52.4	21.6	48.8	21.2
1968	17,511	841	8,216	1,071	906.54	18.22	398.89	23.41	51.8	21.7	48.6	21.9
1969	17,843	801	8,324	1,136	922.13	17.40	402.05	24.99	51.7	21.7	48.3	22.0
1970	18,361	841	8,675	1,244	945.78	18.38	415.88	27.29	51.5	21.8	47.9	21.9
1971	18,999	932	8,700	1,367	970.09	20.52	413.60	30.10	51.1	22.0	47.5	22.0

Source: See text for derivation.
a. Comparable to earlier years.
b. Comparable to later years.

Table F-2. Nonagricultural Self-Employed and Unpaid Family Workers: Employment and Hours by Sex and Full-Time or Part-Time Status, 1952–71

Calendar year	Employment (thousands)				Total weekly hours (millions)				Average weekly hours			
	Males		Females		Males		Females		Males		Females	
	Full-time (1)	Part-time (2)	Full-time (3)	Part-time (4)	Full-time (5)	Part-time (6)	Full-time (7)	Part-time (8)	Full-time (9)	Part-time (10)	Full-time (11)	Part-time (12)
1952	3,567	837	2,216	1,413	215.48	17.35	133.65	28.50	60.4	20.7	60.3	20.2
1953	3,790	898	2,549	1,625	228.73	18.62	147.94	32.78	60.4	20.7	58.0	20.2
1954ᵃ	3,845	908	2,746	1,750	234.58	18.80	168.85	35.30	61.0	20.7	61.5	20.2
1954ᵇ	3,890	863	2,792	1,704	237.41	17.87	170.17	34.46	61.0	20.7	61.0	20.2
1955	3,828	910	2,853	1,822	231.59	18.86	170.78	36.73	60.5	20.7	59.9	20.2
1956	3,832	821	2,913	1,801	235.67	17.02	177.66	36.42	61.5	20.7	61.0	20.2
1957	3,967	793	3,035	1,746	245.12	16.51	184.74	35.41	61.8	20.8	60.9	20.3
1958	3,852	746	2,885	1,671	236.51	15.55	175.81	33.77	61.4	20.8	60.9	20.2
1959	3,886	716	2,956	1,584	237.59	14.92	182.68	32.11	61.1	20.8	61.8	20.3

Year											
1960	3,868	701	3,004	1,585	236.53	14.62	183.72	32.05	61.2	20.9	61.2	20.2
1961	3,839	640	2,929	1,488	234.10	13.34	177.91	30.10	61.0	20.8	60.7	20.2
1962	3,838	571	2,740	1,453	227.25	11.90	161.47	29.19	59.2	20.8	58.9	20.0
1963	3,859	618	2,808	1,464	227.84	12.95	164.18	29.69	59.0	21.0	58.5	20.3
1964	3,903	594	2,885	1,459	229.34	12.36	167.16	29.63	58.8	20.8	57.9	20.3
1965	3,862	591	2,838	1,584	225.43	12.34	163.44	32.20	58.4	20.9	57.6	20.3
1966	3,909	588	2,866	1,631	227.43	12.41	163.96	32.88	58.2	21.1	57.2	20.2
1967a	4,123	587	3,062	1,628	239.75	12.24	174.56	33.02	58.2	20.8	57.0	20.3
1967b	4,168	542	2,806	1,884	245.20	10.89	155.90	38.75	58.8	20.1	55.6	20.6
1968	4,412	499	2,904	1,793	255.85	10.57	162.54	37.42	58.0	21.2	56.0	20.9
1969	4,503	477	2,942	1,826	260.36	10.17	163.93	38.64	57.8	21.3	55.7	21.2
1970	4,526	466	2,944	1,807	260.24	9.75	161.42	38.09	57.5	20.9	54.8	21.1
1971	4,460	486	2,854	1,861	256.45	10.30	157.00	39.16	57.5	21.2	55.0	21.0

Source: See text for derivation.
a. Comparable to earlier years.
b. Comparable to later years.

Table F-3. *Agricultural Workers: Employment and Hours by Sex and Full-Time or Part-Time Status, 1952–71*

Calendar year	Employment (thousands)				Total weekly hours (millions)				Average weekly hours			
	Males		Females		Males		Females		Males		Females	
	Full-time (1)	Part-time (2)	Full-time (3)	Part-time (4)	Full-time (5)	Part-time (6)	Full-time (7)	Part-time (8)	Full-time (9)	Part-time (10)	Full-time (11)	Part-time (12)
1952	4,880	1,800	3,876	2,838	252.15	36.97	189.65	56.82	51.7	20.5	48.9	20.0
1953	4,939	2,067	3,912	3,117	253.57	41.03	192.08	60.75	51.3	19.8	49.1	19.5
1954	4,955	1,879	3,931	2,930	256.82	38.01	193.84	57.78	51.8	20.2	49.3	19.7
1955[a]	4,796	2,131	3,987	3,132	249.63	42.24	197.48	60.76	52.0	19.8	49.5	19.4
1955[b]	4,883	2,044	4,036	3,083	264.56	40.00	206.68	60.06	54.2	19.6	51.2	19.5
1956	4,801	1,955	3,811	3,048	258.92	38.28	195.54	59.38	53.9	19.6	51.3	19.5
1957	4,753	1,714	3,845	2,848	258.04	33.58	198.59	55.48	54.3	19.6	51.6	19.5
1958	4,531	1,668	3,756	2,754	247.39	32.59	196.33	53.70	54.6	19.5	52.3	19.5
1959	4,166	1,607	3,614	2,685	227.80	31.43	188.69	52.30	54.7	19.6	52.2	19.5

1960	4,152	1,598	3,525	2,684	229.15	31.32	184.25	52.31	55.2	19.6	52.3	19.5
1961	4,081	1,471	3,501	2,577	221.39	28.73	182.86	50.17	54.2	19.5	52.2	19.5
1962	4,016	1,406	3,380	2,535	214.09	27.49	172.08	49.38	53.3	19.6	50.9	19.5
1963	3,649	1,469	3,150	2,452	191.97	28.60	158.82	47.52	52.6	19.5	50.4	19.4
1964	3,484	1,369	3,064	2,395	182.77	26.57	155.13	46.77	52.5	19.4	50.6	19.5
1965	3,290	1,376	2,840	2,394	171.15	26.72	142.17	46.16	52.0	19.4	50.1	19.3
1966	3,188	1,328	2,767	2,261	165.20	25.94	137.63	43.77	51.8	19.5	49.7	19.4
1967a	3,137	1,240	2,713	2,200	169.27	24.25	142.35	43.19	54.0	19.6	52.5	19.6
1967b	3,414	963	3,108	1,805	189.27	19.11	168.55	36.57	55.4	19.8	54.2	20.3
1968	3,297	960	2,964	1,856	177.41	19.41	156.06	38.12	53.8	20.2	52.6	20.5
1969	3,256	918	2,879	1,734	174.78	18.76	151.46	36.08	53.7	20.4	52.6	20.8
1970	3,105	816	2,662	1,659	164.97	16.89	138.34	34.59	53.1	20.7	52.0	20.8
1971	2,820	759	2,411	1,519	150.48	15.91	126.48	31.88	53.4	21.0	52.5	21.0

Source: See text for derivation.
a. Comparable to earlier years.
b. Comparable to later years.

Table F-4. *Total and Average Hours Worked per Week in Nonresidential Business, 1952–71*

Calendar year	Total weekly hours worked (millions) (1)	Number of persons employed (thousands) (2)	Weekly hours worked per person employed (3)
1952	1,565.87	34,166	45.83
1953	1,653.97	36,308	45.55
1954a	1,700.37	36,742	46.28
1954b	1,702.21	36,742	46.33
1955a	1,733.81	37,851	45.81
1955b	1,755.01	37,851	46.37
1956	1,819.03	38,535	47.20
1957	1,898.47	39,626	47.91
1958	1,919.40	39,922	48.08
1959	1,937.82	40,161	48.25
1960	1,992.60	41,170	48.40
1961	1,999.22	41,374	48.32
1962	1,996.47	41,974	47.56
1963	1,991.43	42,277	47.10
1964	2,018.95	42,822	47.15
1965	2,037.93	43,658	46.68
1966	2,087.72	44,639	46.77
1967a	2,151.51	45,579	47.20
1967b	2,185.07	45,579	47.94
1968	2,204.44	46,324	47.59
1969	2,220.75	46,639	47.62
1970	2,231.62	47,106	47.37
1971	2,221.96	47,168	47.11

Sources: Column 1, tables F-1, F-2, and F-3; column 2, column 3 of table 3-4; column 3, column 1 ÷ column 2.
a. Comparable to earlier years.
b. Comparable to later years.

ment in each of the three main categories, because it is adjusted to the table 3-4 aggregates, is a continuous series but estimates by sex and full-time or part-time status are not.

Table F-4 shows total and average hours worked in nonresidential business as a whole. Total hours can be obtained by summing the components of tables F-1, F-2, and F-3. Because breaks in the series for total employment were eliminated, the breaks between overlapping series shown in this table result only from measurement changes that affect average hours.

Nonresidential Business: Hours and Age-Sex Composition Indexes

THIS APPENDIX describes the labor input indexes shown in columns 2 through 6 of table 4-3.

Average and Total Hours Worked

The indexes of average and total hours worked shown in table 4-3, columns 2 and 3, are computed from table F-4, columns 3 and 1. The indexes are linked wherever table F-4 shows overlapping estimates for the same year.

The Age-Sex Composition Index

The index shown in table 4-3, column 4, is based on the classification of persons employed in the business sector among the ten age-sex groups shown in table G-1. To calculate the age-sex composition index, two kinds of information are needed. One is differentials in hourly earnings among the ten age-sex groups. The other is annual distributions of total hours worked, by age and sex.

Earnings by Age and Sex

Various surveys in Japan agree that among wage and salary workers the average monthly or annual earnings of females are just over one-half of the average earnings of males. Among them, the most satisfactory source for estimates by age as well as sex is the Basic Survey on Wage Structure of the

Table G-1. *Estimated Earnings in Japan, by Sex and Age, 1971, and Comparison with the United States, 1966–67*

Sex and age	Average monthly earnings (thousands of yen) (1)	Average monthly hours (2)	Average hourly earnings (yen) (3)	Index of hourly earnings (all employees = 100)	
				Japan (4)	United States (5)
Males[a]	97.0	205	472	115	113
15–19	43.7	199	220	54	36[b]
20–24	66.7	207	322	79	77
25–34	96.5	206	468	114	114
35–59	121.8	205	594	145	128[c]
60 and over	75.8	208	364	89	88[d]
Females[a]	49.0	192	255	62	67
15–19	38.2	193	198	48	49[b]
20–24	50.8	191	266	65	59
25–34	54.4	190	286	70	68
35–59	52.8	192	275	67	68[c]
60 and over	44.8	196	229	56	54[d]
All employees[a]	82.0	201	409	100	100

Sources: For columns 1–4, see text; column 5, *Accounting for Growth*, p. 189.
a. Data for these groups are not used as weights in the computation of quality indexes.
b. Data refer to persons fourteen to nineteen.
c. Data refer to persons thirty-five to sixty-four.
d. Data refer to persons sixty-five and over.

Ministry of Labor. This survey covers wage and salary workers employed in establishments with ten or more regular employees. Industrial coverage is reasonably close to that which we desire (the business sector). Excluded are agriculture, forestry, and fisheries, which employ few wage and salary workers; public administration, which is not in the business sector; and services, where most wage and salary workers are not in the business sector though some are. The main limitation of these data is the omission of self-employed and unpaid family workers; in effect we impute to all employed persons differentials among age-sex groups observed for wage and salary workers. This limitation would be difficult to remedy because there is no suitable method by which to allocate the earnings of an unincorporated enterprise among the individual proprietors and family workers associated with it. Because agriculture employs an exceptionally large proportion of females, is an industry in which average earnings are especially low, and employs self-employed and unpaid family workers almost exclusively, we may somewhat understate the male-female differential by basing it on wage and salary workers alone.

Column 1 of table G-1 is the sum of "monthly contractual earnings" (regular and overtime) in June 1971 and one-twelfth of "annual special earnings" in the year ended December 1970 (June 1971 for new workers). Column 2 is average hours worked in June (including overtime hours). Column 3 (the quotient of columns 1 and 2) is average hourly earnings. Because females work shorter hours than males, the differential between the sexes is smaller in hourly than in monthly earnings. All these data are from *Year Book of Labor Statistics, 1971,* page 144, except that (1) data given for more detailed age groups were consolidated, and (2) within the fifteen-to-nineteen age group of each sex, the weight of persons fifteen to seventeen years of age was raised relative to that of persons eighteen to nineteen so as to accord with Census of Population data for total employment by age.[1]

In column 4 hourly earnings are expressed as a percentage of average hourly earnings of all employees. Column 5 provides similar indexes for the business sector in the United States. For the most part the pattern of wage differentials is similar in the United States and Japan (and in Western Europe as well) when age groups of this breadth are used. The average male-female differential is moderately bigger in Japan. Relative earnings of males thirty-five to fifty-nine years of age in Japan exceed those of men thirty-five to sixty-four in the United States; the difference in the upper age limit is only partially responsible.[2]

The use of sixty as the lower limit for the top age bracket in Japan was determined partly by the classification followed in the available earnings data. However, we wished to use an age lower than the sixty-five adopted for the United States (we would have preferred fifty-five to sixty) because of a peculiarity of the Japanese labor market, which artificially lowers the productivity of many workers when they reach fifty-five or so. Wage and salary workers are customarily "retired" from their regular jobs at an early age—most often at fifty-five, though it is increasing—and must then find a new job, usually at less skilled work for which their previous experience has little pertinence and, correspondingly, at sharply reduced earnings.[3] Consequently, average earnings drop sharply as this milestone is passed.

1. The average earnings of all age groups combined were also adjusted downward by increasing the weight of persons fifteen to seventeen.
2. Within this age bracket, earnings of males rise more sharply, up to retirement age, in Japan than in the United States.
3. Few leave the labor force: participation rates for older workers are not low in Japan. Financial circumstances would not permit many to cease work if they wished to do so. Public pensions are small, private pensions rare, and employers' lump sum payments at retirement equal no more than three or four years' pay even for employees with the longest service with the employer.

Table G-2. *Nonresidential Business: Percentage Distributions of Hours Worked and Labor Input, by Sex, 1952–71*

Calendar year	Total weekly hours		Total labor input	
	Males (1)	Females (2)	Males (3)	Females (4)
1952	62.16	37.84	74.77	25.23
1953	61.99	38.01	74.59	25.41
1954a	61.38	38.62	74.20	25.80
1954b	61.68	38.32	73.99	26.01
1955a	60.88	39.12	73.66	26.34
1955b	60.88	39.12	73.67	26.33
1956	61.16	38.84	73.88	26.12
1957	61.33	38.67	74.09	25.91
1958	61.10	38.90	73.86	26.14
1959	61.45	38.55	74.15	25.85
1960	61.64	38.36	74.40	25.60
1961	61.50	38.50	74.32	25.68
1962	62.08	37.92	74.65	25.35
1963	62.18	37.82	74.74	25.26
1964	62.36	37.64	74.95	25.05
1965	62.69	37.31	75.23	24.77
1966	62.78	37.22	75.38	24.62
1967a	62.50	37.50	75.00	25.00
1967b	62.92	37.08	75.58	24.42
1968	62.96	37.04	75.62	24.38
1969	63.20	36.80	75.83	24.17
1970	63.45	36.55	76.04	23.96
1971	64.08	35.92	76.53	23.47

Sources: Columns 1 and 2, computed from tables F-1, F-2, and F-3; columns 3 and 4, see text for derivation.
a. Comparable to earlier years.
b. Comparable to later years.

Distributions of Hours Worked and Computation of the Index

Total hours worked by persons of each sex who were employed in nonresidential business were obtained by combining data from tables F-1, F-2, and F-3. Percentage distributions of aggregate hours, by sex, are shown in table G-2, columns 1 and 2.

Distributions of hours by sex and age are shown in table G-3. To secure the estimate for any year, the nonresidential business percentage for each sex that year was allocated among the five age groups in proportion to the products for the age groups of employment in the whole economy that year and average hours in the whole economy in 1972. Average hours are not

Table G-3. *Nonresidential Business: Percentage Distributions of Total Hours Worked, by Sex and Age, 1952–71*

Cal-endar year	Males (by age group)					Females (by age group)				
	15–19	20–24	25–34	35–59	60 and over	15–19	20–24	25–34	35–59	60 and over
1952	6.11	7.37	16.42	26.50	5.76	5.81	5.97	8.61	14.72	2.73
1953	6.24	7.34	16.35	26.73	5.34	5.34	6.03	8.70	15.22	2.71
1954[a]	5.66	7.19	16.01	27.02	5.50	5.17	6.11	8.82	15.68	2.84
1954[b]	5.64	7.16	15.94	26.92	5.47	5.21	6.15	8.87	15.78	2.86
1955[a]	5.90	7.23	16.12	26.10	5.52	5.22	6.22	8.98	15.81	2.90
1955[b]	5.92	7.23	16.10	26.09	5.54	5.25	6.19	8.94	15.80	2.94
1956	5.65	7.40	16.48	26.13	5.51	5.01	6.24	9.01	15.77	2.80
1957	5.38	7.51	16.72	26.34	5.38	5.02	6.18	8.91	15.76	2.80
1958	5.37	7.58	16.88	25.90	5.37	5.07	6.23	8.99	15.84	2.77
1959	5.30	7.71	17.17	25.98	5.29	5.03	6.17	8.90	15.75	2.70
1960	4.97	7.31	17.21	26.60	5.55	4.80	6.07	8.87	15.86	2.76
1961	4.53	7.35	17.59	26.42	5.61	4.58	6.36	8.65	16.05	2.86
1962	4.47	8.37	17.84	25.97	5.43	4.48	6.75	8.44	15.75	2.50
1963	4.29	8.43	17.80	26.18	5.48	4.25	6.79	8.28	16.00	2.50
1964	3.95	8.67	17.54	26.69	5.51	3.96	6.89	8.02	16.23	2.54
1965	4.02	8.57	17.48	27.06	5.56	3.92	6.65	7.79	16.45	2.50
1966	4.37	8.03	17.33	27.55	5.50	4.28	6.19	7.63	16.63	2.49
1967[a]	4.02	7.62	17.67	27.72	5.46	4.23	6.19	7.85	16.71	2.53
1967[b]	4.03	7.71	17.80	27.91	5.47	4.19	6.07	7.70	16.61	2.51
1968	3.73	7.88	17.70	28.26	5.39	3.83	6.38	7.57	16.90	2.36
1969	3.16	8.08	17.73	28.76	5.47	3.26	6.68	7.47	17.00	2.39
1970	2.74	8.60	17.47	29.20	5.45	2.89	6.99	7.19	17.06	2.41
1971	2.52	9.15	17.09	29.84	5.48	2.57	7.21	6.68	17.09	2.37

Source: See text.
a. Comparable to earlier years.
b. Comparable to later years.

regularly available by age; the procedure assumes that differentials among age groups of the same sex are stable.[4] It also assumes, for each sex, that employment distributions and hour differentials by age are similar in business to those in the whole economy.

The employment distributions by age (and the 1972 data on hours by age) are from the Labor Force Survey. Age brackets in the employment distributions by age from the LFS do not entirely correspond to those of table G-3; when necessary, LFS labor force distributions were used to adjust the LFS employment distributions to the desired age classes. (The LFS provides age distributions of the labor force in sufficient detail to match the age classes used in both the LFS employment tables and in table G-3.) LFS data for 1967–72 (new series) are from the 1972 *Report on the Labor Force Survey*, those for 1955 to 1967 (old series) from the 1968 *Report on the Labor Force Survey*, and those for earlier years from the *Report on Revised Figures of the Labor Force Survey* (published November 1957) and *Report on the Labor Force Survey*, no. 2 (published March 1955). Fourteen-year-olds included in LFS data for the early years were eliminated.

The percentage shown each year in table G-3 for each age-sex group was multiplied by the weight shown in table G-1, and the products summed. The resulting series of weighted averages was converted to a time series index (1965 = 100) to secure column 4 of table 4-3. The index was linked wherever overlapping estimates are shown in table G-3.

A percentage division between males and females of the sum of the age-sex weights entering into the index is shown in table G-2, columns 3 and 4. These percentages are needed in the computation of the remaining labor input indexes.

Effect on the Efficiency of an Hour's Work of Changes in Hours Resulting from Intragroup Changes and Specified Intergroup Shifts

Multiplication of the age-sex composition index by the indexes of employment and average weekly hours worked (table 4-3, columns 1, 2, and 4) would yield the same index as would be obtained by measuring the total hours worked by each age-sex group and weighting the total hours of each group by average hourly earnings. If we were to stop here in measuring labor input, we would assume that when the average hours worked by persons employed

---

4. Hours are available by age for wage and salary workers covered in the Basic Survey on Wage Structure, but the pattern of differentials by age does not resemble that for all workers obtained from the Labor Force Survey.

in business change for any reason a proportional change occurs in work done.[5]

We do not believe this would be a correct appraisal of the situation, and the indexes described in this section introduce different assumptions. They are constructed in exactly the same way as the corresponding indexes for the United States, which are discussed at length in *Accounting for Growth,* pages 35–43 and 218. We provide here a brief explanation and refer the reader to *Accounting* for details of calculation.

In the framework of the twelve-way classification of workers in tables F-1 to F-3, average hours, as shown in table F-4, may change for any of five main reasons. When hours change for only three of these reasons do we consider it appropriate to assume that labor input is altered in proportion to the change in average hours. These three are changes in the proportions of full-time and part-time workers, changes in the proportions of male and female workers within the full-time categories, and changes in the average hours of part-time workers (including changes due to the distribution of part-time workers among the six part-time groups shown in the tables).

Intragroup Changes in Hours for Full-Time Workers

A fourth reason that average hours in nonresidential business change is that the length of the average hours of one or more of the six groups of full-time workers distinguished in tables F-1 to F-3 may change. If it does, what are the effects?

The general shape of a curve relating hours to output for any given category of workers can be described with some assurance. If working hours are very long, the adverse effects of fatigue upon productivity are so great that output per worker increases if hours are shortened (and output per hour increases much more). The effects of fatigue are reinforced by a tendency for absenteeism, which is costly, to be excessive when hours are long, and by important institutional factors. If hours are shortened further, a point is reached below which output per worker declines while output per hour continues to increase. At this stage, increases in output per hour only partially offset the reduction in hours worked. Finally, if hours become very short, the proportion of time spent in starting and stopping work may become so great that even output per hour declines as hours are shortened.

The difficulty in deriving such a curve empirically is that evidence about the location of the critical points is inadequate. Nevertheless, it is impossible to measure labor input at all, or to analyze sources of growth, without intro-

5. If the change is accompanied by an altered age-sex distribution of total hours, the average value of an hour's work is altered, of course, but this is a separate point.

ducing assumptions about such curves.[6] In Japan, we believe, the great length of hours worked by all groups of full-time workers throughout the 1952–71 period makes it unlikely that shortening hours had much adverse effect on output per worker. It is possible, of course, that the effect was favorable. Indeed, the Japanese Ministry of Labor computed a production function for manufacturing industries, based on 1960–69 data, which indicates that each 1 percent decrease in actual average hours worked raised output per hour worked by 2.57 percent.[7] Although we regard a small favorable effect as by no means unlikely, we consider one of this magnitude improbable.

Our exact assumptions are the same as were used for the United States in *Accounting for Growth*. We assume that within the range observed in 1952–71 changes in the average hours of full-time agricultural workers of either sex do not change labor input (or output), implying that changes in average hours are fully offset in output per hour. We make the same assumption for nonagricultural self-employed and unpaid family workers. We also make the same assumption for nonagricultural wage and salary workers so long as average weekly hours of males do not fall below 52.7 and those of females below 49.0 (based on the levels of the "new" series for 1967 forward).[8] Average hours of nonagricultural wage and salary workers in Japan in fact stayed above these levels until about 1967, except for two years in the case of hours for females. As hours drop from these levels toward levels ten hours shorter—42.7 for males and 39.0 for females—declines in average hours are estimated to be partially offset by changes in work done per hour, the offset gradually decreasing from 100 percent to zero as hours shorten. The offset is nearly complete at the upper end of the range, which is all that is observed in Japan up to 1971.

The index of the "efficiency of an hour's work as affected by changes in hours due to intragroup changes" is so constructed that it effectuates the desired assumptions when it is multiplied by the average-hours series. It offsets changes in average hours in nonresidential business as a whole that are due to changes within the six groups, except that the offset for nonagricultural wage and salary workers is less than complete toward the end of the period.

The preceding sentence must be qualified in one respect. Because the age-

6. Available evidence and a number of opinions are discussed in *Why Growth Rates Differ*, pp. 59–64.

7. Ministry of Labor, *White Paper on Labor—1972*, pp. 320–21.

8. Note that full-time hours of agricultural workers and nonagricultural self-employed and unpaid family workers were always longer than this when the levels for early years are adjusted for consistency with hours for later years. See tables F-2 and F-3.

sex index introduced different weights for hours worked by males and females, it is necessary to construct separate indexes for the efficiency offset to intergroup changes for males and females, compute the annual percentage changes in each, weight them by the percentages of labor input supplied by males and females (as given in table G-2, columns 3 and 4) to obtain the combined percentage change each year, and then compute the final index for both series combined by linking the percentage changes.[9] Because weighting by sex is introduced after the computation of the average-hours index but before computation of the index for the efficiency offset to intergroup changes, the two are not exactly consistent. When both are multiplied by the age-sex index, however, the desired measure for labor input is secured.

Changes in the Composition of Full-Time Employment for Each Sex

The fifth principal reason that average hours in nonresidential business change is that the distribution of full-time employees of each sex among the three types of employment we distinguish may change. Because average hours vary among the three types, such changes in "mix" alter average hours. Despite the unusually large decline in the agricultural share of full-time employment that has occurred in Japan, mix changes of this type have had less effect on average hours than in the United States or most other Western countries. The reason is that hours of nonagricultural wage and salary workers fall below those of agricultural workers by a much smaller amount in Japan than they do in the other countries.

We regard full-time workers with the same personal characteristics as the same amount of labor input if they work the average hours of their group, whether that group is nonagricultural wage and salary employment, nonagricultural self-employment (including family workers), or agricultural employment. Consequently, we do not allow labor input to decline if, for example, a full-time agricultural worker, working the average hours of his group, becomes a full-time nonagricultural wage and salary worker, working the average hours of his new group. The index labeled "efficiency of an hour's work as affected by changes in hours due to specified intergroup changes" is so calculated as to offset the effect on average hours of such changes in the mix of full-time employment. (Note that effects of changes in the composition by sex of full-time employment are not canceled out.)

As in the case of the index for "intragroup changes," annual changes were calculated separately for each sex, and combined by use of labor input weights.

9. In principle separate treatment should be accorded each age group, but this is impractical.

APPENDIX H

Nonresidential Business: The Education of Employed Persons

THIS APPENDIX describes the derivation of the education component of the index of labor input in nonresidential business (table 4-3, column 7) and of table 6-1, which shows distributions of employed persons not in school by amount of education, the weight used for education groups, and related data. Part 1 describes the weights and part 2 the distributions by amount of education and the computation of the index.

This introductory section briefly describes the Japanese educational system. We must be concerned with the structure back to the time when the oldest persons employed in 1950 were of school age.

A modern school system was first promulgated in 1872. Education was made compulsory in 1886, when a four-year requirement was established. However, no claim is made that the compulsory education requirement was fully enforced before 1900, and enrollment data show full compliance with the four-year requirement actually was not approached before 1909.[1] In

1. The statement that full enforcement of compulsory education was completed in 1900 appears on p. 26 of Ministry of Education, *Japan's Growth and Education: Educational Development in Relation to Socio-economic Growth* (July 1963). However, the same source (p. 160) shows that in 1900 the percentage of children of compulsory school age who were enrolled in school was still rising rapidly. From 49 percent as late as 1890 it increased to 73 percent in 1899, 81 percent in 1900, and 88 percent in 1901. Not until 1909 did it attain 98 percent. Percentages were much higher for males than for females until both approached 100.

1908 the education requirement was extended to six years and in 1947 to nine years, where it has remained. Most persons ended their education with the compulsory years until after World War II, but opportunities for further education have been present throughout the period of interest, have expanded, and have been increasingly grasped by students. The major breakthrough occurred in the postwar years.

Since 1947 the structure of the Japanese educational system has been similar to that in the postwar United States: six years of elementary school, three of junior high, three of senior high, and four of college or university (or two of junior college). Graduate school curricula vary in length.

In the decades before 1947 too, the ordinary elementary school was six years but the rest of the structure was different. Alternative progressions existed. After ordinary elementary school a student might go to middle school for five years, followed by college preparatory school for two (or the division between the two schools might be four years and three). Then came university for three years (again, followed by graduate courses of varying length). Alternatively, after completing ordinary elementary school the student could spend two years in an upper elementary school, followed by three years in a higher vocational school. Or from ordinary elementary school he could proceed to a youth training ("vocational continuation") school for up to three years. There were also colleges and normal schools which could be entered after four years at middle school, and other normal schools which could be entered after a third year at upper elementary school. This summary pertains to the situation from about 1919, before which there were various differences in the structure. Most important is that ordinary elementary school was only four years from 1886 to 1908 while upper elementary school was still two. Earlier, these six years of elementary school were divided between primary and intermediate divisions, each of three years.[2]

Part One: Weights by Education Class

We seek differentials in average earnings between groups of workers who differ in amount of education and in the length of their work experience as a consequence of differences in length of education, but who are similar in characteristics that are not the consequence of education. The data should refer to all persons working in the business sector.

2. Detailed charts of the prewar school system appear in ibid., pp. 24, 25.

Earnings by Broad Education Groups

The most pertinent earnings data are from the Basic Survey on Wage Structure conducted by the Ministry of Labor; its coverage is described in appendix G. The data are reasonably representative of nonagricultural wage and salary employment in the business sector.[3] However, agricultural, self-employed, and unpaid family workers are excluded. As in the computation of age-sex weights, average monthly earnings were calculated as the sum of "monthly contractual earnings" and one-twelfth of "annual special earnings." Average hourly earnings are the quotient of average monthly earnings and average monthly hours.

The surveys provide data cross-classified by sex, age (nine classes, but we discard two), and education. However, only four education classes are distinguished for males and only two for females. This is too few for our needs, but we work with these broad groupings at first and divide them later.

Table H-1 shows average earnings in each education group as a percentage of average earnings of persons with a "lower secondary" education or less.[4] The percentages are shown separately for each age-sex group. The upper panel shows monthly earnings, the lower hourly earnings. The indexes are averages of similar indexes for three dates: June 1967, June 1970, and June 1971. The reason for averaging the three sets of indexes is minimization of sampling error; the number of persons and hence the size of the sample in some sex-age-education cells is small. We use the indexes as representative of a date around 1970.

The earnings indexes for Japan show the same characteristics as similar data for the United States and other countries. Earnings are higher the greater the amount of education in all age groups except the youngest, and the differ-

---

3. Exclusion of the "services" industry division from the survey has the fortunate effect that teachers and religious workers are omitted. Of all the groups of wage and salary workers outside the business sector, these probably are the two whose inclusion would most distort differentials in the sector.

4. Persons seventeen and younger, for whom the source reports earnings for only the lowest education class, and those eighteen and nineteen, for whom only the two lowest classes are reported, are omitted. In analysis of the United States, where information refers to annual earnings, the twenty-to-twenty-four and sixty-five-and-over age groups were also omitted because it was impossible to derive comparable earnings data for time actually worked by different education groups of the same age. For Japan this is not a problem because data refer to monthly earnings of employed persons and average hours worked are reported. Also, average age is available, and in the twenty-to-twenty-four and sixty-and-over age groups these data show an absence of significant age differences between the education groups.

entials widen persistently with age (except for the sixty-and-over age class). There are probably two main reasons that differentials widen as age increases.

First, persons with more education have less experience than persons of the same age with less education because extra schooling delayed entrance into the full-time labor market. Additional education raises earnings while less experience depresses earnings. The importance of the experience differential diminishes as age increases. The difference between the two years of experience typically held by senior high school graduates at twenty-one and the five years held by junior high school graduates at the same age has, as would be expected, a much greater effect on earnings than the difference at forty-one when it is between twenty-two and twenty-five years of experience.[5] Though the junior high school graduates still have an advantage of three years, the percentage difference in experience dwindles from 150 to 14. On the other hand, the benefit to earnings of additional education seems to increase with age. The differential in years of education remains constant (the three-year difference between persons with twelve and nine years of education remains 33 percent) while the impact of additional education on earnings (and, we believe, on the worker's contribution to output) increases as education interacts with experience.

In a direct sense, the rather rigid wage structure in Japanese firms, which is based mainly on education, experience, and sex, must greatly influence the earnings pattern we observe. But the pattern is so similar to that which emerges in other countries as to suggest that Japanese firms have codified a pattern which would be present in much the same form in any case (though, probably, with more variation among individuals of the same experience, education, and sex).

In the derivation of education weights for the United States, the first step was to secure earnings differentials by amount of education, separately for persons cross-classified by sex, age, race, geographic region, and attachment to agricultural or nonagricultural industries. Differentials in these groups were then averaged, using total earnings as weights for age groups, to secure combined differentials.[6] The reason for separate treatment of each category is that education differs among these groups, and earnings differ for reasons

5. I refer here to total work experience. Experience with the present employer is also an earnings determinant and continuity of employment is positively associated with education. The lowest education group has the most service with present employer among persons twenty to twenty-four, but less than the second education group at twenty-five to twenty-nine and less than any other group at thirty to thirty-four even though it has the longest total work experience.

6. Actually, calculations were made only for males. Differentials for males were also used for females.

Table H-1. *Indexes of Monthly and Hourly Earnings by Level of Education, by Sex and Age*[a]
Earnings of persons of the same sex and age having "lower secondary and below" education = 100

| | Indexes for males, by education group | | | | Indexes for females, by education group | | Addendum: percentage distributions of total earnings, by age | |
	Lower secondary and below (1)	Middle school (old) and senior high (2)	College preparatory (old) and junior college (3)	University and post-graduate (4)	Lower secondary and below (5)	Middle school (old), senior high, and above (6)	Males (7)	Females (8)
Age group								
			Monthly earnings					
20–24	100.0	96.5	91.7	93.5	100.0	109.6	9.19	19.28
25–29	100.0	103.4	104.9	110.8	100.0	123.2	12.55	11.81
30–34	100.0	111.7	117.4	136.6	100.0	134.3	14.00	10.39
35–39	100.0	118.1	135.9	158.7	100.0	136.9	15.29	12.34
40–49	100.0	123.1	166.3	191.8	100.0	149.0	25.73	23.98
50–59	100.0	131.0	182.0	224.5	100.0	166.8	15.62	14.91
60 and over	100.0	129.7	160.3	182.1	100.0	172.8	7.62	7.29
Weighted average[b]	100.0	117.6	142.2	164.2	100.0	139.7	100.00	100.00

	Hourly earnings							
20–24	100.0	101.1	95.0	100.3	100.0	112.2	9.19	19.28
25–29	100.0	109.7	109.4	121.0	100.0	125.2	12.55	11.81
30–34	100.0	118.2	125.3	151.9	100.0	135.8	14.00	10.39
35–39	100.0	123.8	145.7	178.9	100.0	138.7	15.29	12.34
40–49	100.0	128.4	181.9	216.3	100.0	152.2	25.73	23.98
50–59	100.0	136.9	198.7	253.2	100.0	173.6	15.62	14.91
60 and over	100.0	133.4	168.3	194.5	100.0	180.7	7.62	7.29
Weighted average[b]	100.0	123.1	153.0	183.0	100.0	143.2	100.00	100.00

Source: Computed from Ministry of Labor, *Basic Survey on Wage Structure*, 1967, 1970, and 1971. See text for method of calculation. Earnings refer to wage and salary workers employed in establishments with ten or more regular employees. Workers in agriculture, forestry, fisheries, and service industries and those under twenty years of age are excluded.

a. Indexes are averages of similar indexes for June of 1967, 1970, and 1971.

b. Weights are the percentages of total earnings shown in columns 7 and 8.

other than education, so that failure to standardize data in this way would ascribe to education differentials that are caused by other earnings determinants (or obscure differentials that education introduces). In Japan race can safely be ignored and regional differences seem unlikely to be important. Our data exclude agriculture, so earnings differentials are unaffected by differences in the proportion of agricultural workers in the various education categories. In standardizing the data we can consequently ignore race, region, and attachment to agricultural or nonagricultural industries. However, we must assume that, within age-sex groups, earnings differentials among education groups in agriculture, and also in nonagricultural self-employment, are the same as they are among education groups in nonagricultural business wage and salary employment.

In the framework of the labor input estimates of this study and of *Accounting for Growth* the differentials should be based on hourly earnings for complete consistency with other labor input components. In the United States it was necessary to use earnings per full-time equivalent person employed instead of hourly earnings. Given the detailed standardization procedure adopted, it was believed that there was little difference between the two types of differentials.[7]

For Japan it is possible to compute differentials in hourly earnings among education groups. In general, hours are longer for the less educated wage and salary workers than for the more educated in Japan, so that percentage differentials in hourly earnings exceed those in monthly earnings. This is apparent from a comparison of the upper and lower panels of table H-1.

The last row of each panel shows weighted averages of the indexes for the age groups. The weighted indexes are computed by use of total earnings as weights, which are adopted to represent total labor input. They are shown in the last two columns of table H-1. For each sex, the percentage distribution of total earnings among age groups, used for weighting, is proportional to the products of total employment (all categories, from the Labor Force Survey, monthly average for 1970) and average monthly earnings of wage and salary workers covered by the Basic Survey on Wage Structure for June 1970. The procedure assumes, for each sex, that the age distribution is the same for total business employment as for total employment.

The weighted average differentials correspond roughly to those of persons around thirty-seven to thirty-nine years of age, if we can judge by interpolation of the estimates by age group in table H-1. The youthfulness of the Japa-

---

7. Without standardization or reduction of employment to full-time equivalence, and with all classes of workers included, hours per worker and amount of education are positively associated in the United States.

nese labor force causes the education differentials to be narrower than they would otherwise be. The greater weight of young age groups in female than in male employment reduces the education differential for females relative to males. (Lack of detail for females in any case prevents a direct comparison in table H-1.)

Derivation of Weights

The differentials may overstate the effect of education on earnings. This will be the case if persons with more education have greater academic aptitude than those with less education and, in addition, persons with greater academic aptitude earn more than their counterparts—persons of the same age and sex who have the same amount of education—who have less academic aptitude. It will also be the case if persons from a high socioeconomic background both receive more education on the average and earn more without additional education than persons of lower socioeconomic status. It was estimated that in the United States differences in academic aptitude and socioeconomic status would cause earnings of persons in any education group to exceed those of persons with four fewer years of education by 2.67 percent even if the difference in education were absent. This is equivalent to an increase of 0.66 percent for each year of additional education. In the absence of any information on which to base such an estimate for Japan, we shall use the same figure.[8]

Column 2 of table H-2 shows the estimated average number of years of education held by males in each of the four education groups in 1970. (These averages are calculated from the detailed percentage distributions in column 1 and the estimated average number of years of education in each detailed group, shown in column 2; derivation of the distributions is described in part 2 of this appendix.) These averages and the assumption of the previous

8. The estimate that in the United States workers at each level of education would earn only 0.66 percent more than workers with one less year of school, if all had the same education, applies only up to the college graduate level. The reason the percentage is small despite large differences in noneducational characteristics is that earnings at a given level of education do not vary much with academic aptitude (as measured by indicators such as rank in class or score on IQ test). College graduates are an exception to this generalization; their earnings vary considerably with academic aptitude. Because of this, combined with a considerable difference in aptitude between college graduates and those with graduate work, academic aptitude accounts for a much bigger difference between earnings of college graduates and those with graduate work. Since we combine college graduates and those with more advanced study in Japan an estimate of the difference in Japan is unnecessary. See *Accounting for Growth*, pp. 228–42, for a discussion of the effects of academic aptitude and socioeconomic status in the United States.

paragraph permit calculation of an index of the variation in earnings that would exist between persons in different education groups because of differences in academic aptitude and socioeconomic status, even if education did not affect earnings. Thus the second group averaged 3.73 more years of school than the first; at 0.66 percent per year, the second group would earn an average of 2.46 percent more than the first. The index is shown in column 4.

Division by this column of the previously computed index of standardized hourly earnings (which is repeated in table H-2, column 3) yields an index of the effects of education on earnings (table H-2, column 5). This column would provide the weights we need if the education classes were more detailed. But the two lower classes are much too big (the first, alone, included 73 percent of employed males in 1950 and 55 percent even in 1970). We have therefore estimated indexes for more detailed classes.[9] These indexes are, of course, so selected that the weighted average (using column 1 as weights) of the indexes for component detailed groups equals the index for a broader group. In selecting indexes we have tried to be consistent with the differentials among the broader groups, and have considered differentials in other countries, especially the United States. Column 6 shows the final indexes, or education weights, which are subsequently used to calculate the time series index. These weights have been calculated, throughout, with the earnings of men in the "lower secondary and below" category equaling 100. On this scale, earnings of men with eight years of education can be estimated at 100.[10] Hence, this final column can be regarded as measured with earnings of men with eight years of education equaling 100.

We use the same weights for detailed groups throughout the 1950–70 period, in the absence of clear evidence of a change in standardized earnings differentials. It should be noted that constant weights for detailed groups imply that standardized earnings differentials between the broad education groups were narrowing. This is because of a changing mix of the educational distribution within them. The implied weights for broad groups of men, when

9. The need for estimation could not be obviated by use of more detail in the collection and tabulation of earnings statistics. When there is a change in the amount of compulsory education (as from four to six years) or a change in educational structure, such as that from middle school to high school, representative individuals of the same age are not present for both educational levels so that actual earnings cannot be compared. We can only infer what the difference would be if the same age groups contained persons with both types of education who were similar in other characteristics.

10. Eight years is one-third of the distance between the average years of education of the seven-and-eight- and nine-year groups, while 100 is one-third of the distance between the weights of these two groups.

Table H-2. *Derivation of Weights for Education Groups, Males*

Kind of school and years completed	Percent of employed males, 1970 (1)	Average years of school (2)	Stan- dardized earnings[a] (3)	Effect of noneduc- cational[b] deter- minants[a] (4)	Effect of education[a] (5)	Final weights[a] (6)
Lower secondary and below	54.60	7.85	100.00	100.00	100.00	
0	0.24	0.00	...	...	70.00	70
1–3	0.31	2.00	...	...	80.00	80
4	0.85	4.00	...	...	86.00	86
5–6	5.21	5.80	...	...	91.00	91
7–8	25.06	7.50	...	...	96.53	97
9	22.93	9.00	...	...	106.94	107
Middle school (old) and senior high	31.57	11.58	123.13	102.46	120.18	...
10–11	10.16	10.70	...	...	117.19	117
12	21.41	12.00	...	...	121.60	122
Junior college and col- lege preparatory (old)						
13–15	4.04	14.00	152.96	104.10	146.94	147
University and postgraduate						
16 or more	9.79	17.00	183.04	106.16	172.42	172

Sources: Columns 1 and 2, table 6-1; broad groups computed from detail. Column 3, table H-1. Columns 4 and 6, see text. Column 5, column 3 ÷ column 4; see text for detailed groups.

a. Index, hourly earnings of men in the "lower secondary and below" category = 100. In column 6, this is the same as earnings of men with eight years of education = 100.

b. Academic aptitude and socioeconomic status.

earnings of men with "lower secondary and below" education are equal to 100, are as follows:[11]

	1950	1960	1970
Elementary, junior high, and youth training	100	100	100
Middle school (old) and senior high	124	121	120
Junior college and college preparatory (old)	155	149	147
University and postgraduate	181	175	172

Data from the Basic Survey on Wage Structure do show a tendency for such differentials to have narrowed.[12]

11. These calculations are based on the distributions of men in table H-3.

12. It did not seem feasible, however, to derive detailed weights for different dates from the Basic Survey on Wage Structure that could be used with confidence that changes were significant. Tsunehiko Watanabe, after examining data from 1954 through 1969, reached the following conclusion. "From these observations it is possible to say: (1) the relative wage structures by age and education have been substantially stable

The data for the two female education groups were analyzed, but we abandoned the attempt to secure independent weights for females. Instead, we use the male weights for females as well.

Actually, percentage differentials for females are almost surely as great, and probably greater, than those for males. After the procedure to eliminate the effects of academic aptitude and socioeconomic status was applied to females, it appeared that earnings of females with old middle school education or more exceeded earnings of those with less education than this by 39 percent because of the difference in education, whereas the comparable difference for males was only 34 percent. This was so even though the difference between the two education groups in average amount of education was smaller in the case of females. If female earnings were a constant fraction of male earnings in all detailed education groups, the higher of the two broad female education groups would have earned only 25 percent more than the lower group as against the actual 39 percent.

The 1973 Basic Survey of Wage Structure, which became available after our estimates were completed, provides more detail for females than earlier surveys. Percentage differentials in hourly earnings between senior high school and college graduates were about the same for the two sexes from fifty to fifty-nine years old, much greater for females from twenty through forty-nine and in the sixty-to-sixty-four age bracket, and greater for males only after sixty-five.

The characteristics (notably the age distribution) of female wage and salary workers covered in the Basic Survey of Wage Structure differ greatly from those of all employed females so caution in making inferences about all females from these data is indicated, but it seems probable that, overall, differentials for females are at least as big as those for males.

Part Two: Distributions by Amount of Education

The next task is to derive distributions of employed persons by sex and amount of education, using a ten-way education breakdown corresponding to that for which weights were estimated. To do so we rely mainly upon data from the decennial Censuses of Population and on knowledge of the historical changes in the structure of Japanese education that have taken place in the period since the oldest members of the 1950 labor force were educated. These were summarized at the beginning of this appendix.

---

during the last twenty years (those by sex are of a similar nature), and (2) no significant changes have been found in the relative wage structure by education." "Improvement of Labor Quality and Economic Growth—Japan's Postwar Experience," *Economic Development and Cultural Change,* vol. 21 (October 1972), p. 40.

The distributions we develop refer to all employed persons, not, as they should, to those employed in the business sector alone. Chiefly because teachers are employed in general government and nonprofit institutions, the percentage of persons in the highest education categories is doubtless smaller in business than in the whole economy; the percentage in the lowest education categories probably is smaller also, due in part to omission of private households. It is unlikely, however, that the time series index computed from the educational distributions would be much different if the distributions were confined to the business sector.

Distributions Based on Census Data

The 1950, 1960, and 1970 Censuses of Population distribute the total population and employed persons, fifteen years of age and over, by amount of education. Both population and employment distributions are cross-classified by sex. The 1960 and 1970 distributions of the total population are further cross-classified by age. Persons who were still in school have been eliminated from both the population and employment distributions we use.[13]

The 1950 Census classification was based on number of years of school completed. The classification was quite detailed, with separate data reported for persons with 0, 1–3, 4, 5–6, 7–8, 9, 10, 11, 12, 13, 14–15, 16, and 17 or more years of education. In table H-3, data in columns 1 and 5 appearing in rows identified by number of years of school are (with some consolidation) directly from the Census. The groupings and the descriptive labels referring to kinds of school, however, are not from the Census but represent the combinations of the data by years of school which descriptions of the school system would suggest are required for comparability with 1960 and 1970 data. However, as explained below, the 1950 data for males at the upper levels were subsequently adjusted for comparability with 1960 and 1970 (as shown in the "1950 adjusted" column).

Instead of reporting the number of years of school completed, the 1960 and 1970 Censuses reported the highest school completed.[14] For the total population 1960 data were reported for nine categories: (a) elementary

13. The 1950 employment data include employed fourteen-year-olds who were not still in school but this difference from 1960 and 1970 is immaterial because such cases must have been few.

14. Persons who did not complete a school were supposed to report the next lowest school, but in schools above the elementary level the numbers who did not complete a school after attending it for a year or more are said to be trivial. From comparison with 1950 Census data it appears that persons who attended but did not complete elementary school were classified in the elementary rather than the "no school" category despite the general instruction.

Table H-3. *Distributions of Employed Persons Fifteen Years Old and Over Who Have Completed School, by Sex and by Kind and Years of School Completed, 1950, 1960, and 1970*

Thousands

Kind of school and years completed	Males				Females		
	1950						
	Re-ported (1)	Ad-justed (2)	1960 (3)	1970 (4)	1950 (5)	1960 (6)	1970 (7)
No school	339	339	144	77	648	259	111
Elementary, junior high, youth training[a]	15,448	15,448	17,569	17,119	10,086	12,457	12,911
1–3	429	429	182	97	424	169	73
4	1,149	1,149	862	268	855	485	142
5–6	3,262	3,262	1,930	1,640	3,260	2,519	2,292
7–8	8,901	8,901	8,980	7,892	4,492	4,731	4,419
9	1,707	1,707	5,615	7,222	1,055	4,553	5,985
Middle school (old) and senior high	3,758	4,323	6,159	9,944	2,594	3,880	6,241
10–11	2,943	3,508	3,542	3,200	2,272	2,005	1,889
12	815	815	2,617	6,744	322	1,875	4,352
Junior college and college preparatory school (old)							
13–15	1,507	841	1,067	1,271	223	322	830
University and postgraduate							
16 or more	477	578	1,438	3,082	14	73	268
Total (added)	21,529	21,529	26,377	31,493	13,565	16,991	20,361

Sources: Census of Population and estimates by authors. See text for explanation.
a. Includes elementary school, high elementary school (old), junior high school, and youth training school (old).

school; (b) higher elementary school (old); (c) junior high school; (d) youth training school (old); (e) middle school (old); (f) senior high school; (g) college preparatory (higher) school (old) and junior college; (h) university, including postgraduate; and (j) never attended school.[15] Tabulations for employed persons were less detailed; they combined (b) with (c), and (e) with (f). With the further consolidation of (a) and (d) with (b) and

15. To avoid confusion we follow Census lettering. The letter "i" was used for persons still attending school, whom we have omitted. The word "old" refers to types of schools eliminated by the 1947 reorganization of the school structure.

(c), the 1960 Census data are shown in the kind-of-school rows of table H-3.[16]

The 1970 Census data are similar to those for 1960. However, at the time of estimation education data were available only for the whole population (classified by sex and age), and it was necessary to estimate 1970 distributions for employed persons of each sex. To do so, the number of employed persons of that sex in each age group in 1960 and 1970 (also obtained from the Censuses of Population) was distributed among education categories in the same proportions as the total population in that age-sex group, and the age groups were added to secure totals by education category. For each education category, the ratio to this total for 1960 of the known 1960 number of employed persons who had completed school was multiplied by the corresponding total for 1970 to secure the estimated 1970 number of employed persons who had completed school. The resulting 1970 estimates for the education groups were adjusted proportionally to agree with a control total obtained by application of a ratio for all education groups.

Detailed Distributions, and Adjustments

We next describe the derivation of the more detailed distributions for 1960 and 1970, comparable to those for 1950, which are shown in table H-3. For brevity, the 1970 estimates just described will be referred to as "reported" even though the employment data were derived from those for population; they are "reported" in the sense that the Census reported data for that education category. Unless otherwise noted, the following description refers to each sex separately.

No School

Data for this category, which consists chiefly of persons already elderly in 1950, are reported in the Census in all years.

One to Three Years

The reported 1950 number in this group was extrapolated to 1960 and 1970 by the number in the no-school group because the age distribution can be assumed to be similar. Neither category met even the pre-1908 compulsory education requirements.

16. The sum of the entries for 1–3, 4, and 5–6 years equals the Census figure for (a) elementary school.

Four Years

This category consists almost entirely of persons who completed compulsory education by 1908. If they started school at eight years of age, members of the last such class were twelve in 1908, fifty-four in 1950, sixty-four in 1960, and seventy-four in 1970. The number employed in 1950 is reported. The 1960 figure is assumed to equal 70 percent of all employed persons sixty-five and over in 1960, and the 1970 figure 70 percent of all employed persons seventy-five and over in 1970.

Five to Six Years

The 1950 figure is reported. The 1960 figure is obtained by subtracting the numbers with 1–3 and 4 years of education from the Census total for the (a) elementary school category. A 1970 figure for persons with 5–8 years was obtained by subtraction of the 1–3-, 4-, and 9-year groups from the Census aggregate for groups (a) to (d). The number of males with 5–8 years fell 12.6 percent from 1960 to 1970, the number of females 7.4 percent. The numbers with 5–6 years presumably fell somewhat more: we suppose males by 15 percent and females by 9 percent. These figures imply declines in the 7–8 year group of 12.1 percent for males and 6.6 percent for females.

Seven to Eight Years

The 1950 figure is reported. The 1960 total with 7–9 years is the sum of the Census figures for (b) higher elementary school (old), (c) junior high school, and (d) youth training school (old). Those with 7–8 years are mostly from (b) and finished their education before 1948, whereas those with 9 years are mostly from (c) and finished their education after 1948.[17] Almost all new entrants to the 7–9 category after 1950 were junior high school graduates with 9 years, whereas those leaving employment, except a certain number of young women, were overwhelmingly in the 7–8 category. The percentage of the 7–9 group who had 7–8 years of education in 1960 was estimated to be equal to the corresponding percentage in 1950 minus the percentage of employed persons in 1960 who were fifteen to twenty-four years old. The rest were allocated to the 9-year category. The 1970 figure for the 7–8 group is explained in the "5–6 years" description.

17. Youth training school graduates, a relatively small group, also finished their education before 1948; over four-fifths were thirty to forty-four years old in 1960. They may be in either the 7–8- or the 9-year groups.

Nine Years

The 1950 figure is reported. The 1960 number is explained in the "7–8 years" description. The 1970 number is equal to the 1960 number (which includes almost exclusively young people) plus the estimated number of employed persons fifteen to twenty-four years of age in 1970 who had 0–9 years of education (all of whom are presumed to have 9 years, the legal minimum).

Ten to Eleven Years and Twelve Years, 1960 and 1970

Persons shown with 10–11 years of education are those who completed the old middle school, before 1948, whereas those shown with 12 years are senior high school graduates, who graduated after 1948. It is more accurate to use type-of-school rather than number-of-years descriptions. We defer description of the 1950 estimates until the next section.

The number of senior high school graduates (not still in school) in the population in 1960 was available from the Census of Population, classified by age. Only the four five-year age groups within the range from fifteen to thirty-four contained senior high school graduates, and few of these were thirty to thirty-four. We estimated the percentage of high school graduates in each age group that was employed, multiplied by the number of high school graduates, and summed the products for the age groups to obtain the total number of employed high school graduates in 1960. The 1960 number of old middle school graduates (who appear only in age groups thirty to thirty-four and older) was obtained by subtraction.

The number of old middle school graduates in the population in 1970—all of whom were then thirty-five years old or more, but with only a small population over sixty-five—was estimated by a variant of the cohort method. The number in each age group in 1970 was multiplied by the 1960 ratio for the same cohort (i.e., for persons ten years younger) of the number of persons with a middle school education to the total population. The products were added to secure the percentage of middle school graduates in the population in 1970. The percentage change from 1960 to 1970 in the number of middle school graduates in the population was applied to the number of employed middle school graduates in 1960 to secure the number in 1970. The number of senior high school graduates in 1970 was then obtained by subtraction of middle school graduates from the combined number of middle school and senior high school graduates.

Junior College and College Preparatory School (Old), and University and Postgraduate, 1960 and 1970

Data for each of these groups in 1960 and 1970 are reported.

Middle School and Above, 1950

Above the elementary or junior high school level it is difficult to associate total number of years of school with a given level of educational attainment. Indeed, it is not customary to collect data in this form, which was used in the 1950 Japanese Census. In the United States, for example, although it is customary to say that persons who have completed 1 to 3 years of college have had 13 to 15 years of education, what is actually reported to the Census is the number who have completed the first through third years of college. Persons in this group often had more, and occasionally less, than 12 years of education prior to college and hence often attended school something other than 13 to 15 years. What is meant by this term is that they attained the level reached after 13 to 15 years by individuals who followed the typical progression each year.

We accept the total number with 10 or more years of education reported in the 1950 Japanese Census as equivalent to the total number reported in the upper three broad education groups (i.e., old middle school and above) in the 1960 and 1970 Censuses. Initially, as shown in column 1 of table H-3, we divide them in accordance with the nominal number of years required to complete each type of school: 10–11 for middle school, 12 for senior high school, 13–15 for junior college and college preparatory school (old), and 16 or more for university.

For at least two groups of males, however, the change from 1950 to 1960 that is implied is improbable. With no new middle school graduates in this decade, an increase from 2,943,000 to 3,542,000 in the 10–11 year education category is not plausible. Also, the huge drop from 1,507,000 to 1,067,000 in the junior college and college preparatory school group is inexplicable. We therefore develop 1950 estimates independent of the Census detail.

We first estimated the 1950 number of each sex in the university and postgraduate group by a variant of the cohort method, working back from the 1960 and 1970 estimates of employment by education and age which had been calculated in order to get the 1970 estimates. The 1950 number of employed university graduates in the twenty-five to thirty-four age range, for example, was estimated to differ from the number of employed university graduates thirty-five to forty-four years of age in 1960 by the same percentage that the number twenty-five to thirty-four in 1960 differed from the number thirty-five to forty-four in 1970. A similar procedure was followed for other age groups up to fifty-four (in 1950). Older age groups are estimated to account for less than one-ninth of the total. The number fifty-five to sixty-four in 1950 was assumed equal to all the male and half the female university graduates in the whole population who were sixty-five to seventy-four in 1960. The number sixty-five and over in 1950 was assumed equal to twice the number of male and all of the female university graduates in the whole population who were seventy-five and over in 1960. The numbers in the age groups were then added. A small final adjustment was required; the total was multiplied by the 1960 ratio of the Census number in the category to the sum of the estimates for the age groups that were developed for the projection to 1970 (see above, page 209).

We next estimated for 1950 the number of each sex in the junior college and college preparatory school (old) category by use of a similar procedure.[18] These cohort estimates compared with the Census figures as follows (in thousands):

	Cohort estimates		Census		
Category	Males	Females	Years	Males	Females
Junior college and college preparatory school (old)	841	331	13–15	1,507	223
University and postgraduate	578	13	16 or more	477	14

The cohort estimates yield a reasonable-appearing increase from 841,000 in 1950 to 1,067,000 in 1960 in the number of males in the junior college and college preparatory school (old) category. The 1950 estimate is below the Census number with 13–15 years of education by 666,000. The cohort estimate for the university and postgraduate group indicates that 101,000 of

18. The percentages of 1960 data used in estimating the numbers of males fifty-five to sixty-four and sixty-five and over in the university category were used for both males and females in estimating the numbers in the junior college and college preparatory school category.

this number should be transferred to the university group. The remaining 565,000 must be moved to lower education categories. The next lowest category, senior high school (12 years), cannot reasonably be increased because the number (815,000) is already surprisingly big; senior high schools were new in 1950. Instead, we increase the middle school (10–11 years) category. The number in this category now rises only 34,000 from 1950 to 1960 (from 3,508,000 to 3,542,000), much more reasonable than the initial increase of 599,000. The final 1950 estimates for males are shown in column 2 of table H-3.

The cohort estimates for females are 13,000 for university and postgraduate and 331,000 for junior college and higher professional school. These compare with Census figures of 14,000 for 16 or more years of education and 223,000 for 13–15 years. The following considerations led us to retain the Census figures. The differences are too small to affect labor input appreciably; the cohort estimates are less reliable for females than for males because employment is intermittent; and it seems unreasonable to raise the Census figure for females in the 13–15-year group while lowering the figure for males.

Detailed Distributions and Education Indexes

Table 6-1 shows percentage distributions of employed persons who were not still in school among the ten education categories for which weights were developed in table H-2 and numbers of persons in table H-3. Also shown are the approximate average number of years of education held by persons in each education category and by all employed persons of each sex. Finally, the average weight for employed persons of each sex (with the weight of persons having 8 years of education equaling 100) is calculated. Time series indexes of the average number of years of education and of the average weight are also shown.

Over the twenty years from 1950 to 1970 the average number of years of education held by employed males increased by 25 percent, the number held by females by 29 percent. Reasons for these very substantial increases are of three main types. First, among persons who ended their schooling upon completion of legal requirements, new entrants into the labor force had 9 years of education whereas those who left had 0, 4, or 6. Second, and only partially overlapping the first, the restructuring of the school system had the effect of adding a year or two to the length of education received by many persons. Students who completed high school after 12 years of education were the same type who previously had completed middle school after 10 or 11. Similarly, junior high school graduates with 9 years of education were similar to persons previously completing upper elementary school after 8 years. These were 1947 changes. Much earlier, the 3-year "primary division" of elementary school had been succeeded by the 4-year ordinary elementary school, and attendance at the latter was subsequently changed to 6 years without shortening time spent at higher schools. Third, the proportion of students who continued school beyond the compulsory attendance period rose, especially in the postwar period. This was due to expanded educational opportunities, matched by increasing desire and financial ability of students to defer entry into the full-time labor market to continue their studies. The addition of hundreds of new colleges and universities in the postwar period is especially noteworthy.

The change in average years of education cannot, of course, be used as a measure of the change in labor input. It would count an hour worked by a person with 12 years of education, for example, as three times as much labor as an hour worked by a person with 4 years of education, whereas our estimate of earnings differentials between comparable persons indicates the correct figure to be 1.42 times (122 divided by 86). An index for males constructed with the weights derived in table H-2 increased by 11.39 percent from 1950 to 1970, a similar index for females by 10.69 percent.[19] Growth rates of the index, by sex and decade, follow:

	1950–60	*1960–70*
Males	0.53	0.55
Females	0.56	0.46

To compute the annual index for the education component of labor input it was assumed that, for each sex, the percentage change in the index in each year from 1952 to 1960 was the same as the 1950–60 growth rate, and in each year from 1960 to 1971 was the same as the 1960–70 growth rate.[20]

19. These indexes, it should be noted, are computed from distributions of employment rather than from total hours worked because hour series for all employed persons classified by amount of education are lacking. However, this could scarcely affect the index unless differentials in average hours between education groups changed substantially.

20. This is probably satisfactory, because the rates are not very different in the two periods. In the United States the corresponding index has a cyclical element in its behavior (because the less educated are most subject to unemployment) which this procedure would miss, but in Japan fluctuations in unemployment have been insufficient to influence the education index much.

The percentage changes for the two sexes in each pair of years were weighted by their shares of earnings in nonresidential business in the second of the paired years (the weights are from table G-2). These percentages were then linked to secure a continuous index. The growth rate of this final index is 0.54 in 1952–60 and 0.53 in 1960–71.

Our estimate of the increase in the index from 1950 to 1960 is close to that obtained by Chung in previous research.[21] However, our index increases more than those for various postwar time spans computed by Watanabe, Watanabe and Egaizu, Kanamori, and Ohkawa and Rosovsky.[22] We believe the main reason these investigators secured smaller increases is that they worked with very broad education groups, corresponding generally to the five broad groups of table H-3. Most of the change in the distribution is eliminated by consolidation into such broad groups (one of which absorbs much more than half of all employment).

Watanabe's distributions are also higher pitched than ours, and he obtains higher estimates for average number of years of school, even though he too relies upon the Census of Population. The difference between our averages is biggest in 1950, the year in which the Census data are reported as years of school completed. (Ohkawa and Rosovsky report almost the same figures as Watanabe.) Watanabe has informed us that he narrowed the coverage of the data to persons in the prime working ages. Elimination of the oldest and youngest employed persons raises the average educational level, and this explains at least part of the difference between the averages.

The education index for Japan makes no allowance for changes in frequency of absenteeism from school or in the length of the school year and may rise too little on this account. In this respect it differs from Denison's indexes for the United States and some European countries.[23] It is likely that the content of a year's education increased over time, if only because of the

21. William K. Chung, "Study of Economic Growth in Postwar Japan for the Period of 1952–1967: An Application of Total Productivity Analysis" (Ph.D. dissertation, New School for Social Research, New York, 1971).

22. Tsunehiko Watanabe, "Improvement of Labor Quality and Economic Growth—Japan's Postwar Experience," *Economic Development and Cultural Change*, vol. 21 (October 1972), pp. 33–53; estimates by Watanabe and F. Egaizu from the Japanese language *Economic Studies Quarterly* of March 1968 are included. Hisao Kanamori, "What Accounts for Japan's High Rate of Growth?" *Review of Income and Wealth*, series 18 (June 1972), pp. 155–71, and unpublished supplementary "Explanation of Estimation." Kazushi Ohkawa and Henry Rosovsky, *Japanese Economic Growth: Trend Acceleration in the Twentieth Century* (Stanford University Press, 1973), p. 51.

23. See Denison, *Why Growth Rates Differ*, pp. 90–91, and *Accounting for Growth*, p. 46.

reduction in childhood illnesses.[24] We have been unable to obtain information that permits an adjustment to be attempted, but doubt that any appropriate adjustment would be appreciable.

24. Even from the 1959 to the 1970 fiscal year the percentage of students who missed 50 days or more of school dropped from 0.65 percent to 0.33 percent in elementary school and from 1.50 percent to 0.62 percent in junior high schools. This suggests that the decline in total absenteeism even in this recent period might have been appreciable; the decline is continuous in 1959–70, and probably had gone on for a long time. Available information indicates a decline since at least 1951–53, and also points to illness and dislike of school as the leading reasons for absenteeism. Data from Ministry of Education, *Zu de miru wagakuni kyōiku no ayumi—Kyōiku tōkei hachijū-nen-shi* [Evolution of Educational Systems in Japan Illustrated by Graphs—An 80-Year History of School Statistics] (1957), p. 56; unpublished tables for 1959–70 from Statistical Survey Division, Ministry of Education.

Information concerning changes in the scheduled length of the school term that we have uncovered refers to decrees of the Ministry of Education concerning minimum standards. For example, middle or junior high schools had to operate at least 32 weeks of 23 to 30 hours a week in 1881, more than 40 weeks in 1886, no less than 200 days with 28 to 30 hours a week in 1901, and more than 35 weeks in 1958. This information was obtained from Ministry of Education, *Gakusei hyaku-nen-shi* [A Hundred-Year History of School Systems in Japan] (1972). We have not obtained data on average actual practice.

Nonresidential Business: Estimates of Capital Stock

THIS APPENDIX describes the estimates of inventories and of structures and producers' durable goods. The data refer, in general, to the private portion of the nonresidential business sector. Assets are valued in 1965 prices. The following aspects of the coverage of the data should be noted.

1. Assets of general government and of private nonprofit organizations are omitted, as is desired.

2. Assets of government enterprises are also omitted, even though such enterprises are in the nonresidential business sector, because they receive only trivial weight in national income. Their inclusion would lower growth rates of the capital stock series, and understate the estimated contribution of capital to output growth by incorrectly applying part of the weight of private capital to these slower growing series.

3. The series for fixed capital exclude dwellings except those which are owned by firms and used to house their own employees. We were unable to eliminate the latter type of housing, but it is small relative to the capital stock aggregate.

4. Livestock are included in fixed capital and omitted from inventories.

5. The series for fixed capital exclude construction work in progress.

Inventories

For the value of inventories in constant (1965) prices we adopted the series from which the Economic Planning Agency computes the increase in stock in private enterprises. The EPA provided the value at the end of 1965

Table I-1. *Private Inventories: Accumulation and Stock, 1951–71*

Billions of 1965 yen

Calendar year	Increase in stocks (1)	Value of stocks		Index of yearly average (1965 = 100) (4)
		Year-end (2)	Yearly average (3)	
1951	n.a.	2,275.7	n.a.	n.a.
1952	297.0	2,572.7	2,424.2	25.87
1953	160.0	2,732.7	2,652.7	28.31
1954	67.5	2,800.2	2,766.5	29.52
1955	344.9	3,145.1	2,972.6	31.72
1956	415.8	3,560.9	3,353.0	35.78
1957	674.0	4,234.9	3,897.9	41.59
1958	228.5	4,463.4	4,349.1	46.41
1959	393.5	4,856.9	4,660.1	49.72
1960	505.7	5,362.6	5,109.8	54.52
1961	1,367.4	6,730.0	6,046.3	64.52
1962	410.9	7,140.9	6,935.4	74.00
1963	895.8	8,036.7	7,588.8	80.97
1964	1,023.4	9,060.1	8,548.4	91.21
1965	623.3	9,683.4	9,371.8	100.00
1966	813.1	10,496.5	10,090.0	107.66
1967	1,847.1	12,343.6	11,420.0	121.85
1968	1,943.6	14,287.2	13,315.4	142.08
1969	1,952.8	16,240.0	15,263.6	162.87
1970	2,946.7	19,186.7	17,713.4	189.01
1971	1,689.8	20,876.5	20,031.6	213.74

Sources: Column 1, Economic Planning Agency, *Revised Report on National Income Statistics, 1951–1967*, pp. 82–83, and *Annual Report on National Income Statistics, 1973*, pp. 58–59. Column 2, year-end 1965 from EPA worksheets; other years cumulated from column 1. Column 3, average of prior-year and current-year figures from column 2. Column 4, computed from column 3. n.a. Not available.

from its worksheets, and we reconstructed the complete series by cumulating the published annual changes. Table I-1 displays all the data.

Fixed Capital Stock

The EPA maintains quarterly series of the gross capital stock of private enterprises, and of gross fixed capital formation and retirements. The series are prepared on two bases: with construction work in progress included, and with it excluded. We have used, and in columns 1, 4, and 5 of table I-2 show annual data from, the series excluding construction work in progress. The estimates are expressed in 1965 prices.

Table I-2. *Fixed Capital Stock of Private Enterprises[a] and Related Series, 1951–71*
Billions of 1965 yen

Calendar year	Gross stock			Gross fixed capital formation (4)	Retirements (5)	Depreciation (6)	Net stock			
	Year-end (1)	Yearly average (2)	Index of yearly average (1965 = 100) (3)				Year-end (7)	Yearly average (8)	Index of yearly average (1965 = 100) (9)	Index of capital input (1965 = 100) (10)
1951	16,850b	n.a.	n.a.	n.a.	n.a.	n.a.	8,166	n.a.	n.a.	n.a.
1952	17,229	17,018	39.83	872b	470b	439	8,600	8,383	35.17	38.66
1953	17,720	17,474	40.90	964	474	544	9,020	8,810	36.97	39.92
1954	18,485	18,103	42.37	1,243	478	713	9,550	9,285	38.96	41.52
1955	19,131	18,808	44.02	1,117	471	804	9,863	9,707	40.73	43.20
1956	19,946	19,538	45.73	1,308	494	856	10,315	10,089	42.33	44.88
1957	21,214	20,580	48.16	1,697	429	884	11,128	10,722	44.99	47.37
1958	22,609	21,912	51.27	1,830	434	976	11,982	11,555	48.49	50.58
1959	24,179	23,394	54.75	2,082	512	1,133	12,931	12,457	52.27	54.13
1960	26,425	25,302	59.21	2,782	537	1,360	14,353	13,642	57.24	58.72
1961	29,309	27,867	65.22	3,659	775	1,694	16,317	15,335	64.34	65.00
1962	32,875	31,092	72.76	4,248	681	2,020	18,544	17,431	73.14	72.86
1963	36,622	34,749	81.32	4,616	869	2,418	20,743	19,644	82.42	81.60
1964	40,634	38,628	90.40	5,076	1,064	2,959	22,860	21,801	91.48	90.67

1965	44,825	42,729	100.00	5,245	1,055	3,299	24,806	23,833	100.00	100.00
1966	49,069	46,947	109.86	5,580	1,336	3,753	26,634	25,720	107.92	109.38
1967	54,578	51,823	121.28	6,820	1,310	4,222	29,232	27,933	117.20	120.26
1968	61,512	58,045	135.84	8,426	1,492	5,088	32,570	30,901	129.66	134.30
1969	69,694	65,603	153.53	10,262	2,080	6,060	36,772	34,671	145.47	151.52
1970	79,718	74,706	174.84	12,176	2,152	6,918	42,030	39,401	165.32	172.46
1971	89,885	84,802	198.46	12,533	2,366	7,682	46,880	44,455	186.53	195.48

Sources: Columns 1, 4, and 5, from Economic Planning Agency, "Minkan kigyō sōshihon sutokku no suikei" [Estimates of Gross Capital Stock of Private Enterprises: Quarterly Data for the Period June 1952–September 1972] (February 1973; processed). Columns 2 and 8, average of prior-year and current-year figures from columns 1 and 7, respectively. Columns 3 and 9, computed from columns 2 and 8. Column 6, EPA current price series for "provisions for the consumption of fixed capital" less "depreciation allowances: dwellings" less "depreciation allowances, enterprises, government" deflated by implicit deflator for "gross domestic fixed capital formation, by private, others"; data from *Revised Report on National Income Statistics, 1951–1967*, pp. 60–61, 86–87, and 258–59, and *Annual Report on National Income Statistics, 1973*, pp. 36–37, 62–63, and 240–41. Column 7, see text for 1955; other years cumulated from 1955; annual change equals column 4 minus column 6. Column 10, weighted average of column 3, weighted 3, and column 9, weighted 1.

n.a. Not available.

a. Construction work in progress is excluded; see text for full description of coverage.

b. Estimate; EPA series begins April 1, 1952.

The EPA gross stock series is obtained by the perpetual inventory method modified by the establishment of an independent benchmark at the end of 1955 and a special method of estimating retirements. Except in agriculture, forestry, and fisheries, the EPA obtained for each industry division a benchmark net stock value at the end of 1955, in 1955 prices, from the 1955 National Wealth Survey. A special sample of 7 percent of the schedules from the same survey provided gross–net ratios for corporations which were applied to the net stock estimates to secure corporate gross stock. (The 1960 National Wealth Survey was used for unincorporated enterprises.) Indexes of asset prices prepared by the EPA were used to convert the estimates from 1955 prices to, first, 1960 and, subsequently, 1965 prices. For agriculture, forestry, and fisheries, the EPA obtained gross stock by adjustment of estimates made by the Agricultural Policy Research Committee.

The gross capital formation series is the same as that which enters the Japanese estimates of gross national product except that the net increase in construction work in progress was deleted. Retirements ("removed" assets in the Japanese translation into English) by corporations are based on changes between national wealth surveys and ratios from the Corporation Enterprise Survey. Retirements by unincorporated enterprises are assumed to be matched by acquisitions of used assets from corporations and hence are omitted. The change in gross stock each year equals gross capital formation less retirements (table I-2, columns 4 and 5).[1]

The EPA does not provide a net stock series. To secure the series shown in table I-2, column 7, it was first necessary to establish the 1955 year-end benchmark. In each industry division the 1955 corporate ratio of net stock to gross stock in current prices was multiplied by the gross capital stock (including unincorporated enterprises) in 1960 prices to obtain net stock in 1960 prices. Except for the net–gross ratio in agriculture, forestry, and fisheries, all data are from the EPA.[2] For the year-end ratio of net stock to gross stock in agriculture, forestry, and fisheries, we used data valued in 1934–36 prices from Ohkawa and others.[3] (We excluded their data for planted forest in the forestry industry.) Industry data were combined, and the all-industry ratio of net stock to gross stock in 1960 prices was calculated.

1. This description is based mainly on Economic Planning Agency, Economic Research Institute, *Estimation of Gross Fixed Capital Stock of Private Enterprises, 1952–1964* (1967).

2. Ibid., pp. 4, 10.

3. Kazushi Ohkawa, Shigeru Ishiwata, Saburo Yamada, and Hiromitsu Ishi, "Capital Stock," vol. 3, of Kazushi Ohkawa, Miyohei Shinohara, and Mataji Umemura, eds., *Estimates of Long-Term Economic Statistics of Japan since 1868* (Tokyo: Tōyō keizai shinpō sha, 1966), pp. 153, 159.

This ratio was multiplied by the EPA estimate of gross stock at the end of 1955 in 1965 prices to secure net stock at the end of 1955 in 1965 prices. The change in net stock each year is equal to gross capital formation less capital consumption allowances. The capital consumption allowance series was described in appendix C. (See also the sources to table I-2, column 6.)

Because of their complex derivation, it is not possible to describe the capital stock series as conforming to a particular set of assumptions as to length of service lives or patterns of depreciation or discarding. However, it may be observed that annual retirements have stayed in the range of 2 to a little over 3 percent of gross stock on January 1, with little or no trend in the percentage. Depreciation, on the other hand, has risen persistently from about 3 percent of the January 1 value of the gross stock in 1952–53 to nearly 10 percent in 1969–71. If depreciation were computed by the straight-line formula (as in data for other countries with which comparisons are made), these percentages would imply that the average service life of capital goods in the gross stock fell from over thirty years to little more than ten. A decline has been observed in most countries as producers' durables became more important relative to longer-lived structures, but this drop seems too big. The implied service life at the start of the period seems too long, that at the end of the period too short, but we had no basis for altering the depreciation series.

The net stock, as estimated, grew faster than the gross stock from 1952 to 1963, when the net–gross ratio peaked at 0.565 (0.580 in industries other than agriculture, forestry, and fisheries), then grew less fast from 1963 to 1971. Over the whole period from 1952 or 1953 to 1971 the net stock grew moderately more.

The index of input of fixed capital is a weighted average of the indexes of gross and net stock, with the gross stock assigned three-fourths of the weight. With this weighting the index is not very different from the index of gross stock alone, and not very sensitive to plausible errors in depreciation or inconsistencies between depreciation and the other series.

Gains from Reduced
Misallocation of Resources

THIS APPENDIX describes the statistical derivation of the indexes of gains from reallocation of resources shown in columns 2, 3, and 4 of table 4-5. Procedures are quite similar to those used for other countries in *Why Growth Rates Differ* and *Accounting for Growth,* so their rationale will not be developed here.

Part One: Gains from the Reallocation of Labor from Agriculture

Estimation of the gains in output per unit of input from the reallocation of labor from agriculture followed closely the procedure adopted for the United States. This required that labor input in nonresidential business be divided between agricultural and nonagricultural industries. To do this, total labor input in the sector, taken as 100 percent, was first divided by sex, based on table G-2, columns 3 and 4. The annual labor input percentage for each sex was then divided between part-time workers and full-time workers in proportion to the total number of hours worked by part-time and full-time workers of that sex. (In this and subsequent steps data from tables F-1, F-2, and F-3 were utilized.) The percentage for part-time workers was divided between agricultural and nonagricultural industries in the same proportion as total hours worked by part-time workers, while the percentage for full-time workers was divided between agricultural and nonagricultural industries in proportion to the numbers of full-time workers.[1] The components were

---

1. This procedure is consistent with our measurement of the effects on labor input of changes in hours, especially the convention that differences in hours between otherwise similar full-time agricultural and nonagricultural workers do not imply differences in labor input.

then combined so as to obtain a preliminary division of the labor input provided by each sex between agriculture and nonagriculture.

A final adjustment for education and age differences was made by applying a constant adjustment ratio in all years. From the 1960 Census of Population, distributions by level of education of agricultural workers and of nonagricultural workers (excluding those in the education and public administration industries) were obtained. When the education weights of table H-2 were applied, the education index for agricultural workers was found to be 91.5 percent of the index for nonagricultural workers in the case of males, and 93.8 percent in the case of females. On the other hand, application of age weights to age distributions for each sex yielded (for the year 1970) weights that were higher in agriculture than in nonagricultural industries by 1.5 percent in the case of males and by 0.6 percent in the case of females—chiefly because there are few young persons in agriculture. Combination of the educational and age adjustments indicated that the ratio of labor input in agriculture to that in nonagricultural industries should be lowered by 7.1 percent for males and 6.2 percent for females to allow for differences in education and age. After this was done, the agricultural shares for the two sexes were combined.

The final estimates of the agricultural share of labor input in nonresidential business are shown in table J-1, column 2. Incomparabilities in the hours series, handled by overlapping estimates, carry over into this series, as indicated by a footnote to the table.[2] The agricultural share of employment is shown in column 1. Chiefly because of the high proportion of females employed in agriculture and the relatively low education of agricultural workers, agriculture's share of labor input is considerably below its share of employment, even though the new Labor Force Survey series for agricultural employment that we use, which is confined to individuals primarily engaged in agriculture and counts people only in weeks during which they are actually employed, is about the lowest such series available.[3]

2. Labor input is based on employment data adjusted to provide continuous series, so the incomparabilities stem from the division of employment between full-time and part-time workers, and the average hours of each of the groups.

3. The 1967 change in procedures reduced agricultural employment previously reported in the Labor Force Survey itself by about one million persons. Also, the 8,242,000 employed in agriculture in 1970 according to the new Labor Force Survey compare with 14,094,800 with some attachment to agriculture according to data from the Survey of Employment of Farm Household Members. That source shows 8,946,400 persons engaged mainly in farming, 1,971,900 engaged in agriculture though mainly in keeping house or other activities except gainful employment, 2,340,500 engaged in agriculture though mainly in other jobs, and 836,000 engaged in agriculture though mainly in self-employment.

Table J-1. *Nonresidential Business: Agricultural Shares of Employment, Labor Input, and National Income in 1965 Prices, 1952–71*

Percentage of total nonresidential business

Calendar year	Employment (1)	Labor input (2)	National income in constant (1965) prices (3)
1952	39.20	32.76	20.96
1953	38.66	31.85	20.33
1954	37.27	30.98[a]	21.47
1955	37.11	30.59[a]	24.52
1956	35.33	28.80	20.94
1957	33.21	27.06	19.16
1958	31.83	25.67	18.98
1959	30.06	23.75	19.20
1960	29.05	22.83	15.90
1961	28.11	22.10	14.14
1962	27.01	21.13	12.92
1963	25.36	19.50	11.01
1964	24.08	18.36	10.19
1965	22.68	17.07	9.77
1966	21.38	16.10	9.18
1967	20.38	16.14[a]	8.97
1968	19.59	15.34	7.96
1969	18.84	14.85	6.78
1970	17.50	13.81	5.67
1971	15.92	12.51	4.82

Sources: Column 1, computed from table 3-4; column 2, see text; column 3, computed from table 3-3.

a. Percentages shown are comparable to those for the following year. Percentages comparable to those shown in the table for the preceding year are: 1954, 31.08; 1955, 30.45; 1967, 15.39.

The method adopted to calculate gains from reallocation uses the agricultural percentages of constant-dollar national income and of labor input shown in table J-1. A calculation is made for each year of the percentage by which national income in constant prices (and consequently output per unit of input) originating in the nonresidential business sector would have been raised if labor input in the sector had been distributed between agricultural and nonagricultural use in the following year's proportion. Two estimates are required. First, it is estimated that if labor input used in farming in any year had been smaller by 1 percent, agricultural output would have been smaller by 0.25 percent. The selected ratio, one-quarter, is much below the labor share in agriculture (0.65 to 0.75) because labor could be withdrawn from many farms with little loss of output (and it was, of course, from such farms that it predominantly was drawn). The second estimate is that if labor input in nonagricultural nonresidential business had been larger by 1 percent, non-agricultural output would have been larger by a fraction of 1 percent equal to the labor share in that subsector (0.72 to 0.82 percent, depending on the year). Appendix E describes the income share estimates. No allowance is made for any change in output resulting from a shift in the distribution of capital and land.

The procedure may be illustrated by the following calculation, which yields my estimate that the shift of resources from agricultural to nonagricultural use raised sector national income by 0.78 percent from 1963 to 1964:

	Agri- culture (1)	Nonagri- culture (2)	Nonresidential business sector (columns 1 + 2) (3)
1. Percentage of national income in 1965 prices, 1963	11.01	88.99	100.00
2. Percentage of labor input, 1963	19.50	80.50	100.00
3. Percentage of labor input, 1964	18.36	81.64	100.00
4. Change, row 3 − row 2	−1.14	1.14	0.00
5. Percentage change in 1963 labor input if distribution had been that of 1964, row 4 ÷ row 2	−5.85	1.42	. . .
6. Assumed ratio of percentage change in output to percentage change in labor input, 1963 (see text)	0.25	0.7465	. . .
7. Percentage change in 1963 agricultural or nonagricultural national income with 1964 labor distribution (row 5 × row 6)	−1.46	1.06	. . .
8. Percentage change in 1963 national income in sector (row 1 × row 7)	−0.16	0.94	0.78

Similar calculations were made for each pair of years, and the percentage changes were linked to secure the continuous index shown in table 4-5, column 2.

It will be noted that the data for agriculture include agricultural services, because they could not be eliminated, but this industry appears to be of trivial importance in Japan. Forestry and fisheries are classified in the nonagricultural sector. Even though their relative importance, like that of agriculture, has declined sharply, we do not think this gave rise to reallocation gains. Resources used in these industries do not appear to have had particularly low earnings nor is there evidence of underutilization of labor.

Part Two: Gains from the Reallocation of Labor from Nonfarm Self-Employment

Labor input in nonagricultural nonresidential business was first divided between wage and salary workers, on the one hand, and nonfarm self-employed and unpaid family workers, on the other. The procedure was the same as that used to divide labor input in the business sector between agricultural and nonagricultural industries except that the final adjustment for education and age differences was not made. Table J-2 compares the employment and labor input percentages.

We suppose that the decline in the proportion of self-employed and unpaid family workers occurred among those with the lowest value of output and least efficiently utilized. Usually, this means persons in proprietorships with no paid employees. We assume that an increase of only one wage and salary worker—or, more exactly, one unit of labor input—was required to offset the loss of four units of labor by self-employed and unpaid family workers. (Much of the lost work could be absorbed by the remaining self-employed and unpaid family workers.)

The calculation of the percentage gain in nonresidential business output in 1964 will illustrate the procedure. The self-employment share of nonagricultural nonresidential business labor input dropped 0.49 percentage points from 1963 to 1964 and the saving in labor was 75 percent of this, or 0.368 percentage points. Multiplication by the 1963 labor share in nonagricultural nonresidential business, 0.7465, yields 0.275 percent as the amount by which 1963 nonagricultural business national income would have been raised if the 1964 labor input distribution had prevailed. Multiplication by 0.8899, the ratio of nonagricultural to total nonresidential business national income in 1963 (measured in 1965 prices), yields 0.245 percent as the estimated

Table J-2. *Nonagricultural Nonresidential Business: Shares of Self-Employed and Unpaid Family Workers in Employment and Labor Input, 1952–71*

Percentage of total nonagricultural nonresidential business

Calendar year	Employment (1)	Labor input (2)
1952	38.67	33.98
1953	39.79	34.67
1954	40.13	34.87[a]
1955	39.54	34.15[a]
1956	37.59	32.29
1957	36.05	31.09
1958	33.64	28.99
1959	32.55	28.05
1960	31.35	26.91
1961	29.91	25.87
1962	28.08	24.40
1963	27.72	24.07
1964	27.19	23.58
1965	26.29	22.60
1966	25.63	22.00
1967	25.90	22.29[a]
1968	25.80	22.55
1969	25.75	22.55
1970	25.07	22.03
1971	24.36	21.29

Sources: Column 1, computed from table 3-4; column 2, see text.

a. Percentages shown are comparable to those for the following year. Percentages comparable to those shown in the table for the preceding year are: 1954, 34.78; 1955, 34.16; 1967, 22.46.

gain in sectoral national income from the reallocation of nonagricultural labor from self-employment to wage and salary employment.

Similar calculations were made for each year. The percentage changes were linked to secure the index in table 4-5, column 3.

Part Three: Comments on the Size of Gains from the Reallocation of Labor

Professors Kazushi Ohkawa and Tsunehiko Watanabe are among the most experienced and respected observers of Japanese growth. When they first saw our sources-of-growth estimates for Japan their reactions were the same. Both found the estimates reasonable and consistent with those for other countries except that the contribution made by the reallocation of labor was smaller than they had anticipated. The exception naturally disturbed us and led to a review of procedures, but we did not find reason to alter our estimate. It seems to us no more likely to be too low than too high, and it seems improbable that it can be a great deal too low. For other readers whose reaction may be similar to that of Ohkawa and Watanabe we offer the following observations.

1. Our classification must be kept in mind. Our estimate of 0.94 percentage points as the contribution to growth of national income in the whole economy in 1953–71 refers to the contribution that the shift of labor from agriculture and nonfarm self-employment (including unpaid family workers) would have made if the economy operated with constant returns to scale. We estimate that economies of scale contributed 1.94 percentage points, part of which stemmed from the growth of production and markets that was made possible by labor reallocation. If the contribution of scale economies is distributed among other determinants in proportion to the size of their contributions, the contribution of labor reallocation in the economy as a whole is raised from 0.94 percentage points to 1.21 points, and in nonresidential business from 1.14 to 1.49 points.[4]

The shift of labor also affects other determinants. In chapter 7 it is stressed that demand for business investment was stimulated by fast expansion of output for all reasons, including reallocation of labor. Availability of a labor reserve in traditional types of employment may also have strengthened investment by holding down wages and raising the rate of return. On the other hand, in chapter 6 it is pointed out that the decline in farm employment adversely affected labor force participation rates.

2. As explained earlier, our estimates assume that (a) each 1 percent reduction in labor input in farming reduced farm output by one-fourth of 1 percent; and (b) each reduction of four units of labor input by self-employed persons in nonagricultural industries required the addition of one unit by wage and salary workers to offset the production loss. Substitution of the extreme assumptions that neither in farming nor in nonfarm self-employment did the reduction of employment involve any loss of production at all would raise the estimated contribution of labor reallocation in 1953–71 from 0.94 to 1.19 percentage points. Though appreciable, this increase would be insufficient to alter significantly our interpretation of Japanese growth.

3. The expectation of a larger contribution than we show results in part

4. A classification that eliminates economies of scale as a separate growth source, based on the procedure described, was introduced (in addition to the classification followed here) in Denison, *Accounting for Growth*. There is some question about the applicability of the procedure to the Japanese estimates without some adjustment because economies of scale "associated with income elasticity" are related to per capita consumption rather than total output.

from the belief that the shift of labor from agriculture and nonfarm self-employment to nonfarm wage and salary employment was far more important in Japan than it was in Western countries during the periods studied. The shift was, indeed, bigger in Japan, but the prevailing impression of the extent to which this was so may be exaggerated.

From 1953 to 1971 (according to data in table 3-4) nonagricultural wage and salary employment increased from 41.9 percent of total employment to 66.6 percent in Japan, so on the average 1.37 percent of employment shifted each year from agricultural or self-employed status to nonfarm wage and salary status. The first column of the table below shows similar figures for the annual change in the Western countries during the periods studied.[5] The shift was not greatly larger in Japan than in Italy, West Germany, or France. In all but the three lowest of the ten Western countries the shift was in the range from 57 to 88 percent of the Japanese figure.

Country and period	Average annual increase in nonagricultural wage-salary percentage (percentage points) (1)	Contribution of labor force shift to growth rate (percentage points) (2)	Ratio of (2) to (1) (3)
Japan, 1953–71	1.37	0.94	0.69
Italy, 1950–62	1.21	1.26	1.04
West Germany, 1950–62	1.13	0.81	0.72
France, 1950–62	1.00	0.88	0.95
Canada, 1950–67	0.93	0.64	0.69
Denmark, 1950–62	0.89	0.66	0.74
Norway, 1950–62	0.82	0.77	0.94
Netherlands, 1950–62	0.78	0.47	0.60
Belgium, 1950–62	0.56	0.35	0.63
United States, 1948–69	0.53	0.36	0.68
United Kingdom, 1950–62	0.17	0.10	0.59

As column 3 indicates, it is true that the contribution in Japan is estimated to have been smaller relative to the employment shift than it was in Italy, France, or Norway—though bigger than in some of the other countries and not much below the average of all the countries. There are various reasons

5. The armed forces are included in nonfarm wage and salary employment. Data for the United States are from *Accounting for Growth*, p. 165; for the European countries, from *Why Growth Rates Differ*, pp. 46, 48, and 356; and for Canada, from Organisation for Economic Co-operation and Development, *Manpower Statistics, 1950–62, 1954–64, 1959–70,* and *1961–72.* Adjustments for comparability were made where necessary.

for differences in these ratios, two of which are especially pertinent here. First, the higher the ratio of output per worker in farming to output per worker in nonfarm industries, the lower tends to be the contribution. The ratio in Japan was above those for the next three countries in the table though much below those for Belgium, the Netherlands, and the United Kingdom. Second, it was estimated that in Italy the gains from consolidating fragmented farms and plots were so great that the reduction in farm labor had *no* adverse effect on farm output. This judgment is chiefly responsible for the estimate that the contribution in Italy was especially large relative to the size of the employment shift.

4. An estimate in whose preparation Watanabe participated seems actually to be no larger than ours. Watanabe and Egaizu confined their estimate of reallocation gains to the contribution of the shift of employment out of agriculture. They put it at 0.64 percentage points (out of an output growth rate of 10.54 percent) in the 1952–61 period.[6] Our estimate of the contribution of the shift from agriculture is 0.67 points for 1953–61 (table 4-6) and would be 0.66 points for 1952–61, almost the same as theirs.[7] We estimate that the shift from nonagricultural self-employment contributed an additional 0.33 percentage points in 1952–61 (and 0.41 points in 1953–61, as shown in table 4-6).

5. Ohkawa and Rosovsky also estimated the contribution of the shift from agriculture. Their estimate is larger than ours. We believe the main reasons are use of different data rather than different procedures. They include our use of the new employment series from the Labor Force Survey, which was not available when their study was made, and the Economic Planning Agency's change from 1960 to 1965 as the base year for deflation of output.

A precise comparison of the estimates of contributions eludes us because Ohkawa and Rosovsky used moving averages, but if we ignore this difficulty we obtain the following comparisons. Ohkawa and Rosovsky put gains from the movement of labor out of agriculture at 0.76 percentage points in 1952–55, 1.46 points in 1955–61, and 1.07 points in 1961–65.[8] This averages 1.24

6. Tsunehiko Watanabe and F. Egaizu, "Gijutsu shinpo to keizai seichō" [Technological Advance and Economic Growth], in Motoo Kaji, ed., *Keizai seichō to shigen bunpai* [Economic Growth and Resource Allocation] (Iwanami Shoten, 1967), p. 130.

7. However, their procedure seems not to allow for gains in productivity within agriculture as a result of reducing agricultural employment. This is evidently offset by some of the same factors, described under point 5, that give Ohkawa and Rosovsky a higher estimate than we obtain.

8. Kazushi Ohkawa and Henry Rosovsky, *Japanese Economic Growth: Trend Acceleration in the Twentieth Century* (Stanford University Press, 1973), p. 116.

points from 1952 to 1965. They do not estimate gains from the shift out of nonfarm self-employment, but recognize the presence of such gains and indicate they were similar in character to the shift from agriculture.[9] Our estimates for 1952–65 are about 0.70 percentage points for the shift from agriculture and 0.35 points for the shift from nonagricultural employment—or, if an allocated portion of gains from economies of scale is included, 0.90 and 0.45 points, respectively, for a total of 1.35. The effects of reducing the percentage of employed persons engaged as self-employed and unpaid family workers in forestry and fishing is included in their figure for the shift from agriculture and in ours for the shift from nonfarm self-employment.

Part of the difference between the estimates of the contribution of the shift from agriculture derives from the fact that their data show a bigger shift. Their employment series shows the share of agriculture, forestry, and fisheries declining by 19.7 percentage points, from 45.2 percent in 1952 to 25.5 percent in 1965.[10] Our series (table 3-4) shows the share of agriculture declining by only 15.1 percentage points, from 36.0 percent in 1952 to 20.9 percent in 1965.[11] As noted earlier, our series for agriculture is the new, adjusted series from the Labor Force Survey (see page 159 above). Our use of labor input in effect cuts the reallocation by another 5 percent, from 15.1 percentage points to 14.3–23 percent less than the drop of 19.7 percentage points used by Ohkawa and Rosovsky.

Even more important is that we have a much smaller differential than they between agricultural and nonagricultural industries in the value of output per unit of labor. This is partly because of our reliance on labor input rather than employment. By our estimates, as can be calculated from table J-1, in 1961 (for example) constant-price national income per unit of labor input was 55.6 percent as large in agriculture as in nonagricultural nonresidential business, whereas national income per person employed was only 42.1 percent as large. The Ohkawa-Rosovsky estimates for 1961 imply that in 1960 prices net domestic product per person employed was only 17.0 percent as large in agriculture, forestry, and fisheries as in private nonagricultural industries (a more comprehensive series than our nonagricultural business).[12] This would be raised, perhaps to 23.5 percent, if their output series, like ours, were

9. Ibid., p. 117.

10. Ibid., p. 311.

11. Of the difference of 4.6 percentage points in this decline, nearly one-half, 2.2 points, is in the movement from 1952 to 1953, which does not affect our sources of growth tables. As indicated on page 158 above, we regard changes in employment from 1952 to 1953 as highly uncertain.

12. Calculated from Ohkawa and Rosovsky, *Japanese Economic Growth*, pp. 285, 311.

measured in 1965 rather than 1960 prices.[13] The difference in base years for deflation is a legitimate reason for the Ohkawa-Rosovsky ratio to be lower than ours and their estimate of the contribution to be larger; the shift from agriculture actually did contribute more to growth measured in 1960 prices than in 1965 prices. Another legitimate difference is introduced by their measurement of output at market prices. A shift to use of factor cost weights might raise their figure another 15.3 percent to 27.1.[14] The remaining difference, between 27.1 percent and 42.1 percent, presumably flows in large part from the use by Ohkawa and Rosovsky of a farm employment estimate that is much bigger than ours.

We believe our use of labor input to be an improvement, and as nearly as we can judge so is our use of the new series for agricultural employment.

The two estimates of the contribution of the shift from agriculture (before separate allowance for economies of scale) differ only moderately with respect to assumed elasticities of output, and such differences as are present would tend to make our estimate the larger. Both estimates assume that in nonfarm industries the ratio of the percentage increase in output to that in the amount of labor used was equal to the labor share, but the Ohkawa-Rosovsky figure refers to gross output and thus, properly, their ratio is lower than ours, which refers to net output. We assume that in agriculture the ratio of the percentage decline in output to the percentage decline in labor is 0.25 whereas Ohkawa and Rosovsky use 0.355 in 1952–55 and 0.43 in 1955–61 and presumably also in 1961–65, although this is not stated. Our lower ratio would, in itself, tend to give us the larger estimated contribution from the shift. Their estimate that the contribution in 1952–65 was 1.24 percentage points would be raised by 0.14 points, or one-ninth, if they were to substitute our assumption as to the elasticity in agriculture for theirs.

Part Four: Gains from the Reduction of International Trade Barriers

This series (table 4-5, column 4) is described in chapter 9, pages 89–90.

13. According to tables 3-2 and 3-3 above, in the year 1960 national income originating in agriculture was equal to 13.67 percent of national income originating in nonresidential business when output is measured in 1960 prices and 18.91 percent—some 38.3 percent more—when output is measured in 1965 prices. The figure, 23.5 percent, given above equals 17.0 percent raised by 38.3 percent.

14. The 1961 ratio of constant-price output in agriculture to constant-price output in nonagricultural nonresidential business calculated from our table C-3 is 0.1429, 15.3 percent more than the ratio computed from table 3-3 (0.1648).

Irregular Fluctuations in Output per Unit of Input Caused by Weather and Labor Disputes

THE EFFECT on output per unit of input in the nonresidential business sector of irregular fluctuations in farm output and of labor disputes is the subject of this appendix. The statistical series are shown in table 4-5. A third irregular factor, fluctuations in intensity of demand, is discussed in appendix M.

Part One: Irregular Fluctuations in Farm Output

Irregular fluctuations in agricultural national income are mainly attributable to weather, pest infestations, and other natural conditions. The series shown in table 4-5, column 5, measures their estimated effect on nonresidential business national income. This index is the ratio of the index of actual nonresidential business national income in 1965 prices (table 4-4, column 1) to the index of a series for nonresidential business national income in which the five-year moving average of agricultural national income (taken as a rough approximation of "normal") is substituted for actual agricultural national income (table 3-3, column 8).[1]

1. Estimates of actual national income in 1950, 1951, 1972, and 1973, required for computation of moving averages at the beginning and end of the period, are approximations.

Because the index is expressed with 1965 equaling 100, an index value above 100 means that conditions for agriculture were more favorable than in 1965 (not more favorable than in an average year), while a value below 100 means conditions were less favorable than in 1965. Conditions in 1965 were moderately below average.

As time passed the importance of agriculture fell and the effect of equal fluctuations in farm output on nonresidential business national income dwindled. Even so, fluctuations remained appreciable even at the end of the period. The biggest deviation of actual from normal agricultural output occurred in 1955, and the effect on nonresidential business national income was much bigger in 1955 than in any other year. From 1953 to 1955 this determinant increased the sector's national income by 4.8 percent.

The five-year moving average of agricultural production rises until 1960—sharply up to 1957, slightly from 1957 to 1960. It then slides downward until 1964, moves up to a new peak in 1968, and slips again until the end of the period. If viewed more broadly the series could be regarded as rising sharply until 1957 and then remaining essentially stable.

Part Two: Work Stoppages Caused by Labor Disputes

In Japan so little time has been lost from work as a result of labor disputes that not much effort need be devoted to estimation of the effects of disputes on output per unit of input. We simply adopt the procedure used for the United States in Denison, *Accounting for Growth*.[2] This procedure assumes that output per unit of input in nonresidential business is reduced by a percentage three-tenths as large as the percentage that time lost by persons in establishments involved in labor disputes represents of the sum of the time available (worked and not worked).[3]

For man-years worked in nonresidential business we use our employment series from table 3-4, column 3. For man-years not worked we divide by 300 the series for working days lost which is prepared by the Japanese Ministry of Labor.[4]

2. See pp. 65–66 and 291–94.
3. For the United States, a special adjustment was made for strikes with exceptionally large secondary effects. We are aware of no strikes in Japan which would necessitate such an adjustment.
4. Ministry of Labor, Minister's Secretariat, Statistics and Information Department, *Year Book of Labor Statistics, 1971* (1972), p. 330, and earlier publications. The series covers only participants in labor disputes, hence may be slightly narrower in scope than the Bureau of Labor Statistics series for the United States, which covers all persons employed in establishments involved in labor disputes who are idled by the dispute.

Fluctuations in the series are trivial and do not affect growth analysis except perhaps short-period analysis involving the year 1952. In that year work stoppages in mining yielded a much larger aggregate for time lost than was experienced in any subsequent year, but time lost was still only 0.15 percent of available time. This compares with 0.04 percent in the base year 1965.

Nonresidential Business: Gains from Economies of Scale

GAINS FROM economies of scale were estimated in two parts, corresponding to columns 8 and 9 of table 4-5. The first, gains from economies of scale with output measured in U.S. prices, is sufficiently described in chapter 10. The second, gains from economies of scale associated with income elasticities, needs further elaboration.[1]

The starting point for this series was the estimate that in 1967 per capita consumption in Japan was 33.0 percent of per capita consumption in the United States when consumption in both countries was valued in Japanese prices, and 47.8 percent of the United States when consumption in both countries was valued in U.S. prices.[2] The relationship between the two figures is close to that implied by a regression obtained from comparisons of eight European countries with the United States in 1950, and supported by other comparisons. That regression states that

$$\log y = 0.5871 + 0.7096 \log x$$

when x and y represent per capita consumption in a lower consumption

1. A much fuller explanation of the procedure as applied to European countries appears in Denison, *Why Growth Rates Differ*, pp. 235–51.

2. The source of the estimate (which refers to consumption as defined in the standardized system of national accounts) is the preliminary version of Irving B. Kravis and others, *A System of International Comparisons of Gross Product and Purchasing Power*, United Nations International Comparison Project: Phase One (Johns Hopkins University Press for the World Bank, 1975). The final estimates of the project (ibid., p. 181) were 32.6 and 47.5, too close to the preliminary results to warrant recalculation of our series. This source also provides estimates for 1970. Use of the 1967 estimates was preferred because that year is closer to the base year for deflation of Japanese output, 1965. The 1967 estimates also fit better the European pattern described in the text.

country expressed as a percentage of per capita consumption in a higher consumption country, based on price weights of the lower consumption country and the higher consumption country, respectively. When x equals 33.0, the 1967 figure for Japan, the regression yields 46.2 as the value of y; this is not far from the actual figure of 47.8.

A time series index of U.S. per capita consumption, measured in U.S. prices of 1958, was calculated with 1965 equaling 100. An index for Japan, also with per capita consumption in the United States in 1965 equal to 100, was secured by starting in 1967 with 33.0 percent of the U.S. figure for 1967, and extrapolating by Japanese per capita consumption measured in Japanese prices of 1965. The ratio of the second index to the first provided annual estimates of Japanese per capita consumption as a percentage of U.S. per capita consumption based on Japanese price weights.[3] This series was inserted into the regression formula to secure a preliminary series for Japanese per capita consumption as a percentage of U.S. per capita consumption based on U.S. price weights; this series was then used to extrapolate the 1967 benchmark.

The two series for Japanese per capita consumption as a percentage of U.S. per capita consumption were then converted to indexes with 1965 equal to 100. Division of the first index by the second yields a third index which measures the amount by which the rise in Japanese per capita consumption valued in Japanese prices exceeds the rise in Japanese per capita consumption valued in U.S. prices because of systematic differences in quantities and prices which are related to income elasticities.[4]

We assume that such a systematic association between series based on Japanese weights and U.S. weights is confined to consumption. The percentage change in this index each year is therefore reduced by multiplying it by the ratio of private consumption expenditures to the net national product of nonresidential business, both valued in 1965 prices. The resulting reduced percentage changes were linked to obtain the index of the contribution of economies of scale associated with income elasticities to the growth of national income in nonresidential business (valued in 1965 Japanese prices).

A case could be made for eliminating the effects of irregular factors from the income and expenditure data before computation of the two indexes of economies of scale, or else smoothing the indexes themselves.[5] However,

3. This assumes that an index of U.S. per capita consumption is the same whether Japanese or U.S. price weights are used. See *Why Growth Rates Differ*, p. 243.

4. Random differences between Japanese-weighted and U.S.-weighted series are also to be expected, but we do not wish to count these as effects of economies of scale. For this reason we do not adjust the series to conform to the 1970 estimates by Kravis and others, *A System of International Comparisons*, p. 176.

5. See *Accounting for Growth*, pp. 75–76, 315–17.

irregularities seemed insufficient to affect analysis very much (although a few year-to-year movements are erratic), and a satisfactory basis for smoothing the data was not readily available until the estimates described in appendix M were developed.

Sources of growth tables for European countries in *Why Growth Rates Differ* show estimates for the contribution made to growth by a third type of economies of scale, those associated with the "independent growth of local markets." This referred to increased concentration of local markets as a consequence of population shifts and the spread of automobile ownership. Such an entry was omitted in *Accounting for Growth* and this study because of the extreme difficulty of estimating it and the possibility that, by the procedures now adopted, its effects may be captured in other series. In comparative tables, the contributions to European growth of economies of scale associated with "independent growth of local markets" and with "growth of national market measured in U.S. prices" are combined.

Nonresidential Business: Advances in Knowledge and Fluctuations in Intensity of Demand

DIVISION of the index of output per unit of input in nonresidential business by the product of the indexes of the effects of the seven output determinants measured in columns 2 through 6, 8, and 9 of table 4-5 yields an index of the effects of the remaining determinants, which is shown in column 1 of table M-1. Conceptually, such an index has two very different ingredients; these were presented as separate indexes in Denison, *Accounting for Growth,* and must now be separated in the estimates for Japan.

One index is a cyclical variable which causes large short-term fluctuations in output per unit of input but has little or no long-term trend. It measures the effect of fluctuations in the intensity with which employed resources are used as a result of variations in the pressure of demand. Output per unit of input tends to be high when demand is strong and total output is large relative to potential supply, and low when demand is weak and total output small. The reason is that input series measure the labor, capital, and land that are present in business establishments and available for use. In the United States, even though labor input drops in contractions and increases in expansions as workers are laid off or hired and hours varied, labor input contains such a substantial element of overhead that it fluctuates much less than output. Fixed capital and land input, as measured, vary scarcely at all with fluctua-

Table M-1. *Nonresidential Business: Indexes of the Effects on Output per Unit of Input of Advances in Knowledge and Miscellaneous Determinants and of the Intensity with Which Employed Resources Are Used as a Result of Variations in the Intensity of Demand, 1952-71*

| Calendar year | Indexes of stated output determinants (1965 = 100) | | | Deviation of nonlabor share from 5-year average (4) | Index of intensity of demand, postwar average = 100 (5) |
	Combined effects (1)	Advances in knowledge and miscellaneous (2)	Intensity of demand (3)		
1952	81.18	77.55	104.68	−0.15	100.64
1953	82.89	78.91	105.04	−0.45	100.99
1954	84.60	80.30	105.36	1.00	101.30
1955	85.62	81.70	104.79	−1.21	100.75
1956	87.34	83.14	105.05	−1.55	101.00
1957	89.52	84.60	105.81	2.27	101.73
1958	87.41	86.09	101.53	−0.63	97.62
1959	88.01	87.60	100.46	−1.90	96.59
1960	93.86	89.14	105.29	1.68	101.23
1961	95.91	90.72	105.72	1.88	101.64
1962	96.72	92.32	104.77	0.18	100.73
1963	99.22	94.48	105.01	−0.44	100.96
1964	100.78	97.20	103.68	0.26	99.68
1965	100.00	100.00	100.00	−1.45	96.14
1966	102.48	102.87	99.62	−1.01	95.78
1967	108.01	105.83	102.06	0.23	98.12
1968	114.58	108.86	105.25	0.58	101.19
1969	119.07	111.99	106.32	0.48	102.22
1970	122.94	115.20	106.72	0.94	102.60
1971	122.09	118.50	103.03	−0.95	99.06

Sources: Column 1, table 4-5, column 1 divided by the product of columns 2, 3, 4, 5, 6, 8, and 9; column 2, see text; column 3, equals column 1 divided by column 2; column 4, estimates described in appendix D; column 5, computed from column 3.

tions in output. In Japan employment and working hours have responded only very moderately to changes in demand. Hence the great bulk of the effect of fluctuations in total output due to demand changes must have been felt in output per unit of input, rather than being divided between input and output per unit of input as in the United States. This difference would make fluctuations in the "demand intensity" index larger in Japan than in the United States if fluctuations in total output were of equal amplitude in the two countries. The stability of labor input in Japan must affect the time pattern as well as the amplitude of fluctuations in output per unit of input. Because input is not affected much, cyclical fluctuations in output per unit of input may be expected to be approximately coincident with those in total output. In the United States, in contrast, output per unit of input tends to lead total output because fluctuations in labor input, which are substantial, lag behind fluctuations in total output.

The second series that must be isolated is a measure of the effect on output per unit of input of the incorporation of advances in knowledge into the production process, together with the effects of a miscellany of unmeasured output determinants which are believed to have only minor effects. We expect this index to have a pronounced upward trend. We also expect it to move fairly smoothly in the short run, although occasional irregular movements are certainly possible.

For the United States the first of the two series was directly measured. The principal statistical ingredient of the measurement procedure was the non-labor share of national income originating in corporations—or, more exactly, the deviation of the nonlabor share from its trend.[1] Output per unit of input was then divided by this first index and by the indexes for other measured components of output per unit of input to secure a series for the effects of advances in knowledge and miscellaneous determinants.

We do not follow this procedure for Japan. The reasons are that we lack confidence in the annual movement of the series for income shares that we have been able to derive and that it is very difficult to fit trends to the series we do have, which reveal a substantial rise in the nonlabor share but not one that occurs in a regular fashion. We have thought it better, instead, to adopt a procedure which involves working back and forth from one index to the other.

The combined series we wish to subdivide is shown in table M-1, column 1. On the basis of the similar estimates for the United States as well as a priori reasoning, we expect, as already indicated, that the series for "advances in knowledge and miscellaneous" should move rather smoothly. To secure a smoothly moving series by fitting a trend line to the whole period would not be satisfactory, however, because inspection of a chart of the combined series indicates that a single growth rate over the whole period will not accurately describe the data. At least this is so if, as seems certain, the 1971 observation is cyclically lower than those for the immediately preceding years. It seems to us best to divide the period in two. This leaves open the dividing point. If 1965 to 1967 were not cyclically low compared to the preceding and follow-ing years, one might divide the period around 1966 and secure a very high

1. See appendix O, part 3, of *Accounting for Growth*.

growth rate for the short following period. It seems to us much more probable, however, that productivity (like sector national income) is low in 1965–67 for cyclical reasons and that the period should be divided earlier; we have chosen the end of 1962.

To secure our series we have assumed that the index of the effect of intensity of utilization due to demand pressure has the same average value for the two years 1952 and 1953 as for the years 1962 and 1963 and for 1970 and 1971; that the index for the effect of advances in knowledge and miscellaneous determinants moved smoothly from 1952 until the end of 1962 at the growth rate (1.79) observed for the combined index from 1952–53 to 1962–63, and thereafter at the rate (2.83) observed for the combined index from 1962–63 to 1970–71. The resulting index for advances in knowledge and miscellaneous is shown in column 2 of table M-1. The series that it implies for the effects of fluctuations in intensity of demand is shown with 1965 equal to 100 in column 3 and with the 1952–71 average equal to 100 in column 5.

This procedure, it is to be noted, throws irregularities in the movement of output, which result from determinants not separately measured or from errors of estimate, into the series for the effects of fluctuations in intensity of demand rather than into the series for advances in knowledge and miscellaneous as is the case with the U.S. estimates.

We have no great confidence in the precision of the series for the effects of fluctuations in the intensity of demand, but neither have we any particular reason to reject it. The years 1958–59, 1965–67, and 1971 are estimated to be those in which productivity was most adversely affected by weak demand. The small declines in the index from 1958 to 1959 and from 1965 to 1966 may surprise some readers because 1959 and 1966 are regarded as lying in recovery periods. But the economy probably operated further below its capacity in 1959 and 1966, taken as a whole, than it did in the immediately preceding years. This is suggested by the fact that national income originating in nonagricultural nonresidential business, the sector most appropriate to this examination, increased by less than average percentages in both 1959 and 1966.

Column 4 of table M-1 shows the deviation of the nonlabor share from its five-year moving average that was calculated in the derivation of income share weights. Comparison with column 5 shows that the expected positive relationship between the demand intensity index and the deviation of the nonlabor share from its trend, though loose, is definitely present; it appears despite the inaccuracies of the share data and the inadequacy of the five-year average as a measure of trend when a series of years is cyclically high or low.

Table N-1 in the following appendix permits additional examination of the implications of the intensity-of-demand series.

Of particular concern in the present study are growth rates of the series for advances in knowledge and miscellaneous determinants. The reliability of the rate for the whole 1953–71 period is not greatly qualified by the problem of eliminating cyclical variations but that problem does make the date and the amount of acceleration in the rate rather uncertain. However, contributions to growth in the particular periods chosen in the general analysis—1953–61 and 1961–71—would not be greatly changed if the combined index in column 1 of table M-1 were not judged to be depressed in 1965–67 by low intensity of utilization or other irregular influences and the trend was therefore assumed to accelerate later than we have judged.

Standardized National Income

TABLE N-1 shows an annual series for standardized national income—national income with the effects of three irregular factors on output per unit of input removed—and the adjustments to actual national income which were made to obtain it. The concept is the same as in table 4-7, although an entry for the effects of work stoppages on output per unit of input is omitted from table 4-7 because the estimate is zero in both 1953 and 1971. Unlike table 4-7, which is confined to growth rates, preparation of table N-1, which presents absolute figures, requires acceptance of some standard from which deviations of the indexes for the irregular factors are to be measured. We have used the average values of the indexes for irregular factors over the twenty years from 1952 through 1971. Our first step was therefore to recompute the indexes in table 4-5, columns 5 to 7, with the 1952–71 average, instead of 1965, equal to 100. All of the indexes for irregular factors, it will be recalled, refer only to the nonresidential business sector.

Column 2 of table N-1 measures the effect on output of deviations from the average in intensity of utilization of employed resources resulting from fluctuations in intensity of demand. To obtain it, national income originating in nonresidential business (table 3-3, column 7) was multiplied by the number of percentage points by which the demand intensity index (1952–71 equal to 100) exceeds or falls short of 100. This column is one of two series that would have to be subtracted from actual annual national income if one wished to secure potential national income defined as the national income which would have been obtained if utilization of available resources had been at the average postwar rate.[1] The other, which we have not estimated, represents

---

1. The unemployment rate in Japan is so insensitive that it cannot be used in a definition of potential output in the way that a 4 percent (or some other) unemployment rate has been used in the United States. The average Japanese unemployment rate in 1952–71 was actually only 1.6 percent.

Table N-1. *Actual and Standardized National Income in Constant Prices, 1952–71*

Billions of 1965 yen

Calendar year	Actual national income^a (1)	Effect of fluctuations in intensity of demand^b (2)	Partially standardized national income (col. 1 − col. 2) (3)	Effect of weather on farm output^b (4)	Effect of work stoppages^b (5)	Standardized national income (col. 3 − col. 4 − col. 5) (6)	Column 1 as percent of — Column 3 (7)	Column 1 as percent of — Column 6 (8)	Percentage change from prior year in — Column 1 (9)	Percentage change from prior year in — Column 6 (10)
1952	9,446	43	9,403	−25	−2	9,430	100.5	100.2	...	...
1953	10,170	73	10,097	−109	0	10,206	100.7	99.6	7.7	8.2
1954	10,855	104	10,751	−34	0	10,785	101.0	100.6	6.7	5.7
1955	11,705	66	11,639	285	0	11,354	100.6	103.1	7.8	5.3
1956	12,313	94	12,219	−37	0	12,256	100.8	100.5	5.2	7.9
1957	13,533	183	13,350	−93	0	13,443	101.4	101.7	9.9	9.7
1958	14,136	−265	14,401	−23	0	14,424	98.2	98.0	4.5	7.3
1959	15,233	−413	15,646	139	0	15,507	97.4	98.2	7.8	7.5
1960	17,305	173	17,132	14	0	17,118	101.0	101.1	13.6	10.4
1961	19,007	256	18,751	−8	0	18,759	101.4	101.3	9.8	9.6
1962	20,617	12	20,605	36	0	20,569	100.1	100.2	8.5	9.6
1963	22,370	180	22,190	−86	2	22,274	100.8	100.4	8.5	8.3
1964	24,434	−66	24,500	−41	0	24,541	99.7	99.6	9.2	10.2
1965	25,613	−833	26,446	−78	0	26,524	96.9	96.6	4.8	8.1
1966	27,900	−1,004	28,904	−98	2	29,000	96.5	96.2	8.9	9.3
1967	31,607	−511	32,118	118	3	31,997	98.4	98.8	13.3	10.3
1968	35,840	374	35,466	142	3	35,321	101.1	101.5	11.3	10.4
1969	39,596	778	38,818	53	0	38,765	102.0	102.1	10.5	9.8
1970	43,848	1,021	42,827	−39	0	42,866	102.4	102.3	10.7	10.6
1971	46,193	−387	46,580	−185	0	46,765	99.2	98.8	5.3	9.1

Sources: Column 1, table 3-3. Other columns, see text.

a. Estimates based on U.S. deflation procedures.

b. Value of national income under actual conditions minus value under average conditions. Adjustments are made only for effects on output per unit of input, not on input.

the amounts of national income that would be added or deducted if labor input were at a standardized rate. These additions and subtractions probably would be small relative to the productivity adjustment because the amplitude of fluctuations in employment and labor input are small relative to fluctuations in output per unit of input. Also, correspondence between their movements and those in output, though present, is not close. But the suggestion that cyclical movements in input did not affect output very much can be made only hesitantly because of the difficulty of isolating cyclical from other movements.

Standardized national income can be expected to move more smoothly than actual national income, and comparison of columns 9 and 10 of table N-1 shows that it does. Fairly pronounced irregularities nevertheless remain even in standardized national income, especially in the early years. (The first seven annual percentage changes average 7.4 and range from 5.3 to 9.7; the last twelve changes average 9.6 and range only from 8.1 to 10.6.) By method of estimate, these irregularities are ascribable to output determinants *other* than the three specified irregular factors and "advances in knowledge and miscellaneous." All these other determinants were measured directly so the sources of irregularities in the movement of standardized national income can be traced. Increases of erratic size in employment (including but not limited to those due to the business cycle) seem to be most frequently responsible.

Columns 2, 4, and 5 of table N-1 refer entirely to the nonresidential business sector, in which no distinction is drawn between Japanese and American deflation procedures. Consequently, they can be subtracted from actual nonresidential business national income or from actual national income in the whole economy based on Japanese deflation procedures to secure standardized series for these aggregates. "Actual" data in 1965 prices for both series appear in table 3-3.

National Income
per Person Employed
and Its Determinants:
Comparison of Japan and
the United States, 1970

THIS APPENDIX supplements the description that chapter 11 provides of the Japanese-American comparison of national income per person employed and its determinants. The procedures closely approximate those used in Denison, *Why Growth Rates Differ,* to compare Europe with the United States in 1960. However, the isolation of nonresidential business permitted some improvements in methodology. On the other hand some minor shortcuts were introduced. United States data are chiefly from Denison, *Accounting for Growth.* Because that book ends with 1969, it sometimes was necessary initially to use 1969 data for the United States and then to introduce a rough adjustment to secure a 1970 comparison.

Table O-1 serves as a summary and worksheet for the explanation. Most of the discussion, both here and in chapter 11, concerns the derivation of column 1, and we shall return to it for a line-by-line description. For input components this column shows the value of the index for that particular input (or that particular characteristic of labor input) in Japan as a percentage of the index for that particular input in the United States. For components of

Table O-1. *Derivation of Estimates of Contributions to Gap between United States and Japan in National Income per Person Employed, 1970*[a]

Determinant	Index: Japan as percent of United States[b] (1)	U.S. weight (2)	Contribution to gap (3)	Pseudo growth rate (4)	Weight × pseudo growth rate (5)	Contribution to gap (6)
1. National income per person employed	54.8	...	45.2	...	...	45.2
2. Dwellings	31.7	0.0425	2.9	...	...	2.9
3. International assets	-7.4	0.0056	0.6	...	...	0.6
4. All other determinants	...	...	41.7	...	...	41.7
5. Hours of work	107.0	0.7962	...	-0.338	2.913[c]	-3.9
6. Age-sex composition	96.0	0.7962	...	0.204	0.162	2.3
7. Education	95.6	0.7962	...	0.225	0.179	2.6
8. Nonresidential structures and equipment	59.0	0.0937	...	2.673	0.250	3.6
9. Inventories	56.0	0.0304	...	2.942	0.089	1.3
10. Land	59.2	0.0316	...	2.656	0.084	1.2
11. Overallocation to agriculture	92.0	...	...	0.418	0.418	6.0
12. Overallocation to nonagricultural self-employment	95.5	...	...	0.230	0.230	3.3
13. Use of shift work	99.7	...	...	0.015	0.015	0.2
14. Economies of scale	95.2	...	...	0.246	0.246	3.5
15. Labor disputes	100.1	...	...	-0.005	-0.005	-0.1
16. Irregularity in pressure of demand	106.2	...	...	-0.300	-0.300	-4.3
17. Irregularity in agricultural output	100.0	...	...	0.000	0.000	0.0
18. Lag in the application of knowledge, general efficiency, and errors and omissions	69.8	...	...	1.814	1.814	26.0

Sources: Column 1, see text of chapter 11 and appendix O. Column 2, see text of appendix O. Column 3, row 1, 100 minus column 1; rows 2 and 3 (100 minus column 1) × column 2; row 4, row 1 minus rows 2 and 3. Column 4, growth rate required to move from column 1 to 100 in 20 years. Column 5, rows 5 to 10, column 2 × column 4; rows 11 to 18, column 4. Column 6, rows 1 to 4, column 3; rows 5 to 18, row 4 distributed in proportion to column 5.
a. Based on U.S. price and earnings weights.
b. See text.
c. Sum of rows 5 to 18.

output per unit of input, column 1 shows output in Japan as a percentage of what output would be if that determinant were the same in Japan as in the United States.

Column 2 of table O-1 shows U.S. input weights, expressed as percentages of national income in the whole economy. They were obtained in two steps. Computed first was the percentage distribution of national income in 1969 among earnings of dwellings; net earnings of international assets; compensation of labor employed in general government, households, and institutions; and national income orginating in nonresidential business. (Data are from *Accounting for Growth*, table 3-1, page 18.) The last component was then allocated among labor, nonresidential structures and equipment, inventories, and land in accordance with the distribution of their weights within nonresidential business in 1967–68 (*Accounting for Growth*, table J-2, page 262).

The derivation of the remaining columns of table O-1 was explained in chapter 11. It is also specified in the sources to the table. The implication of the pseudo-growth-rate method of allocating the gap in national income per worker may be further clarified by a simplified illustration. Suppose we dealt with only two determinants, input per worker which was 89 percent as big in Japan as in the United States and output per unit of input which was 62 percent as big. The shortfalls, 11 percent and 38 percent respectively, would add to 49 percent, but the actual shortfall would be only 44.8 percent because actual output per worker would be 55.2 percent as big as in the United States (89 times 0.62). If the calculation is reversed, it is seen that input per worker was 12.36 percent bigger in the United States than in Japan and output per unit of input 61.29 percent bigger—adding to 73.65—while actual output per worker would be 81.23 percent bigger.

Our procedure would be to compute the growth rates that would be required to move from 89 to 100 and from 62 to 100 in twenty years; the rates are 0.584 and 2.419, respectively. The 44.8 percentage point gap would then be allocated in proportion to these growth rates: 8.7 points to inputs and 36.1 points to output per unit of input. (For simplicity the modification for dwellings and international assets is ignored here.) Allocation by the original percentages, 11 and 38, would have assigned 10.1 points to inputs and 34.7 to output per unit of input. Allocation by the reversed percentages, 12.36 and 61.29, would have assigned 7.5 points to inputs and 37.3 to output per unit of input. Use of pseudo growth rates yields estimates about midway between these extremes. The numbers assumed in the calculation are close to the actual ones so they indicate the degree to which results are sensitive to the choice of allocation method.

Multiplication of the growth rates of the individual inputs by constant shares (table O-1, column 5) is equivalent to assuming unit elasticity of substitution among the factors as the gap between U.S. and Japanese input levels closes. This explains why the difference between contributions before and after allowance for interaction is smaller for nonresidential structures and equipment and inventories than for labor input components. The estimates before interaction imply that the relative marginal products of the factors are unaffected by differences in factor proportions, which are large in this comparison.

We now describe the derivation of the estimates in column 1 of table O-1.

National Income per Person Employed

Gross domestic product per person employed, valued in U.S. prices, was 55.2 percent as large in Japan as in the United States, according to table 2-1. The percentage for domestic national income was assumed to be the same. The figure for each country was multiplied by the ratio of total national income to national income minus net earnings of international assets. (Data for Japan are from table 3-2.) This provided an estimate that Japanese national income per person employed was 54.8 percent of the U.S. figure.

Dwellings and International Assets

These estimates are adequately described in chapter 11.

Hours of Work

Other things being equal, differences in hours of work would have made labor input per person employed in Japan equal to an estimated 107.0 percent of labor input per person employed in the United States. This result was obtained as follows.

Total hours worked by full-time and part-time workers in each of six groups in nonresidential business were divided by the average hours of full-time workers in the group to secure full-time equivalent employment. This was done for Japan in 1970 (using data from tables F-1, F-2, and F-3) and the United States in 1969 (using data from *Accounting for Growth*, tables G-1, G-2, and G-3).

Labor input per full-time equivalent worker was then estimated to be 8.33 percent greater in Japan than in the United States for males in the category of nonagricultural wage and salary workers and 12.70 percent greater for females in this category; these are the amounts by which labor input when full-time hours are at the Japanese level differs from labor input when hours are at the U.S. level, according to the curves relating output to labor input that were used in time series analysis. These percentages are much smaller than the differences between average full-time hours themselves. Japanese full-time equivalent employment estimates for wage and salary workers in nonagricultural business were raised by these percentages and the adjusted figures were added to actual full-time employment in other categories to secure a number for nonresidential business comparable in labor input content to actual full-time equivalent employment in the United States. This is appropriate because our assumptions for agricultural workers and nonagricultural self-employed and unpaid family workers imply no difference in labor input between workers employed at Japanese full-time hours and those employed at U.S. full-time hours.

The following table shows (in thousands) the results of these calculations, together with other employment data from the same sources:[1]

	United States, 1969	Japan, 1970
Nonresidential business		
Full-time and part-time employment	63,062	47,106
Full-time equivalent employment	57,151	43,061
Labor input (employment and hours only)	57,151	45,796
General government, households, and institutions		
Full-time and part-time employment	20,552	4,183
Whole economy		
Full-time and part-time employment	83,614	51,289

Business employment in Japan is 74.70 percent of that of the United States (47,106 divided by 63,062); with account taken only of employment and hours, labor input in business in Japan is 80.13 percent of that of the United States (45,796 divided by 57,151); and labor input per person employed is 107.28 percent of that of the United States (80.13 divided by 74.70). (For comparison, it may be observed that average hours per person employed in business in Japan were 122.2 percent of those of the United States. Total hours worked in business were 91.3 percent of those of the United States.)

The United Nations output comparisons for general government (as defined in that study) are obtained by dividing annual employee compensation by international price ratios that are based on *annual* salary schedules,[2] so

1. Labor input (third row) is expressed relative to full-time equivalent employment in the United States.

2. Irving B. Kravis and others, *A System of International Comparisons of Gross Product and Purchasing Power,* United Nations International Comparison Project: Phase One (Johns Hopkins University Press for the World Bank, 1975), p. 163.

they assume that differences in full-time hours do not affect output per worker.[3] We assume this to be the case for general government, households, and institutions as we define them. Consequently, to measure labor input in the whole economy, we compare total full-time and part-time employment in the United States (83,614) with the sum (54,718) of full-time and part-time employment in general government, households, and institutions (4,183) and 107.28 percent (50,535) of full-time and part-time employment in business (47,106). Total labor input (taking account of employment and hours only) in Japan is then found to be 65.44 percent of that of the United States. Since the employment percentage is 61.34 (51,289 divided by 83,614), the percentage for hours is 106.69 (65.44 divided by 61.34).[4] We have rounded up to 107 to allow for the fact that the U.S. data used referred to 1969 instead of 1970.

Age-Sex Composition of Hours Worked

This component is fully described in chapter 11 except that the adjustments for general government, households, and institutions may need amplifying. The output comparisons for this sector do not distinguish by sex—at least, not explicitly—in applying the assumption that output per worker is the same in the two countries, and we therefore use an index of 100 for this sector. Combining the indexes for the two sectors, 95.62 for business and 100 for government, etc., in the same way as the corresponding indexes for hours were combined, we secure 96.0 as the index for the age-sex composition component of labor input in the whole economy in Japan when the U.S. index equals 100. It is assumed that the result would have been the same if the U.S. data referred to 1970 instead of 1969.

Education

Chapter 11 adequately describes this component. The adjustment for general government, households, and institutions is similar to that for the other components of labor input.

3. Since salary scales are for full-time employees, differences in the proportion of part-time workers would affect the output comparison, but we have not attempted an adjustment.

4. The same result could be obtained by weighting the percentage for business (107.28) by business employment (47,106) and the percentage for general government, etc. (100.00), by employment in that sector (4,183).

Nonresidential Structures and Equipment

Per capita gross investment in the United States and Japan in 1970 measured in U.S. prices was computed from table 13.7 and appendix table 13.7 in Kravis and others, pages 176 and 210, as the sum of their line numbers 113–16, 119–20, 122–23, and 125–46. Included are (1) nonresidential business construction—approximated as the sum of "nonresidential buildings" and "construction excluding buildings" other than "educational buildings," "hospital buildings," "roads, highways," and "land improvement" —and (2) "producers' durables." Per capita investment was multiplied by population to secure total investment in each country. Total investment in Japan was 58.8 percent of total investment in the United States. (Measured in Japanese prices it was 50.8 percent as large.)

The ratio of investment during the twelve years from 1960 through 1971 to investment in 1970 was calculated for each country from series for investment in its own constant prices and multiplied by its 1970 investment in 1970 U.S. prices to obtain estimated total 1960–71 investment valued in 1970 U.S. prices. For the United States it scarcely mattered whether or not construction and producers' durables were calculated separately; for Japan they could not be handled separately. The Japanese aggregate was 41.6 percent of the U.S. aggregate. We assume that this represents the relative size of the net stock of private business nonresidential structures and equipment at the end of 1971.[5] The figure for each country was multiplied by the ratio of net stock in 1970 (annual average) to net stock at the end of 1971, according to series for net stock valued in the country's own constant prices. This yielded an estimate that the Japanese net stock was 36.7 percent of the U.S. net stock in 1970. Division by total employment in 1970 provided an estimate that the net stock of nonresidential structures and equipment owned by private business, per person employed in the whole economy, was 59.0 percent as large in Japan as in the United States.[6] We use the same percentage for gross stock and therefore for capital input in the form of nonresidential structures and equipment.[7]

5. This ratio corresponds to gross investment during the previous twelve years. In *Why Growth Rates Differ*, ratios based on gross investment during the previous sixteen years and the previous eight years were averaged.

6. This is in U.S. prices. Similar calculations yield 50.9 as the percentage in Japanese prices.

7. The estimates used for time series analysis show a lower net–gross ratio in Japan than in the United States, but we believe this results from differences in estimating procedures.

Inventories

In 1969 the average value of private business inventories in the United States, valued in current dollars, was $220.2 billion (*Accounting for Growth*, table J-4, page 265). In 1969 the average value of private business inventories in Japan, measured in 1965 yen, was ¥15,264 billion (table I-1). The annual-average price of the stock of inventories in Japan was 6.0 percent higher in 1969 than in 1965 (calculated from Economic Planning Agency, *Annual Report on National Income Statistics, 1973*, page 153), so in current prices the 1969 value was ¥16,180 billion. This figure excludes livestock, and we raise the total by 1 percent to ¥16,342 billion to allow for this omission.

Kravis and associates (appendix table 13.7, page 210) put the purchasing power of the dollar for inventories at 326 yen, which is the weighted average of the purchasing power parities for producers' durables and the commodity components of consumption (that is, consumption excluding services). (See Kravis and others, *A System of International Comparisons*, page 159.) This rate is used to convert the value of the change in inventories but conceptually is more appropriate for conversion of the stock of inventories, which is less concentrated by commodity than a single year's investment. Kravis and associates treat the increase in stocks as a single item so that the same purchasing power parity (326 to 1) is used to derive gross domestic product whether U.S. or Japanese price weights are used. On the assumption that this ratio was 326 to 1 in 1969 too, the dollar value of Japanese inventories in 1969 was 50.13 billion. In each country's own constant prices, the value of inventories increased from 1969 to 1970 by 16.05 percent in Japan (table I-1) and by 2.84 percent in the United States (computed from *Accounting for Growth*, table 5-2, page 54, and underlying data, and *Survey of Current Business,* July 1974, page 13). Hence, in 1970 the value of inventories was $58.2 billion in Japan and $226.5 billion in the United States, both measured in U.S. prices of 1969. Per person employed in the whole economy, inventories were then 41.3 percent as large in Japan as in the United States according to this calculation.

This estimate is crude, particularly because of the wide margin of error for the purchasing power parity entering into it, and we must ask whether the result is reasonable. The estimate implies that inventories per person employed in nonresidential business were 34.4 percent as large in Japan as in the United States. This figure refers to comparisons in both Japanese and U.S.

prices, as already noted. Table 2-1 shows that gross domestic product per person employed in Japan was 55 percent of that of the United States on the basis of U.S. weights, 44 percent on the basis of Japanese weights, and 50 percent on the basis of the ideal index (their geometric mean). Relative output per person employed in nonresidential business is unlikely to differ much from the relationship in the whole economy, especially when output is measured in U.S. prices. If it does not, the implied ratio of inventories to non-residential business output is much lower in Japan than in the United States: 38 percent lower on the basis of U.S. weights for output and over 30 percent lower on the basis of the ideal index. In the 1960 comparisons of the United States with European countries, ratios of inventories to output in the European countries were found to be about the same or larger than in the United States, so this result for Japan does not accord with the general pattern. Geographic isolation from sources of supply would, if anything, lead one to expect a higher ratio in Japan.

We compromise between our expectation that the ratio of inventories to output in nonresidential business is about the same in the two countries (when both output and inventories are measured in U.S. prices) and the statistical result that the ratio was 38 percent lower in Japan by assuming the ratio was actually 15 percent lower in Japan. This implies that private inventories per person employed in nonresidential business were 47 percent as large in Japan as in the United States and that per person employed in the whole economy they were 56 percent as large. The latter is the estimate needed for our analysis.[8]

Nonresidential Land

The procedure is the same as in *Why Growth Rates Differ*. The total weight of nonresidential land in the U.S. national income was divided into three parts. Of the total, 34.5 percent was assigned to agriculture. This is the estimated percentage that the earnings of agricultural land represented of the total earnings of private nonresidential land in 1969; the data are from worksheets underlying *Accounting for Growth*.[9] The remainder was allocated be-

---

8. If the estimate of inventories in each country's own prices were correct, this would be equivalent to using a purchasing power parity for holdings of inventories in 1969 of 239 yen to the dollar (instead of the initial 326), which seems low. However, the estimates in national prices may not be comparable.

9. See pp. 260–72 for a description of the estimates.

tween mineral land and land whose economic rent derives from its site value in the same proportions as was done in 1960 in *Why Growth Rates Differ*, page 183. This assigned 7.9 percent of the total weight to mineral resources and 57.6 percent to nonresidential sites.

Japan had 4.0 percent as much total land area as the United States, 1.5 percent as much agricultural land, and 3.2 percent as much arable land. To measure land input in agriculture, we have counted the arable land plus one-third of permanent meadows and pastures; this yields 2.3 as the Japanese percentage of the U.S. input. Per person employed in the whole economy, the Japanese percentages of the United States were 6.4 for all land, 2.4 for agricultural land, 5.2 for arable land, and 3.7 for agricultural land input. The lowest percentage of the United States obtained for agricultural land input per person employed in any European country in 1960 was much higher: 9 in Belgium, the Netherlands, and the United Kingdom.

Mineral resources in Japan were put at 2.3 percent of the United States in total and 3.7 percent per person employed in the whole economy. This comparison was based on 1970 output of the mineral products listed in *Why Growth Rates Differ*, page 185, and a few additional products. Each product was valued at U.S. unit prices. Data are from the *United Nations Statistical Yearbook, 1973*, pages 166–98. They were checked against the *U.S. Minerals Yearbook, 1972* (vol. 1, table 2, for the United States and vol. 3 for Japan). The figure for Japan of 3.7 percent of the United States per worker compares with 2 percent for Denmark, 5 percent for Italy, and at least 10 percent for the other European countries in 1960.

The other main use of land is for sites. Input of nonresidential sites, except in agriculture and mining, is assumed to be the same, per person employed, in Japan (like Europe) as in the United States. The reasoning is that such sites require only a small fraction of total land area, generally represent a use superior to agriculture or even housing, and for the most part require no special physical characteristics not readily available in all countries.

The weighted average of the three indexes (3.7, 3.7, and 100.0) is 59.2.

This properly is less than the indexes obtained for all the European countries in 1960, which ranged from 76 to 81, but the difference is exaggerated because the weights used are inconsistent. According to the latest estimates (underlying *Accounting for Growth*) the 1960 agricultural share of land input comparable to the 34.5 percent in 1969 used in the comparison with Japan was 35.8. In *Why Growth Rates Differ,* however, only 17 percent of the weight was assigned to agriculture. Consequently, more weight was allocated to nonresidential sites, for which indexes of 100 were used, and this led to higher land input indexes in Europe.

Overallocation to Agriculture

Our estimate derives from the assumption that the ratio of output per unit of input in Japan to that in the United States would be the same in all industries combined (excluding the services of dwellings and property income from abroad) as it is in all nonagricultural industries combined (with the same exclusions) if overallocation to farming were equally costly in the two countries.

With the services of dwellings and property income from abroad excluded, assume that total input per person employed is 20 percent higher in nonagricultural industries than in agriculture; the ratio of Japanese to American output per unit of input was then 0.651 in nonagricultural industries and 0.599 in all industries.[10] With the services of dwellings and property income from abroad included, the ratio for all industries becomes 0.603. It would have been 0.653 if the ratio for all industries except the services of dwellings and property income from abroad had been 0.651 instead of 0.599. We therefore calculate that greater misallocation than in the United States reduced Japanese national income per person employed by $(0.653 - 0.603) \div 0.653$, or 7.7 percent. This probably is a slight underestimate for two reasons. In the calculations agriculture was assumed to be the same percentage of Japanese national income in U.S. prices as in Japanese prices but actually the former percentage almost surely is lower; and the calculation was based on the farm percentage of employment in the United States in 1969 instead of the lower 1970 percentage. We round to 8 percent to allow for these biases and secure an index of 92.0.

Overallocation to Nonfarm Self-Employment

Self-employed and family workers made up 25.07 percent of employment in the nonagricultural nonresidential business sector in Japan in 1970 (table 3-4) and 11.52 percent in the United States in 1969 (*Accounting for Growth*, table C-1, page 165). However, we assume that demand patterns in Japan are more favorable to use of such labor and that the allocation would have been no more costly in Japan than in the United States if the Japanese percentage had been as low as 15. This would have transferred 3,913,000 Japanese workers from self-employed to paid status. By the assumptions used in the time series analysis, an increase of only one-fourth as many in paid

10. Data used for Japan are from tables 3-2 and 3-4 and appendix J. Data for the United States are from *Accounting for Growth*, table 3-1, and appendix N. For a discussion of the assumption, see *Why Growth Rates Differ*, pp. 220–21.

employment would offset the output lost from the reduction in self-employ-ment, so there would have been a gain equivalent to adding 2,935,000 workers to nonagricultural nonresidential business employment. This is 8.17 percent of such employment with this number deducted. The labor contribu-tion to nonagricultural nonresidential business national income was 71.28 percent of this sector's national income of ¥46,072 billion, or ¥32,840 billion. It would have increased 8.17 percent, or ¥2,683 billion, with the alternative allocation. Total national income would have been raised from ¥57,520 billion to ¥60,203 billion. Actual national income was therefore 4.5 percent less than, or 95.5 percent as large as, what national income would have been with the assumed allocation.

Use of Shift Work[11]

The percentage of plant workers in U.S. manufacturing establishments located in metropolitan areas who worked on other than the first shift was about 26.6, based on surveys conducted from July 1969 to June 1971.[12] The percentage of all workers in Japanese manufacturing establishments with thirty or more employees who worked on other than the first shift was, at most, about 8.7 in September 1970. The figure is maximal because it was calculated on the assumption that half of any group of workers employed on a two-shift system and two-thirds of any group employed on a three-shift system work on other than the first (biggest) shift whereas the true fractions are certainly smaller.[13] It probably also is too big because small enterprises are omitted. We assume that 7 is the Japanese percentage of manufacturing plant workers employed on other than the first shift that is comparable to 26.6 in the United States. We have no comparative data for other industries, but we do know that in Japan 5.0 is the maximum percentage—comparable to 8.7 percent in manufacturing—in selected nonmanufacturing industries (mining, construction, wholesale and retail trade, finance and insurance, real estate, transport and communications, and electricity, gas, and water).

In 1960, we estimated, the percentage for manufacturing production workers was around 23 in the United States, 10 in all of the Northwest Euro-

11. The procedure follows that described in *Why Growth Rates Differ*, pp. 173–74. See also pp. 152–55 of that book.

12. U.S. Department of Labor, Bureau of Labor Statistics, Bulletin 1685-92, *Area Wage Surveys: Metropolitan Areas, United States and Regional Summaries, 1970–71*, p. 81.

13. Data are from Ministry of Labor, *Chingin rōdōjikan seido sōgō chōsa hōkoku* [Report on a General Survey of the Structure of Wages and Hours of Work] (1970), p. 313.

pean countries, and 16 in Italy. So the figure of around 7 percent for Japan in 1970, as compared with 26.6 percent in the United States, is quite low.

The latter comparison means that in Japan structures and equipment were used by manufacturing production workers 15.5 percent less than in the United States (19.6 divided by 126.6) because of shift work, provided capital per worker is the same in manufacturing establishments where shift work is used as where it is not. Suppose (as was done in the comparisons between Europe and the United States) that the prevalence of shift work outside manufacturing is the same in the United States and Japan, and that manufacturing production workers use one-fifth of all fixed enterprise capital. Fixed enterprise capital as a whole is then used about 3.1 percent less in Japan than it would be if shift work were as common as in the United States. The difference may be treated as equivalent to a similar difference in the quantity of capital. Multiplication by the share of structures and equipment in the U.S. national income (9.37 percent) yields an estimate that Japanese national income per person employed is 0.3 percent lower (before allowance for interaction) because of less shift work than in the United States.

Economies of Scale

This component is adequately described in chapter 11.

Labor Disputes

The procedure used for time series analysis assumed that output per unit of input in nonresidential business is reduced by a percentage that is three-tenths as large as the percentage of time that is lost due to labor disputes. On this assumption, it was 0.13 percent lower in 1970 in the United States than it would have been in a year of average strike intensity whereas in Japan 1970 was an average year.[14] This implies that national income per person employed in the whole economy would have been 100.1 percent as large in Japan as in the United States if this special characteristic of 1970 had been the only difference between the two countries.

Irregularity in Pressure of Demand

This determinant happened to be unusually important in 1970. The index measuring the estimated effect of intensity of demand on Japanese output

14. For sources see appendix K and *Accounting for Growth*, pp. 291–93. The 1970 estimate for the United States allows for nonstrikers idled by the General Motors strike.

per unit of input was the highest of the postwar period and 3.0 percent above
the 1961–70 average. The comparable American index was apparently the
lowest of the postwar years up to that time; on the basis of a preliminary
estimate, it was 4.0 percent below the 1961–70 average.[15] When the differences are reduced to take account of the weight of the other sectors, which are
not affected by demand intensity, output per unit of input was 2.6 percent
above the ten-year average in Japan and 3.4 percent below it in the United
States. The difference would put Japan 6.2 percent above the United States,
so we use an index of 106.2.

Irregularity in Agricultural Output

The nonresidential business index for the effect of weather on farm output
was estimated to have been below a ten-year average by 0.02 percent in Japan
and by 0.04 percent in the United States, a trivial difference that becomes
still smaller when related to the whole economy, so no difference between the
countries in the 1970 level of output is ascribed to this determinant. The
Japanese index is from table 4-5. The U.S. index through 1969 is from
Accounting for Growth, table 6-1, page 62; the index was extended to 1970
for this calculation.

Lag in the Application of Knowledge, General Efficiency, and Errors and Omissions

An index of total factor input per person employed, 88.6, was calculated
by weighting all inputs in column 1 of table O-1 by their weights in column 2.
Division of the index of national income per person employed, 54.8, by 88.6
and then by the product of the indexes for all other components of output
per unit of input, 88.7, yields this index, 69.8. Like the other entries in
column 1 of table O-1, this index refers to the whole economy, inclusive of
the services of dwellings and international assets. For nonresidential business
alone it would be lower.

15. It was 3.9 percent below the level estimated to be consistent, on the average, with
a 4 percent unemployment rate.

Index

Advances in knowledge: contribution to growth of national income, 47, 48, 49, 78–83, 117; effect on output per person employed, 53, 54, 110–11, 262; factors contributing to, 82–83; index of, 241–45; international comparison of, 79–80, 81

Age-sex composition of labor force: contribution to growth, 47, 57–59, 122–23; earnings differentials by, 58–59; index of, 29–30, 187–92; per person employed, 101–02, 254

Agriculture: capital consumption in, 153; GNP originating in, 153; government support for, 87; interest income, 168; irregular fluctuations in output of, 235, 262; land input per person employed, 107; national income originating in, 163, 166, 170; overallocation to, 108, 259; production, 11; reallocation of labor from, 47, 50, 84–87, 117–18, 224–28, 229–34

Appliances, market for household, 14–15

Automotive industry, 14

Basic Survey on Wage Structure, 70, 187–88, 198, 206

Belgium: contributions to growth, 79, 80, 81, 87, 232; growth rate, 39, 45

Bergson, Abram, 7

Bonuses, 70, 71n, 165, 170

Bureau of Statistics (Japan), 23, 158, 161

Canada: contributions to growth, 80, 81, 231; GDP per person employed, 6; growth rate, 39, 41n, 45

Capital consumption. See Capital stock, depreciation of

Capital input, contributions to growth of, 47, 48, 63–76, 123–25; in nonresidential business, 33–34; per person employed, 52, 104–06; ratio to labor input, 73, 75. See also Capital stock; Dwellings service sector; Gross private investment; International assets sector; Inventories; Nonresidential structures and equipment

Capital stock, 34; depreciation of, 72–75, 145, 153–54; derivation of series for, 219, 222–23; growth rate, 49, 63, 64; international comparison of, 73–74

Center for Econometric Data Development and Research (CEDDR), 134, 136, 139, 141, 158, 161

Chemical industry, 16

Chung, William K., 26n, 216

Cohn, Stanley H., 7n

Consumption per capita, 7, 92, 93

Contributions to growth, by sector, 18–20, 35–39. See also Growth rate; Sources of growth

Corporation Enterprise Survey, 165

Credit, expansion of, 11

Crowley, James B., 11n

Daly, D. J., 7n

Deflation procedures, 20–21, 39, 45, 154–56

Demand intensity, 34–35, 39, 100, 241–45, 261–62

Denison, Edward F., 3n, 26n, 57n, 74n, 79n, 88n, 91n, 92n, 109n, 162n, 216n, 230n, 238n, 249

Denmark: contributions to growth, 79, 80, 81, 231; growth rate, 41, 45

Depreciation. See Capital stock, depreciation of

Dodge, Joseph, 11

"Dodge Line," 11

263